BROKEN TOYS

*Submissives with Mental Illness
and Neurological Dysfunction*

BROKEN TOYS

*Submissives with Mental Illness
and Neurological Dysfunction*

*Edited by Del Tashlin
and Raven Kaldera*

Alfred Press
Hubbardston, Massachusetts

Alfred Press
12 Simond Hill Road
Hubbardston, MA 01452

Broken Toys: Submissives with Mental Illness and
Neurological Dysfunction
© 2014 by Del Tashlin and Raven Kaldera
ISBN 978-0-9905441-1-1

Cover Photography by John Riedell
Jawniffer Photography http://jawniffer.com/

Printed in cooperation with
Lulu Enterprises, Inc.
860 Aviation Parkway, Suite 300
Morrisville, NC 27560

Dedicated to Joshua, Raven's Aspie boy, and Bradon, Raven's ADHD boy. Mastering you is an amazing learning experience, worthy of gratitude.

Contents

Foreword: Broken Toys
Raven Kaldera

A long time ago, when my slaveboy and I had only been together for perhaps two years, I attended a class on Master/slave relationships that dealt with difficult issues for the master/mistress to face. The facilitator was going around the room, asking us to speak about the most difficult obstacle to our mastery. As soon as he began, I felt a sense of dread, because I knew that I wouldn't be able to come clean about the single biggest problem in my relationship with my slaveboy. I couldn't talk about it in public, because I'd promised him that I wouldn't. It was his depression.

My slaveboy's depression, which we discuss in more detail in our essay "In and Out of the Black Pit" later in the book, was at that time overshadowing everything. Each day was an ordeal of getting him out of bed, assessing what he was—or wasn't—capable of, and herding him through basic activities. Our sex life had plummeted, his service was at a bare minimum, and I spent more time comforting him than taking care of myself. Usually flawlessly obedient, he found it excruciating to obey any orders when he was in the black pit ... and on the way down to the black pit, he would often be irritable, paranoid, and even verbally abusive. There were entire days when I'd have to put him in complete silence except for emergency answers, because he couldn't control himself to speak respectfully or even civilly—and entire days when he lay in bed weeping and couldn't get up.

On top of this, he also had Asperger's Syndrome, and was assaulted by sensory issues on a regular basis, not to mention the raft of emotion-processing problems endemic to autistic-spectrum disorders. He felt broken, and I feared that he was broken. I was very close to feeling completely worthless as a master, and yet I couldn't talk about it. I'd promised him, and my word of honor, at least, was something I still had. I picked a smaller, easier problem, and went to the rest of the conference in a funk.

Years later, when we were in a better place and we began teaching classes on Master/slave relationships, we always looked forward to the time after the class, when people would come up to us and share their problems—often problems too personal to speak up about during the public part of the class. By this time his depression was much more under control, but we still didn't talk about it because it was so much of a humiliation to him. The Universe had other ideas, though. In spite of our ongoing silence, we kept getting people who would come up to us after our classes and ask about how to deal with a submissive or slave who was suffering from some form of mental illness or neurological disorder. It became one of the top five subjects people brought up to us. The dominant party would come up and ask quietly, as if they didn't want anyone else to hear, "Um, I've got this problem. My girl's depressed, and she just lays in bed all day, and I don't know what to do. She tells me I'm the worst master in the world because I can't make it any better. I asked on an Internet list, and they told me that I should just beat her until she gets up and works, but I don't want to do that..." Of course, we'd have to come out to that person, if only to tell them what had worked for us. (And to frantically deep-six the notion that someone could be beaten out of a mood disorder!) Then the next person, and the next ... until finally I told my boy that we needed to do a class on this subject. It is, it seems, badly needed.

Part of the problem is that there is a huge stigma around having mental illness or neurological problems—and an even bigger one around having them if you're involved with kink, or are in a nonstandard relationship. The assumption is that if people talk about their brain glitches, the public will get the idea that everyone in the demographic is a nutjob of some sort—or at least that we are all in this because we are so damaged. We'll bring bad publicity down on our struggling communities. We'll make all our perfectly healthy brothers and sisters look bad ... so we'd better shut up about our various problems. I've had "temporarily abled" organizers tell me up front that classes on handling power dynamic relationships with various disabilities were too "special interest", and wouldn't draw a lot of people. Yet every time we've given classes on power dynamics for people with physical and/or mental challenges, we not only get a huge turnout, we find out later that some people have driven up to five hours to attend. There are a lot more people with these issues than the "poster children" like to believe.

In addition, when one brings up issues like these in the context of power dynamic relationships, all too often the answer is, "Those people shouldn't be in these relationships. If you're with one, dump them or go back to being egalitarian." It's true that being in a relationship with someone with these issues is not an easy thing, and it's also true that we know a number of couples who sadly called off their power dynamic (or broke up) because the s-type could no longer force themselves to obey the M-type, or the M-type was acting too erratically to be safe. Some couples with severe mental illnesses referred to it as "having a polyamorous relationship with Master, slave, and Crazy." Except, they said, that Crazy always wants to be the master, and can't be allowed to take over. We don't deny that sometimes it isn't going to work out. This book doesn't guarantee happily ever after; it's just the voices of people who have learned a few tricks to keep surviving in the face of this invisible onslaught, and want to help others get through the thornbushes faster and more efficiently than they did.

However, the enforced silence and shame around these issues is not helpful or supportive. We need to be able to talk about them without being hushed up or dismissed. Forcing a whole section of one's demographic into isolation and shame, where they will not be able to learn coping skills, is neither a compassionate act nor a way to help the overall health and longevity of power dynamic relationships. There are continual complaints, in the demographic of people who practice power dynamic relationships, that so many of us break up after six months or only a couple of years. While there may be many reasons for this, education is probably our best hope of making a dent in those numbers—and we can't educate anyone about something we're all afraid to talk about. And one of the best tonics for fear and shame is knowing that you're not alone, that there are others out there who are walking the same road and struggling with the same thornbushes—and are still making it work.

Another small chip of fear is the idea that some damaged people might be going into power dynamic relationships because they believe that if they only found the right master (or slave), it would fix all their problems. I don't think that this is any more common than damaged people seeking out egalitarian relationships for the same reason, and they will probably—in most cases—be disappointed. However, it cannot be denied that some of the stories in both this book and its companion volume do tell a different story. Some people with psychological damage or different brains actually do far better in the highly controlled environment of a power dynamic relationship. Often these folks have failed repeatedly in the more open field of egalitarian relationships, but they blossom in this little walled garden. To tell them that they are wrong for doing better with more control and structure is to belittle the fact that they may be, for the first time in their lives, having happy and fulfilled relationships. A crutch? As one therapist friend said to me, "If you have a bad leg and you need a crutch to walk down the aisle at your wedding, pick up the damn crutch and go get married already—you'll be glad you did!" We, of all people, should know better than to disrespect someone else's hard-won happiness with another human being.

We should also acknowledge that these issues are also sensitive for people with the disabilities themselves, and that some of the wording in this book may offend some people. Honestly, there's really no way keep from offending *someone*, and it was important for us to keep the authentic voices of everyone who contributed. Some may object to my use of the term "Crazy" as a metaphor for the invisible force that has come to torment the household. Some may object that people's terminology is not correct to the DSM. Some may nitpick about changing labels, or feel that existing accepted labels are unfair. Some may object, yea verily, to the very title "Broken Toys". It was my decision to use it, in honor of the Broken Toys website that was our first shy attempt to create a resources for masters who had them. I hope that in spite of any random terminologies that offend you, you are able to take something useful from this book.

We also acknowledge that this book is not comprehensive. We were not able to find anyone to write essays or be interviewed about slaves with schizophrenia or psychosis, for example, and our personality disorder section is limited to BPD as we couldn't find anyone to write about other ones. Several slaves offered to write about how their masters deal with their hormonal issues such as PMS or

PMDD, but they could not come through on it. In the end our deadline was more than a year past due and we decided to go with what we had. We hope that our book will still be useful to a fair number of people, even with these shortcomings.

We started the M/s And Disability series for the rest of us, the percentage (large or small) of masters and slaves who have less than perfect bodies and brains. The first two books—*Hell On Wheels: Disabled Dominants* and *Kneeling In Spirit: Disabled Submissives*—were aimed at practitioners with physical issues. This book, and its companion *Mastering Mind: Dominants With Mental Illness And Neurological Disorders,* is our gift to all those people who are struggling with trauma, bad brain soup, and bad brain wiring ... and who don't want to jettison either their partner or their power dynamic.

The single most difficult part of editing this book, for me anyway, was figuring out how to categorize each piece. More than half of the respondents and interviewees have multiple issues, some in very different categories. I seriously considered doing away with the categories altogether, but we also had some very specific essays that could be found a lot easier if there were at least some categories, rather than just one giant muddle of essays and interviews. A functional compromise was reached in that the personal essays and interviews have been sorted into categories by the area which seems to be the main problem, or perhaps the problem which has been most effectively helped by the M/s dynamic. However, if you are looking for articles on s-types with, say, depression, don't just stop with what's in the Mood Disorders section. There may be contributions from individuals with depression as a secondary problem in other areas of the book, and their stories might also be useful to you. Use the index in the back, or just read the whole thing.

These stories are not tragedies, they are triumphs. They are the only maps we've got of how to get through the jungle. Some might be crudely made, but they all show similar wisdom—and they give us hope. If these people found a way, you can too. This is the book I wished I'd had, all those years ago when I was struggling with a slaveboy who had multiple issues, and who is still to this day the most wonderful service animal who ever called themselves my slave. If I'd known then what I know now, I could have saved myself years of feeling helpless and useless as a master. This is my gift to you. Use it wisely, broken toys and owners of broken toys alike.

RAVEN KALDERA
AUGUST 2014

Introduction: Stuck in the Middle

Del Tashlin

(This essay was also published in Mastering Mind.*)*

The very first time I heard the mantra of the kink community—"Safe, Sane, Consensual"—I thought I was doomed to forever be excluded from their reindeer games. Oh, I understood the need for safety; the things we do are by their very nature dangerous and that is why we find them compelling and sexy. I also hold consent as Holy Writ due to some incidents in my past where consent was not sought or given. But the one in the middle—"sane"—there's just no definition of that word that I feel applies to me.

It started as casual conversation where I would ask for opinions on people with mental illness participating in the scene. The answers I got were pretty black and white—either the person felt that mental illness precluded you from ever experiencing sadomasochism or power dynamic relationships, or they themselves had a mental illness and understandably felt that it should not be an impediment to following one's sexual compass into the land of fetish, kink, and leather. There really was no grey area. Those who would exclude someone like me had a hard time conceptualizing any scenario where they felt comfortable with persons who were mentally ill being an active part of their leather families, kink organizations, or really in the community at all. They would almost always include some incredibly long and complicated story about people or couples who caused major rifts in the fabric of their community, or about those unfortunate souls who found themselves attracted to and involved with someone who treated them poorly and made them suffer for their love. Even when asked if there was ever a way for someone who had been diagnosed with a mental illness to overcome their symptoms or manage their behavior so as to be indistinguishable from anyone else, there was still trepidation and fear of a relapse or breakdown.

As persons with mental illness, we have to own some of that. Some of us have decided we no longer needed medication only to find that we really, really do. Others may not have accepted that we were truly sick, and were symptomatic in uncouth and hurtful ways until we came to grips with needing help. There are those who demand that anyone in their life must accept their "idiosyncrasies", whether that be memorizing the several personalities that come and go or bearing witness to repeated cycles of manic-depression because being manic made them feel energized and creative (and usually hypersexual, for a bonus). Even those who feel they are mostly in remission have break-outs when under undue stress or emotional upheaval. But what needs to be made clear about this is that everyone has bad days. How those bad days influence our behavior and whether or not that behavior demands abstaining from being a Master or slave, or even just being a Master or slave in public, that's where the grey area begins.

The ones who were open about their own mental illnesses told stories of how kink helped them heal, gave them new coping mechanisms, and allowed them a little freedom from the shame and isolation that commonly accompanies madness. From cutters who turned to ritualized needle play to reframe their coping mechanism into something beautiful and sexual rather than harmful and shameful, to Masters who were a grounding force when their submissive became manic, I not only heard their stories but became frustrated with that middle concept.

What does it really mean to be "sane"? Is the "sane" in "safe, sane, and consensual" really about the mental stability of those who find D/s attractive? I started asking respected presenters, educators, community leaders, and respected elders what is meant by "sane". Some gave it a very narrow focus that was less about the status of the players and more about indulging in fantasies that are tempered by the constraints of reality. An example given was from a well-known Leather Master/Educator who received requests from anonymous Internet seekers wanting a weekend-long scene culminating in the bottom getting murdered, for real. It wasn't so much his concern about whether the person making the request was mentally ill, as there are many who entertain mental fantasies about toeing the line between a really rough scene and permanent damage. Heck, the snuff film industry exists for a reason! But his real concern was the obviousness that these fantasies overlooked logistical concerns like evading law enforcement. I, myself, have been asked to enact scenes that carry consequences I was unwilling to accept in the name of desire. I am much more willing to accept the concept of sanity when it applies to actions rather than persons.

However, there were others who echoed the idea that there are some people who are just not centered enough even to watch the action in a play space or dungeon. The tales of people whose personality and/or actions became disruptive took on an epic level, including those who seemed to "prey" on a certain person/place/thing by moving from city to city once they had worn out their welcome. However much we're loath to admit it, most of us can think of someone we've met through our local munches, clubs, and parties that isn't playing with a full deck. But does that mean they should be expunged or shunned?

A common explanation for those who prefer the mantra "RACK" (Risk Aware Consensual Kink) over SSC is that many of the scenes you witness or perform in your bedroom or your preferred play space would look absolutely insane to a vanilla or non-kinky observer. The Crucible, the main play space in Washington, DC, hosts both BDSM and swinger events, and even offers separate membership cards for each crowd (even though they bestow the same benefits and can be used for either event type). This sometimes leads to a non-kinky swinger—usually one who learned about the club from the Internet—unwittingly finding themselves surrounded by acts us kinksters take for granted. One such incident I bore witness to was a middle-aged woman who had the wide-eyed stare of someone who had never even thought about BDSM before. She seemed relaxed at first, and just wandered around taking in all the different scenes on display. However, when an expert fire Top began lighting his torches and running them along a very willing bottom, the woman's demeanor changed dramatically. She started frantically looking for "someone in charge", because "that man is setting a woman on fire!"

Now it is time to focus on the topic of this book: the intersection of mental illness and power dynamics. Knowing that there are many M/s or D/s relationships that do not practice any form of kink, and some that don't consider themselves part of the Kink or Leather demographics, I still wanted to start from the concept of action rather than relationship. In a way, power dynamic relationships are a combination of several actions that create bonds and enforce the fantasy of being a Master or a slave. No matter how immersive your D/s or M/s relationship is, indentured servitude is (and will always be) illegal, even if the slave enthusiastically consents. So we rely on a variety of props, costumes, rituals and protocols to breathe life into our preferred way of relating. Most of those things might look as threatening as the fire torches to those who have not been exposed to or do not understand the desire for an unequal relationship.

However, as the following essays and personal stories will reveal, the ability to open up to your partners about your darkest sexual fantasies creates a pattern of communication that makes way for us to talk about other things that might embarrass or shame us. The ability to reinforce the dynamic while also supporting each other during times when coping skills alone aren't cutting it is one of the deepest magics I've witnessed in the M/s community. For Masters to admit that they aren't in control of their emotions a hundred percent of the time, or slaves to know it's expected for them to report any symptoms they may be experiencing without fear of judgment or retribution—these things bring color and complexity that asserts each relationship as functionally unique and powerful. After all, most slaves do not wish to submit to a faceless Master archetype who has no quirks, no need for assistance, no foibles that humanize them. Most masters do not expect slaves to be needless servants who perform sexual favors with the same expression they have for doing the laundry. We all want to find a collection of experiences, memories, outlooks, theories, behaviors, and desires that will continue to enthrall and intrigue us for decades.

To me, there is nothing more sane than wanting and creating a deeply emotional and meaningful relationship where the partners involved support and comfort each other on good days and bad—a relationship where we can take off our public face and be a little dysfunctional without fear or shame. Finding people who care enough to learn when we need a little alone time and when we need to be dragged out of our caves kicking and screaming. Having someone create unusually sexy ways to remind us to take our meds, or write in our journals, or to call our therapists. Honestly, I think the idea of a "sane person" is an unobtainable ideal anyway, if what we mean is "free from emotional distress or chemical imbalances". My idea of a "sane person" is "one who has figured out how to relate to the world with as little distress as possible." And the people who are about to share their stories with you are just that.

I hope you find a treasure trove of ideas, concepts, and structures that will help you enrich your own relationships or help discern the right relationships in the future. I also hope that you recognize a little bit of yourself, your lovers, your friends, your family, and so on, in these stories, to prove that none of us are as "sane" as we think we are. If we deny entry to the world of power dynamics based on sanity, only the ones who fail to recognize their insanity will get to play.

> *The one man in the world who never believes he's*
> *mad is the madman.*
> *–L. Ron Hubbard*

DEL A. TASHLIN
6/18/2014

When You're the Broken Toy
Del Tashlin

Before I begin, I want it known that I suffer with several mental disorders that challenge me on a regular basis. I also engage in an active, healthy, therapeutic kinky sex life. I am here to say it *is* possible, that there are things you can do to make it a part of your life if that's what you desire. It's work, like most things dealing with misfiring brain wires—I am not advising that you just dive into your power dynamic without significant self-reflection beforehand, so you understand what you can about what it offers, what you offer it, and how to make it work with your quirky emotions. Also, I know that I frequently use the word "crazy" or "crazies" to describe my own mental health issues, which can be triggers for some. Please understand that I use that as a badge of pride, that to me it proves that I've been to the very painful loss of control over my life due to these issues, and that I've made it back. To me, it's an act of reclamation, like "dyke" or "fat" being used in a positive way. Please see it as such.

First and foremost, don't self-diagnose. It may be tempting to keep your crazy to yourself, a private matter, and just read a bunch of internet resources and take a test or two and go from there, but part of being a healthy person with mental illness is being responsible and seeking treatment when it's necessary. There are resources on the internet to help you find a kink-friendly therapist—most notably the Kink Aware Professionals site—and really, chances are if they're kink aware, then they're probably hip with polyamory, power exchange, or sadomasochism. Even if you feel like your proclivities are unusual, they'll at least be open to discussing it. Part of self-awareness is knowing when you're not the best man for the job, and when it comes to self-diagnosing you have a big bias—that of being you.

Therapy can take many forms—it doesn't always have to be you, on a couch, talking about your inner workings to some stranger. Seek out therapy that helps, that makes you feel like you're making progress. Talk therapy never worked for me; I'm too analytical and got caught up in the game of "Am I saying the 'right' things?" However, Dialectic Behavioral Therapy (commonly referred to as DBT; sometimes also called Cognitive Behavioral Therapy, or

CBT—as kinksters, we're allowed to chuckle about that) saved my life. You owe it to yourself, and the people you bring into your life, to be actively engaged in addressing your issues in one way or another.

Your Tops and Masters, your Dommes and Daddies, are not responsible for treating your mental illness. Period.

It sounds like common sense, but come on—you and I both know people who rely on friends, lovers, and other non-professionals in their life to help them become or make them functional. Don't be that guy. They love you, and many will go to great lengths to be helpful—most humans like to feel useful—but in the same way that you wouldn't ask a lunch lady to operate on your stomach, don't ask your family to be your mental health professional. This can be extra tempting when you're in a power dynamic, since now (to some degree) you have become reliant on another human being for part of your existence. Remember that your Top/Master is also made of meat, not perfection. The way you can be the best submissive or bottom to them is to take your mental illness on, seek out treatment, pursuing self-awareness about your disorders, and being able to discuss them in a logical way with other people.

This doesn't mean that you can't engage in cathartic play with them; that you can't use your kinky outlets as therapeutic; I found a lot of solace for my particular crazies through BDSM. But this has to be a deliberate choice, something that all parties enter into understanding what they're doing. Just hoping that a scene will open up your head and help rewire you, with no one actively consenting to that, is dangerous at best. The beginning of that consent is self-awareness and self-care. How can you ask for a cathartic scene if you don't know what you need to reach catharsis, or what purpose that catharsis will serve?

Mapping Your Minefield: Finding and Communicating Possible Triggers

When someone starts on this road, I usually ask them to list everything about BDSM that draws them in. What kinds of play do you find yourself attracted to? Sometimes the corollaries are obvious—people who need help healing their inner child may find it soothing to engage in ageplay, for starters—and sometimes there is no corollary at all. If you've established a relationship with a therapist that you can discuss this with, share your list with them. Maybe even other friends in the scene, that aren't your Top or Master, may have helpful input you didn't think of.

What you're really doing with this exercise is surveying a potential minefield. Now, most of us will still stumble onto a mine we didn't expect no matter how much time and energy we spend trying to find them beforehand, but it's an incredibly useful device for both you and your partner if you know what your triggers might be. Honestly, you may want to widen this exercise to everyday activities too, but that's a whole different essay. When you learn of a new trigger, something that brings on symptoms of your mental illness, add it to your list.

This list doesn't have to be a No Go list, either. It's labeling a map, not burning the edges or blurring the boundaries. If you know that impact play with bare hands could trigger abuse flashbacks, you may decide to actively engage in that as part of your healing process. However, it would be incredibly unfair for you not to share that fact with your partner, and wandering into that territory should be a deliberate, not accidental, act. This act can also help you set boundaries to keep you from being triggered when you're not prepared for it. There are some things on my list that are fairly "average" sex acts that I have to be in a very specific headspace to be receptive to; usually in the beginning of a new relationship, I make these hard limits with the option for renegotiation if we're still together in a year. It allows me to explore my boundaries with people I have long term intimate relationships with, as an intentional act, rather than trying to force my way through sex that triggers my crazy.

Knowing these boundaries will also ensure that you find a Top that clicks with what you desire. Nothing is more frustrating than entering into an intense emotional relationship with someone whose major fetish turns out to be one of the triggers to your illness. It makes you a more responsible, responsive bottom, which is a huge turn on for Tops. They like to know that you know what you like, that they can provide that for you. If you're leading them down a primrose path, only to have to safeword out before they get where they want to go, it may feel deceptive to them. So even if you're not ready to have the big revealing conversation where you talk about your daily struggles, it will still be incredibly useful for pickup play to know if certain activities are big illness triggers for you.

It's also incredibly hot for most Masters/Tops when their prospective bottom comes across as someone who really knows who they are—what makes them tick, even the weak underbelly parts. If you're looking to establish a long term sadomasochistic or power exchange relationship, you want to be able to actually offer something other than willing flesh to your Sir/Madam. Being forthright about your diagnoses and how they affect your partner may not sound like phone sex, but the assuredness that you give your partners that you have your shit under control belies a true sense of self.

Don't lie, though. If your life is in upheaval and really you just need a good beating to help cope, don't act like everything is cool. There's a subtlety between non-disclosure with a pickup partner, and lying about where your life is at or what your needs are in a scene. Language I like to use is, "I need a cathartic scene for personal reasons; I need to be able to cry/scream/lose myself for a while. I may have some intense reactions, but that's okay. I have an long term aftercare system already in place." What I'm really saying here is, "I need this scene as a coping mechanism for my depression. It's going to set off some of my triggers, so I may react more strongly than you expect. No worries, I have a therapist." This is much different than actively hiding or misrepresenting what the situation is.

Obviously, this becomes much more important when establishing an enduring relationship with someone. But when's the right time? Do you take them out to Denny's and say, "So, now that you've been fisting me for three weeks, it's time to tell you I'm schizophrenic…"?

Disclosure: Yes, it is any of their business.

Disclosure is a tricky thing. Mental illness still has a lot of stigma in our society, and there are people who will stay away from you because you are honest about your situation. I'm not here to sugar coat that for you. I had someone read an article I wrote about a personality disorder *I didn't even have* and decide that they could never play with me because of it. (That wouldn't have worked out in the long run anyway, so I guess I was better off; still hurt a lot in the short term.) Personally, I have always found it better for me to disclose what is necessary over time. Saying too much too soon infers a sense of intimacy that might make a pick-up play partner overwhelmed, whereas saying too little to someone you have a deep emotional bond with may be read as hiding important information. Deciding what to disclose and when to disclose it is a deeply personal decision, I completely understand. There are parts of my crazy that I'm practically flippant about, and there are parts that I really need to trust you before I can talk about. It's taken me a long time to find that balance. Personally, I made the decision that before I enter into any acknowledged long term arrangement, such as a collar, I have to allow my Sir/Madam to make a fully informed decision—that means full disclosure. It's also a good test—if I'm not ready to share the scarier details of my particular mindmap, I'm probably not really ready to surrender my body, my power, my submission to them.

Part of being honest is knowing how your diagnoses surface for you. What do you look like, act like when you're symptomatic of your illness? Your Master will greatly appreciate tools that will help them recognize when emotional or behavioral changes are tied to your mental illness—otherwise, they may find that they blame themselves for your reactions, or find themselves confused, or even afraid—not a great place to put someone who gets off on control. For me, it's also being very clear about the difference between being depressed but needing coaxing before being sexual, and when the depression is limiting my sexual expression. Yes, it's okay to be up front that depression sometimes eats your sex drive!

This is particularly important if you have symptoms that aren't necessarily emotional. If you self-injure, educating your Mistress about your modality and assuring them that you are careful and take good aftercare of your wounds (you do, don't you?) will keep them from wondering about the invisible cat that keeps scratching your arms. If you strong behavioral changes, physical manifestations, or other changes that could radically change the direction of a scene, it's really the responsible choice to disclose them and discuss them in a non-sexual setting.

It may be tempting to use BDSM as a way to run away from your mental illness. To bury your negative feelings in the sensations, to allow your Master to order you from partaking in maladaptive behaviors, to use sex as an escape from feeling horrible. It works; we wouldn't do it if it didn't work. And sometimes it's an appropriate coping mechanism, just like buying yourself something nice or creating a piece of art that expresses your emotions. However, when we spend all our money, or the shopping trip triggers impulsive behavior, it turns something positive into something negative. Sometimes this happens without warning, and we just have to deal. What is concerning is when it becomes a pattern, when you plan or hope for it to happen as an excuse to indulge those desires, rather than using it as a positive release.

Sex, in particular, can be an incredible way to alleviate the negative emotions that come with depression. I won't be the first one to tell you that anything good, done for the wrong reasons, can become a crutch. Sex is one of those things—you can ride on the feelings of being powerful, desirable, useful, obedient, compliant, etc. on top of the biochemical feelings of euphoria that come with orgasm. It may be just intense enough to make you feel real for the first time. I know, I've been there. But if it's the only time you're feeling that way; if you seek it out more and more often to fill that dark hole in your soul, it becomes like any other drug—before you know it, what used to get you high is now what you need to maintain. What you need to maintain gets larger and larger until it becomes a problem that interferes with the rest of your life.

It's not easy to find the middle ground between the human craving for affection and sex, and when it becomes an issue. However, if you find yourself shirking your everyday commitments and responsibilities to pursue sex (that includes cruising pornography, reading slash, and anything else that is a sex substitute when you don't have a partner handy) is when you need to bring this to the forefront of your consciousness.

This happens with BDSM just as easily. Enduring intense sensations releases endorphins, encourages the manufacture of dopamine within your system, relaxes your muscles, and allows you to enter incredible states of consciousness. It can be a slippery slope you don't even notice, in the beginning, because on top of all of that, there's a sense of belonging and community that comes with coming out as kinky as well. You'll have "scene friends", with whom you can talk about your play; online forums where you can post about your experiences, and thousands of books you can read on everything from technique to philosophy of BDSM. It can be a warm, inviting escape hatch from the difficulties of being crazy.

However, you know as well as I do that your mental illness is waiting for you in the back of the closet, waiting for the worst moment to reappear. The only way to evict that monster from your life is to embrace him and face him head on. This means that if you use your kinky life to run away and refuse to acknowledge other problems in your life, you're only making the monster stronger.

There is an inherent power to owning your illness; stating to someone without fear or hesitation makes it much easier for them to accept. I suggest putting this book in your lap now and just stating aloud, "I have [insert diagnosis here]." Even if you've done it before, to other people. Just being able to state it as though it were the same sort of fact like your name, your relationship orientation, or where you born, takes away some of the stigma of having a mental illness to begin with. The more you're able to talk about it, the easier it gets to disclose to people. I usually recommend having an "elevator speech" to go with it—a short, less-than-one-minute explanation of how my diagnoses impact my life.

"I have Borderline Personality Disorder. I tend to categorize things as all good or all bad, and it's hard for me to see things as emotionally complex. I'm aware of this tendency and I work hard towards seeing the grey in life. Also, I'm a recovered self-injurer; I don't do that anymore but it's part of my history. Finally, I have impulse control issues. Do you have any questions?"

This is especially important if you have a diagnosis that's not as well known as others. I find most people have a general sense of what bipolar disorder is, but may be more confused about Asperger's Syndrome. I always make sure my elevator speech includes at least one statement about the fact that I'm actively addressing the problems that come with my disorder. I want to communicate that it's a process, and that although therapists have said that I'm mostly in remission, it's still a struggle for me from time to time. If they merit more detail, or if they ask questions, I'm well informed about different manifestations about my illness and how it's been portrayed in the media. For me, I usually get a lot of questions about "Girl, Interrupted" because the main character had BPD. I might also be fielding a lot of questions about self-injury, because it's something few people talk about (which is why I added it to my elevator speech to begin with, but your mileage may vary). Of course, I also have a bookmark list in my browser of sites that I like and trust that discuss BPD so when they want even more information I can point them in a direction.

The most difficult part about disclosure is knowing and accepting that just because you tell someone about a behavior, symptom or manifestation of your illness, does not justify allowing yourself to sink into your crazy without a fight, saying, "Well, I told you so." If you're feeling out of control of yourself, it still doesn't excuse disruptive, hurtful behavior. The diagnosis explains why you have a certain tendency; it does not give you permission to engage in it without repercussions. You may have problems with depression, but your partners (and friends, and family for that matter) have a right to get angry with you if you lock yourself in your room for weeks without end. By agreeing to enter into a relationship with another human being, you're also making a promise to be the best version of you that you can be as often as you can. It's okay to struggle, to have difficult times, to feel overwhelmed sometimes. What's not okay is engaging in behavior that alarms, threatens, or worries your Top/Master.

Slave in the Pit: Mood Disorders

When Your Bottom Has Major Depressive Disorder
Del Tashlin

(Note: Although the following points can be applied to anyone with Clinical Depression, or Situational Depression, MDD is characterized by repeated depressive episodes with short periods of relief.)

✦ It's not about you. MDD is primarily a biochemical malfunction, and the sufferer tends to be triggered into depressive episodes very easily. Don't make it a personal issue when your bottom is depressed.

✦ Frequently, persons with MDD do not want to be coddled or left alone until they are well. This is a pervasive and persistent illness, and so encouraging them to engage in life (in this instance, kink and sex in particular) is usually welcome. Letting them know that you'll take their emotional state into consideration is useful.

✦ Chronic pain can be a symptom of MDD, as is heightened sensitivity. When depression is at its worst, you may want to play lighter and more sensually than other times. Be aware of where your bottom's pain (both physical and emotional) resides and do what you can to keep from exacerbating it. Remember that kinky sex doesn't have to have pain elements in it all of the time— knife play, sensual play, light bondage, role play, and the like can all take place when someone is suffering from heightened skin sensitivity to great result.

✦ Persons with MDD also crave bigger, louder, more consuming experiences as a coping mechanism to escape depression. Negotiate these catharses heavily; there will be an emotional release, and it may be bigger and messier than you're prepared for.

✦ Many of the commons drug treatments for depression suppress or lower the sex drive. Even if your bottom is feeing non-sexual, it's important to emphasize that you still find them attractive and think about doing sexy things to them. It's a hard line to toe, though, because you also want to make certain that reminders don't turn into pressure to perform. There will be times where your bottom will be completely disinterested in sex or play. This really isn't personal, and taking it personally when it's not makes things much worse for the bottom.

✦ Although some (usually younger) persons with MDD will eventually develop some form of Bipolar Disorder, learn to recognize the difference between mania and being okay. When you're used to someone feeling sad and depressed and lethargic all the time, normalcy may come across like mania, but the two are very different. You may want to read "When Your Bottom Has Bipolar Disorder" to inform yourself about playing with people with mania.

✦ Seek out support for partners of people with depression. It's a difficult road, and knowing that you're not alone is incredibly helpful.

✦ Negotiate, negotiate, negotiate. People with persistent depression tend towards the road of least resistance, which means that something they agreed to a month ago may have been an attempt to placate the Top, and not something they actually enjoy. With reduced tolerances and a reduced ability to initiate conversation that may be uncomfortable, it's useful to have regular "dates" scheduled to discuss your play, where it is, where it's going, what works and what doesn't.

✦ Recent studies are showing that meditation techniques, some of which are easily incorporated into BDSM, can be useful to someone suffering from depression. Simple breathing exercises, systematic muscle relaxing, mindfulness, Tantric breathing, and many other techniques are frequently taught as part of BDSM; seek these out and use them as a part of your play.

When Your Submissive Has Major Depressive Disorder

Del Tashlin

+ Structure is incredibly useful for persons suffering with depression. Setting clear, attainable daily tasks (even if your dynamic is long distance) can do a lot to keep a depressed mood from becoming inability to get out of bed. In the worst times, it may have to be something as simple as "You must go to work four days out of five every week. You must take a shower every other day before 10:30 p.m." Simple, everyday tasks can be easier to tolerate if they're turned into power dynamic chores, rather than just one more thing they have to try to manage on their own. Professional programs force clients to live by strict rules about when they wake up, when they eat, when they shower, etc, and having those things become automated means that they don't have to make any decisions about it.

+ On the flip side of that, though, is patience. When depression is at its worst, things you don't even consider on a daily basis become arduous tasks. Deciding what to wear can feel like a herculean task, which is why so many who suffer from depression wear their pajamas for days on end. Some of these things can be incorporated into your power dynamic, but you also need to be aware that some days your sub will not be able to achieve these tasks. At that point, you should also have a boundary which, when crossed, makes professional intervention mandatory. (If they cannot hold down simple self-care tasks for longer than a week, and they're not in any sort of professional therapy, this is a good start.)

+ Your submissive may fantasize about total power exchanges, where they're no longer responsible for the simplest of decisions in their life. This is almost always counterproductive if they are actively symptomatic and/or not in treatment. You may use this to your advantage, to encourage active participation in therapeutic processes—the more they engage their treatment, the more power you take from them. It can create some odd exchanges, like, "If you meet all of your therapists' requests this week, I will give you one day where all of your decisions will be made by Me."

✦ Find and use non-sexual ways of establishing your power dynamic. Frequently, depression and the meds used to treat it can kill sexual desire. This does not always lessen the submissive's desire to serve. Perhaps just sitting at your feet and being stroked and comforted when things are at their most challenging helps remind them of the power dynamic without bringing sex into it at all.

✦ Make sure you're spending time with people who aren't depressed. There is an energetic field around those suffering from depression that loves to latch onto others. Frequently, long term partners of depressives seek out therapy so they can maintain their grip on their own functionality while assisting their partner.

✦ Make it clear to your sub that suicide threats will always be taken seriously. You are not a professional (unless you are, and then you're under different strictures) and should not try to differentiate between suicidal ideation (talking about suicide as an option) and planning to kill oneself. Once you take a stand, stick to it no matter how difficult it may be. Fifteen percent of patients with MDD will kill themselves, and many of them will show marked signs of their decision, but won't discuss it before it happens. Know the signs of suicidal tendencies and act when you feel uncomfortable, even if it's just calling your submissive's therapist and discussing your feelings with them.

Into and Out of the Black Pit

Raven Kaldera

The Pit and the Depression Pendulum

Many years ago, I let it be known that I was looking for a boy, and Joshua approached me. He was younger than I normally like them—21—and I did worry that he'd be too young, that he wasn't old enough to know what he wanted and to understand what committing to a long-term master-slave relationship would be about. I'd been burned by youngsters before. But he was intelligent, respectful, articulate, and seemed to be exceptionally self-aware and stable. He was also cute, sexy, passionate, sincerely submissive, and incredibly service-oriented, and perfect for me in many other ways. How could I resist? It was like a godsend, after a line of unsuitable boys who didn't last for one reason or another.

We did a trial period of about eleven months, living apart and seeing each other on weekends, and I found long-distance ways in which he could serve me—building my website, doing research, etc. During this time we got to know each other pretty well, and after a great deal of in-depth negotiation, we determined that what we both wanted was a full-on ownership dynamic, no holds barred. He begged to be allowed to come and join me permanently, and I acceded. He moved in, and for the next year things were wonderful. We fit each other in so many ways, I couldn't imagine a better boy. He couldn't imagine a better master.

Then, after about a year and a half, things slowly began to get less wonderful. Joshua began to have mood swings, getting depressed and tired and down a lot more often. Some days it seemed impossible for him to be happy. We'd discuss it, and I'd ask what was bothering him, and what would help ... and he'd think, and come up with something. Sometimes it was an external problem that couldn't be helped, but often it was something not quite right with our process of M/s—he felt that he needed more micromanagement, or more attention, or more rules, or more structure ... and of course, because by that time we loved each other a great deal, and I wanted to help him to do his job happily, I'd try to make those changes.

Sometimes I'd do them even when they weren't what I wanted to do, telling myself that this was just a temporary thing to help him get his head together. Inevitably, though, that would lead to resentment on my part, and I'd rescind the program. And, truth to tell, these changes didn't seem to be helping beyond a few days anyhow. Making sure that he got a lot of sleep helped, but only because sleep deprivation made things dramatically worse.

The months went on, and my formerly stable and reliable boy became more volatile. He still had the occasional good day, but more often he was sullen, or logy, or weepy. Some days he stayed in bed all day crying, and forcing him up only meant that he staggered around the house in a fog, unable to properly do more than the simplest chores. Some days he was so irritable that processing check-ins became long wild-eyed rants about what a bad master I was, and how if I was only a better master this wouldn't be happening. Other days the rants were mostly self-loathing and concentrated on what a bad boy he was. At first I took these all personally, because the whole situation had caught me off guard. One day, though, just before launching into a tirade of how awful he, I, and everything else was, he said, "I think that I'm hysterical, and I'm not sure if what I'm perceiving is true." That made me blink, and knocked me out of my own negative thoughts about how I was failing as a master. What if his thinking was actually distorted, and it wasn't about me at all?

The final turning point came very soon after that. We were going to church choir practice, being driven there by my grown daughter, who was also in the choir and who was aware of our power dynamic. Joshua went off on one of his negative tirades, and after twenty minutes of this, my daughter pulled the car over the side of the road and said to me, "I'm not driving this car any further until you make him stop." She was clear where the power was supposed to lie in our relationship, and why wasn't I using it? Up until then I'd been caught up between anger at his behavior and pity for his condition, but in that moment I realized that he didn't need pity, he needed control that he couldn't seem to pull up himself, and that was my job. I immediately placed him in silence until further notice (allowing him to say absolutely necessary things like "Hello," and "I need my choirbook,"), and it worked. Not only did he shut up, but after the first few minutes of irritation he felt relieved.

At that point, I finally had to concede the point to the Universe: my boy was suffering from mental illness, and it was getting progressively worse by the month. It took one burden off my shoulders—this wasn't about me, or our relationship, or the M/s—but laid another one squarely on them. If Joshua was my property, I was responsible for him. That meant that this problem was mine to handle and make decisions about.

Brokenness and Chemistry

We talked about it, and I found out how devastating it was to him to see himself as broken, defective, crazy. I also discovered, finally, that this was not a new thing. He'd mentioned offhand that he'd had difficult and stressful periods while in college, but he had not made the absolute truth clear: that he had a recurring problem with severe chemical depression, and had been treated for it before, and that it was likely to recur again. His past coping mechanisms had included promiscuous sex, cocaine, and needling his then-boyfriend into violence in order to feel superior to him. (In fact, my ability to remain calm and closed-off when he would needle me or lash out at me was part of what made him respect me enough to become my slave.)

I felt betrayed by the omission of this important information, because without it, I'd suffered through months of fear that the M/s, or our relationship, had caused these problems. This is a warning for submissives with mental illnesses who are looking for a dominant, especially for a full-time live-in position or for ownership: be up front about what you have, and how it should be handled. It's better to have a dominant say, "I'm sorry, I can't handle that," and send you off, than to have them feel betrayed when they inevitably find out. I didn't send Joshua away—I felt that there was too much good in our relationship and I had a deep hope that he could be fixed—but it would have saved me a lot of heartache if I'd really understood beforehand. It's important that the dominant knows what he can expect from the submissive.

Joshua admitted that he'd been so happy in our relationship, in my service, living as my slave, that he'd hoped that the depression would never recur, and so didn't bring it up. In the past it had recurred during times when there was a plethora of extant issues to blame it on—"I'm depressed because my current boyfriend sucks, or because school is so stressful, or because my family has rejected me for being queer, etc." It was when it recurred when his life was, as he said, the best it had ever been, that he was able to realize that it wasn't externally caused at all. "If everything is so great, why am I miserable? Why is everything great one day and terrible the next, when it really hasn't changed?" Chemical illnesses are confusing things, because you think that there ought to be a reason for the way you feel, and you try to find one. Since the world is an imperfect place, it's not hard to find any number of things that are wrong, but blaming them isn't the real truth, and fixing them doesn't fix the problem.

It was also clear that this recurrence was quickly becoming the worst he'd had yet. There were days when the depression was so bad that he lost touch with reality. We tried adjusting his sleep cycle, and eating better and getting exercise, but nothing seemed to stop the terrifying slide into madness. I wanted to send him to a psychiatrist, but we both had fears about that. He'd been put on SSRIs as a teen and had a bad reaction to them, and feared that the shrink would want to try that again. I worried about finding a psychiatrist who wouldn't be horrified about our relationship. How much of his life would Joshua have to hide from the person who was nominally trying to help him?

Part of the reason that I really wanted a shrink who would respect our power dynamic was that I was clear that this, like everything else about Joshua, was my decision to make and my responsibility to make it. I wanted to have absolute access to information in order to do this. I wanted to be there when the shrink described options, not just hear about them secondhand. I wanted to be able to bring up my concerns and have them addressed. I also didn't want Joshua bullied into agreeing to something that I didn't feel was the right choice.

We lucked out, at a friend's suggestion, and found a psychiatrist who was kink-aware, queer-aware, and fine with all the other things that are unusual about us. Of course, the good ones are always booked, and we barely got an appointment, and only because of a friend's plea. But the psychiatrist put him on Wellbutrin, and within days there was a drastic improvement. I read up on the drug and its side effects, which I suggest that any master who is in charge of your slave's health care should do. All such information is online or in the *Physician's Desk Reference*, or comes in flyers with the medication itself. Become familiar with the way that the drug works, and that way you can see side effects when they come.

I should backtrack for a moment at this point, and say that Joshua was completely opposed to the very idea of taking medication. Over and above his negative experience with it in his teens, taking medication reinforced the idea that he was permanently broken and wouldn't be able to fix it without chemical help. He begged me not to make him do it, to help him find some other way. So for about a year we tried every complementary-health-care alternative that I could find. I am really big on alternative medicine myself, as it's one way that I treat my own physical illnesses, so I was willing and hopeful. But after a year of trying everything, we had to admit defeat. Nothing worked well enough to make the difference when the depression got really bad. There were remedies that helped a little, but didn't fix the underlying problem. So, regretfully, I went back to the idea of psychiatric medication for him.

This caused a huge storm of argument. He hated the idea and was absolutely opposed to it. If he had not been a slave in a total-power owner/property relationship to the point where it had become psychologically all but impossible for him to disobey me, he would have walked out at that point. He would probably still be miserable and fighting depression, unless things would have progressed to the point where he would have needed hospitalization and might have been given drugs then. Instead, I forced him to go to the psychiatrist, and then I forced him to take his medication. Every day, I forced him, giving him absolutely no choice, no matter how angry he was at me.

The results showed immediately, and I was even more determined that this had been the right decision. However, for a good year afterward, he still hated taking the drugs, even though he admitted that they made his life better. Every morning when he took his pills, it was a reminder that he had a mental illness. He desperately wanted to quit, even though he knew intellectually that they were needed. He resented it terribly, and probably would have quit several times if I hadn't ordered it. For the first year, my will was what kept him taking them.

I've heard this as a problem from other medicated individuals. On the drugs, you feel better, so eventually you convince yourself that you're all better and you don't need them, and you quit and slide down into being ill again. I became quite experienced at figuring out when he'd forgotten his medication. By noon, he'd be irritable in that slightly paranoid way. If I asked him, "Have you taken your meds?" he'd react badly, but nine times out of ten he'd go check his med-minder and come back sheepishly. "Took them now. Thanks, sir." If I missed that window, by evening he'd be sliding into despair over ... well, nothing. I've heard some detractors claim that antidepressants are all placebos, but if I could pick out whether he'd taken his or not when he didn't even believe me, I can't buy that theory. These days, he's pretty good about it, and is slowly getting used to the idea. It helps him to remind himself that the Crazy is not him. It's something that is happening to him, but it is not who he really is.

No Solution Is Perfect

Neither of us wanted medication to be the first answer to the problem. Joshua still occasionally cherishes the idea that all his problems could be solved with the application of enough structure, rules, and stern management on my part—in other words, that I could force him out of his mood problems. I've learned, though, that this is not possible. You can't beat someone out of chemical illness. You can't micromanage them out of it. Some things are beyond the control of dominants. When he came down with a ruptured appendix, I didn't try to command him to be better or to attempt major abdominal surgery, I took him to the hospital and had the experts in ruptured internal organs fix the problem. Similarly, treating this as a medical problem and not a character flaw is important for the self-esteem of both master and slave. Part of being in charge is figuring out what you can do yourself and what you need to outsource. As long as it gets done, even if not by you, you've done your job.

But even though the meds help 75% of the problem, they are not a total solution. The problem isn't completely solved; it's an ongoing one. First, sleep deprivation for days at a time can still counteract the medication, as can allergies—and he's one of those people who is allergic to a hundred things. It doesn't help that spending the night at the house of a friend who has cats will negate his meds for the next three days. (Hugely stressful situations, such as school finals, funerals, or confrontations with difficult family members might also temporarily cause chemical overrides.) It does mean that I have to keep an eye on his moods, and ask for daily assessments to see that he's back on track. I am now requiring him to log days when he falls back into that dark place, as his medication may need periodic adjusting. But Joshua is my most prized possession, and I want him to run smoothly. It's worth the work. When he's on his game, he's the best boy I've ever had.

In addition to the med glitches, there is also the problem of what Joshua refers to as the "addiction" part of the disorder. Years of swimming in that bad brain soup can set up negative cognitive patterns, and even if the meds are working, sometimes a no-longer-depressed person can fall back into those patterns because they are so familiar and comfortable. (It's hard to believe that misery can become familiar and comfortable, but a person with depression will tell you that it can.) Then the negative thinking overwhelms them—but this kind of trip to the pit can be overcome with mindfulness and coping mechanisms. This is where my job comes in—I ask him to consider whether this particular bad day is a chemical problem (and we look for the obstacle), or a behavioral one (and we run through the list of "things that work"). He's gotten pretty good at figuring that out. At worst, we can run the "things that work" program, and he either gets better or he doesn't.

If I had to give useful information about dealing with a sub who has mental illness, I'd start with this: Don't give the D/s or M/s dynamic too much credit. Don't assume that it made your sub crazy, and don't assume that it will fix the problem, either. If the problem is chemical, then they would have had it no matter what. Separate it, in your mind, from the dynamic, and how well you are or are not "doing it", in your mind. If you want the power dynamic to help, put it to work making sure that the submissive does what is proven to help, and doesn't slack off. Don't assume that you are inept for not being able to stop it, or that they are weak or intractable for not making it go away and cease to inconvenience you. If they could make it go away, they would have done so. Ordering them doesn't help. Brain chemistry laughs at your orders.

What you can do is to train the slave to be self-aware, and aware of their mood levels. They need to learn to be able to usefully and realistically self-assess, so that they can tell you what you have to work with on any given day. You, the one in charge, are going to have to carefully feel around and find out what can be expected of them at any given level. Sometimes they can be pushed through a bad day. Sometimes it will make them collapse. I'm not going to say that it's easy, because it's not. Patience is your number-one resource here. It will be hard. Kinky sex might help, or it might set them off. It might help one day and set them off the next. Endorphins may aid things, or the illness might make the intense sensations and psychological intensity of S/M unbearable. To say the least, it's going to cramp your style. This is not work for just anyone.

Any slave or submissive, but especially a service-oriented one, may have trouble with feeling useless when they're ill, and it may affect their self-esteem. A good message to give them is this: "We are a team. Right now, the primary job of this team is working together to get you through this and into a more stable space. When you're there, you can serve me. Right now your job is to work hard to get better."

The First Big Decision

Should you release them from the power dynamic in order to give them space to heal? That would depend on the depth and intensity of your dynamic, the severity of their illness, and the promises that you have made each other. I know a good friend who had to release her submissive (diagnosed with psychosis) because her sub was no longer in control of herself enough to obey her mistress's commands, or at least not to fight them. When it gets to that point—when the sub loses touch with reality and with self-control to the point where they cannot prevent themselves from disobeying, or can no longer competently manage the emotional complexities of a relationship—it might be best to let them out of the collar.

Other considerations might include whether there was originally a strong egalitarian relationship to fall back on. If you both started out that way, sometimes it's feasible to backtrack. On the other hand, relationships that were M/s from the start may not survive a transition to egalitarianism. In addition, sometimes the slave may feel that they need the "mastery experience" of handling their life and their illness themselves, and that backing off on the power dynamic will be beneficial for those reasons. Some couples restart the power dynamic later when the slave can come to it without the depression issues, although this doesn't always happen because Life doesn't promise perfection.

If the illness includes paranoia of any sort, please keep in mind that as the center of your slave's life, you will be the main focus of that paranoia. Regular reality checks are in order. That's another reason to be involved with their therapy, especially if there is talk therapy. If you're there regularly as a caring, thoughtful, self-controlled individual who is clearly not abusing them, and who is interested in their treatment and committed to helping them get better, when they launch into paranoid rantings about you whilst alone with the shrink, the shrink is more likely to say, "That doesn't sound like your partner. Are you sure about that?" than to assume that you are the Bad Guy.

I think that there also has to be an out for dominants who simply can't cope with a slave with serious mental illness, and that out has to be blameless. If you can no longer deal with running herd on this person's illness, if it's gone on too long without improvement and you're just Done, you have to be able to step back from it. This is especially true if the situation is now affecting your own mental health. If the stress is getting to you, you won't be able to properly hold down the top side of a power dynamic anyway (which requires self-control, stability, and confidence), and you'll be the opposite of helpful to them. Better that you release them and step back before the illness takes down two people. It's a matter of knowing and admitting your limits. You can't do everything. Sometimes life gives you more than you can handle, and the correct response is to say, "I can't handle this." Besides, masters also have the right to say No, and it has to be all right for them to do that. Consent works both ways.

If the slave starts to become physically abusive to the master—and this does happen, especially with slaves that are physically larger and whose mental illness has gotten out of control—the master needs to keep themselves safe. If the slave becomes violent, or threatens the master's job or family or safety, consider it an emergency situation. Call their shrink if they have one. Call friends to come over and be a buffer. If they are live-in, get them a motel room until things can be worked out, or get yourself one. We know of more than one couple for whom this happened, and in some cases the shame of the master over not being able to control their slave kept them from getting help for far longer than necessary. We also know of communities who are disparaging about "masters who can't control their slaves", and simply have contempt for the master in this situation. We prefer not to associate with such communities, and we suggest the same for you.

If a Master/slave couples does break up for these reasons, it should go without saying that the master will at least make sure that the slave has their basic survival taken care of—shelter, medical care, income if only disability and food stamps. If the slave is so far gone that they refuse this help, then nothing can be done, but even then the master might call some mutual friends and quietly set up a support network to check on and help the slave.

The Second Big Decision

If you've decided to stay together, then the next question is whether you as the master want to take full responsibility for your slave's medical issues. Some masters may not want to take that on, because they feel that it is "above their pay grade", as it were. Some slaves would rather keep responsibility for that, because it helps their self-esteem to know that they are managing their own problems. However, even if you are not managing your slave's medical decisions, you need to be kept in the loop. Telling your slave to "handle it", and then ducking your head and ignoring the problem is not going to help. At the very least, you need to be informed of their decisions and why they made them, and kept up to date on the situation. You certainly need to get them to give you regular assessments (see the list below), because it will affect how you manage them from day to day. You also need to discuss with them the possibility that they may make wrong decisions and/or let things slide in a way that negatively affects your lives, and what is it acceptable for you to do then?

If you do decide to take on their medical issues and make the decisions, stick to that decision. Decide that you have the right to do it, and do it. Don't waver in your conviction. When they are emotionally deregulated, they may try to make you waver. Don't fall for it. But if you take this on, take it on all the way. They will be depending on you; don't let them down. On the other hand, don't get caught up in "I can save them." M/s didn't cause this, and it won't fix it either. It can *help*, but you have to be realistic about that. You are trying to manage them, not save them.

Our reasons for staying together, and for letting me handle his medical issues:

+ Joshua and I have made promises to each other, and I would not abandon him unless I had tried everything and it was the end of the road, and he was beyond the point where I could have a useful effect on him. We are both strongly religious, and we feel that our religion affects our commitment. (If this is present, it can be a comfort for both people.) We are also both, to paraphrase John Adams, "commitments over feelings" people rather than "feelings over commitments" people, and it would have damaged our respective sense of self to abandon ship before everything had been tried.

✦ I'm possessive—he's *my* thing, and I don't like to let go of my things, even when they break. I'd rather fix them and keep them on.

✦ We had no egalitarian relationship to fall back on anyway, and we knew that we wouldn't work out well as egalitarian partners. The M/s relationship was very fulfilling for both of us. It rivaled our sex life as the top two best things about being together. Giving it up would have meant breaking up.

✦ Besides, we honestly figured that I couldn't do worse for Joshua than his previous coping mechanisms! Our deal is that since he agreed to turn all control of his medical issues over to me when he was in a sane state of mind, he couldn't take it back when he was in a crazy space. Sane Josh acknowledged that this was a good idea; Crazy Josh doesn't get a vote. We both agree that things are safest that way.

Things That Worked for Us

We're adding the "for us" part to the long list that we generally just refer to as "things that work", meaning tool and techniques that have helped even a little in this team struggle, because nothing works for everyone. They are very good for pulling Joshua entirely out of the "addictive" part of depression, and even when his chemistry is haywire they can help a little. At the very least, they keep him from self-neglect. We aren't trying to go from 2 to 10 on a bad day, we're trying to make it to 3 or 4, because even small moves are better than nothing. We recommend trying everything and then some, and making your own list of "things that work", which the master then imposes on the slave. A good suggestion might be to have the five best "things that work" as your first go-tos; we recommend that at least one of them be something where they don't have to be emotionally engaged in order to manage but can just do it (like taking a walk), or that has clear secondary benefits (like exercise). This is where having a master can really be a blessing; it can make the difference in motivation to the slave who is not quite able to pull themselves out of bed on their own. Having a force to push you into taking care of yourself can be a great help.

+ **Learn All About It.** This is especially important for the master, and it's part of taking responsibility for a depressed slave. Read everything you can find on depression. Learn to understand which sort your slave has—Dopamine? Serotonin? Hormonal? Thyroid? Share the information with your slave, including personal accounts that will make them feel less alone. As the master, it might be useful to you to read literature for parents of depressed children; this is not because the slave is equivalent to a child, but because you have something in common with people who have full responsibility for depressed human beings, whatever their age. Besides, they may have good tips you haven't thought of.

+ **Assessments.** No dominant can do anything useful for their s-type if they are not receiving clear and thorough information. The s-type needs to be on board with giving an assessment of their day-to-day functioning, on demand. Train them to do this, if they don't come to it naturally. Joshua made a little chart called the "Josh Suck-O-Meter", with numbered phrases from zero to ten. Ten was wonderful and zero was the Black Pit, but in between were levels labeled "Pissy Bitch", "Brain fog", "Walking dead, but hey, I'm walking", "Merely dragging my lifeless corpse about", and so on. Encourage your s-type to think about and delineate the different stages of sliding up and down into the Black Pit. Joshua's Suck-O-Meter was hung on the fridge, and it had a little magnet that he could move up and down as things changed throughout the day. It was also a shared language for understanding what he was capable of at any given time, as we discussed each level and what could reasonably be expected of him when he was there. Once you get this put together, ask for assessments daily. Hourly, if it's a bad or highly fluctuating day.

+ **Assessments Only Work If They're Honest.** Joshua had to learn that it didn't help to pretend that he was Super

Slave in order to disguise how bad off he really was. On the other end of the spectrum, the slave can't be thinking, "If I pretend to be worse than I am, maybe she'll let me stay in bed." Every time a slave gives their master less than truthful or complete information about something this important, they are sabotaging their master's job of managing them, and betraying the foundation of their agreement.

✦ **Assessments Only Work If They're Accurate.** Of course, the slave may not always be able, through the fog of bad brain soup, to assess themselves accurately. It's especially hard to notice when one is sliding down into the pit, so the slave may need to depend on the master's (and other trusted people's) observations. An overreaction to the observation—"Uh, you're kind of being a bitch." "No, I'm not, fuck you!"—may be an indication in and of itself. One of our rules is that Joshua is not to argue about whether he is being bitchy. Arguing about it has been an early-warning sign of deregulation so many times that we both agree he should just shut up and accept it.

✦ **Statements of Truth.** On a good day, the slave should come up with a half-dozen or so affirmations that they can completely get behind. Examples might be: "I'd rather be useful. I'd rather be working." "I have the best master in the whole world." "I'm the luckiest slave in the whole world." "I chose this life for a good reason. That reason hasn't changed." "This is an illness, not a character flaw. The character flaw is giving up." "I believe that I am loved and valued." "Serving makes me happy." Say them every day, but not because it's some kind of New Agey feel-good trick. This is a tool of assessment for your mental state. Notice whether, when they are said aloud, you still really feel like they are true for you. If they don't feel so true, that may be a sign that you are starting a slide down into the Black Pit.

✦ **Actual Affirmations.** The New Agey feel-good trick also works for some people, sometimes. A good one for the slave is "I am not my emotions. This is not me. This is not who I really am." A good one for the master to give to the slave is "I love you, even if you're broken. You are still valuable to me." I encourage Joshua to come to me when he needs a head-pat or a reminder of how much he is valued, in spite of everything.

✦ **Fake it 'Till You Feel it Can Actually Work, Sometimes**. Acting as if you are not depressed can make you feel a little better. At the very least, even a slave who is deep in the pit can be made to get out of bed, shower and take care of personal hygiene, put on clean clothing, and eat healthy food. If that is all they can manage, fine, but at least make them do that. Joshua and I joked about his membership in what he (and a depressed friend) call the "Whiny Sack Of Shit Club", whose club uniform was either a bathrobe and sweat pants, or whatever you were wearing yesterday. Getting him out of the WSOSC uniform and into the one I mandated for him, every day, helped that little bit.

✦ **Sleep.** Whatever's wrong with you, sleep deprivation makes it worse. However, depression can also cause oversleeping. Try to make sure they get enough sleep, but not too much; a sleeping schedule may help. Remember that depression can push someone out of touch with bodily signals, including the need for sleep and food, and the master may have to be that "voice" for them.

✦ **Body Language.** Changing the posture of the body makes minute chemical changes in the brain. Making him stand up straight, put his shoulders back, breathe, and smile even if he didn't feel like it actually helped another tiny bit. This sounds silly, but don't put it down as a useful tool. Keep reminding them—they'll want to go back into the tense slump, but don't let them. Sulking posture is not allowed.

✦ **Useful Work.** If they can do some useful service, even in their bad state, it can help keep from falling into self-loathing. Even little things that please you can help. If you have a wide range of tasks ready, you can pick one for their ability level on any given day. Also, specific tasks can be part of the "fake it till you feel it"; e.g "What would I be doing if I wasn't depressed? Can I do that anyway? See, things can't be that bad, I'm making cookies! Depressed people don't make cookies!"

+ **Restrict Negative Input.** Avoid media that makes the slave wallow, like violent movies or sad songs. Instead, watch positive things (even if it makes the master want to puke) and listen to good music. This is another place where control can be useful—the master can restrict or require access to stimulation, and thus shape their immediate environment to help with their stress levels. The master may also need to restrict them from contact with negative, stressful, unnecessary people—"You can't talk to your fucked-up ex right now." "I'll screen any emails from your abusive relative and tell you if there's anything in there that you absolutely need to know." "You can't read that person's blog because it upsets you and you're in a bad state for hours." Instead, do positive things together. If an activity starts being negative, don't fret, just do something else. Do "fun" things only if you enjoy them, or if they are proven to work.

+ **Beepers.** We've found that using a repeating alarm for Joshua, set to go off every ten minutes, helps during a bad day. When it goes off, he's supposed to check that he isn't obsessing about something negative, and if he is, stop and redirect himself. Joshua has a pocket-sized timer for this, but many phones can be set up for this.

+ **Sex.** Make time for it. Good sex changes brain chemistry and can help a mood. It's one of the top five mood-enhancers for Joshua, although when he's in a bad way, he doesn't believe it will help. We have sex anyway, and it almost always does. However, slaves whose sex drive is more emotional than purely physical may not find that this helps as much. The same goes for SM—for some slaves, the endorphins really help depression, at least for a few hours. Others don't find that it helps. If you're into it, experiment.

+ **Body Contact.** Even if sex is off the table, physical contact can be a comfort to a depressed slave. It can be vanilla-style cuddling, or sitting on the floor leaning against the master's knee. It can be a caress or a firm grip in the hair while their head is held to their master's shoulder. But it helps. I've trained Joshua to come ask for it when he needs it. It's good for me too, and good for our bonding, so I'm almost never unwilling to grant that.

✦ **Exercise.** Whether they like it or not. Exercise also creates positive chemical changes in the brain. Even disabled s-types can do something to move their bodies. Exercise also helps to stretch and release the tense or limp muscles associated with depression.

✦ **Daylight.** Even a nocturnal slave with depression should be made to go outside in daylight at least once a day, perhaps for a short walk. Every day. Really.

✦ **Healthy Food.** A period of depression is not the time to be forced onto radical or restricted diets, but no slave will die from being restricted from junk food and forced to eat healthy meals on a regular basis. Limit caffeine, alcohol, sugar, and other "mood food"—they are too volatile to use as drugs, and have bad "drops" after usage. Food allergies can worsen mood disorders; an elimination diet can help find out what their body doesn't want. (Since an elimination diet may seem to go against the "no radical or restricted diet changes", you might want to do this when they are feeling better.)

✦ **Shut Off Negative Talk.** A mantra can help here, or just a constant discipline of the slave having to step on the ugly voice in the head. If it's coming out the mouth, the master can shut it down; if it's happening inside the slave's head, the slave can say a preplanned phrase to shut it down, or come to the master and say, "Please tell me to shut up the negative voice in my head that is telling me paranoid things!" Sometimes the master's firm command helps here, even with an internal problem.

✦ **No One Is Allowed to Beat You Up But Me, And That Includes You.** In the same vein, self-loathing talk gets stepped on. One of the best tools I ever got from another master was: "Tell me three good things about yourself. Right now." Make them say it in a positive, or at least a neutral, tone. They can be small and inconsequential, so long as they are sincere. You can follow this up with

"Now tell me three good things about me," or "Tell me three good things about your life." To add to this, point out when things go right. Remind them that life isn't all bad. It may not help much in the moment, but it will help when they are asked to "count their blessings" out loud in this way.

✦ **Silence.** Joshua had the kind of depression that took him through an "irritable" phase before landing him in the black pit, and this sometimes meant I had a slave who could not control his verbal outbursts. Placing him in silence, except for brief and absolutely necessary information-giving on his part and the acknowledging "Yes, sir," to orders, was a relief to him. It provided the self-control he couldn't provide for himself. It was difficult for me to do, partly because it felt unfair, and partly because of my background in polyamory counseling where one wants to get everything out as soon as possible. However counterintuitive it may have seemed, though, it worked well and made him feel better.

✦ **Verbal Protocols.** Even when he is not placed in silence, I help shore up his trouble with verbal self-control during deregulated periods by having specific respectful ways in which he can express himself. This helps to keep him from outbursts he will later feel bad about. Remember that restricting behavior and modes of communication is not the same as restricting transparency. You still want to get all that information that is in their head. You are just giving them a framework of doing it that provides a replacement for their temporarily absent sense of discernment and self-control. For example: "You have to answer any question I ask honestly. But you will say it in this way, respectfully *(define that usefully)*, without acting out *(define that too)*. This is how you will volunteer unasked-for information. This is the standard you will run it by before you open your mouth." (The "Is it true? Is it useful? Is it kind?" standard was useful for Joshua.) Remember that even if a particular irritable or depressed behavior doesn't bother you all that much, it may be corrosive to them and their sense of submission, and it may be better for them to make them do it.

✦ **No Relationship Negotiations Under the Influence.**
This was one of the best rules I ever made. At some point
I realized that all discussions about how the relationship
ought to go—and, for that matter, about any major
subject that needed addressing—turned into irrational
arguments when my slaveboy was emotionally
deregulated. So I made a rule that all such processing
had to be put off until he was feeling saner (at which
point he often wondered what the big deal had been,
anyway). While this, too, may seem counterintuitive to
the "talk about it immediately" rule that works in most
relationships, I finally ended up seeing it as similar to
having relationship discussions while drunk or tripping.
If one person is not in their right mind, it's not going to
work. Important issues need to be dealt with "sober".
I've learned to say, "Nothing good can come of talking
about this now. The subject is closed until later." The
catch is, of course, that as soon as he is better I am
obligated to have that discussion, in order to maintain
trust.

✦ **Know Where You Can Take Them.** Don't put a
deregulated slave into a high-pressure public situation
that they are not going to be able to handle at the time.
On the other hand, do take them out for low-stress forays
away from the same wallpaper every day.

✦ **Protect Yourself Emotionally.** When your slave is
having a really bad day, they may not be able to handle
emotional intimacy with you. They may also say hurtful
things that are more about their brain chemistry than the
truth they might express on a saner day. Learn not to
take it personally. Remind yourself that it is Crazy
talking, not your slave and partner. If you have to get
some emotional distance from them and put up some
walls during that time in order to help them, that's all
right. I don't like it when I have to do that, but I consider
it more like getting your own emergency oxygen mask
on before you can help the next person with theirs. If I
am busy being hurt and wounded, I can't help them or
myself. Also, have a support system for yourself, if
possible. It's good to have at least one person to talk to

about all this, both for a reality check for the negative things your slave might say, and emotional support when your slave is not in a place to give you that. You might also want to talk about handling a depressed person with a mental health professional who is not their shrink. (Oh, and be patient, breathe, and get out in the sun daily yourself.)

✦ **Caretaking as Service.** On the other hand, some depressed slaves are helped by focusing on their master's needs and taking care of them. It can be a welcome distraction, and one that makes the most important person in their life happier. If you've got this kind, let them give you emotional support in simple, meaningful ways that don't ask for their advice. This is especially good if, again, it involves physical touch.

✦ **Mental Health Professionals.** This is a tricky area. If you're going to choose your slave's shrink, get references from friends. Check out kink-aware professionals (although at the moment there is a terrible dearth of them in many areas, and being kink-aware doesn't necessarily mean M/s aware). If you can't find a M/s-friendly therapist, both master and slave should show the master as a supportive partner who wants their partner to get better, and will do what it takes to get there. Attend the occasional session, with permission from both the therapist and your slave. You can get your slave to sign a HIPPA form that enables the therapist to talk to you about anything that is discussed. Therapists like it when you as the partner, "help" (read: *order*, but they don't have to know that) your partner to maintain whatever therapeutic protocol they prescribe. Learn the side effects of medications, including the sexual side effects. If sex is a serious part of your relationship and a medication suppresses that, it's OK to ask to try something different. A therapist who will not accept the two of your prioritizing your sex life, especially if sex is high on the "things that work" list, is not the one for you. The two of you might want to keep "therapist-safe" journals, your slave on how the meds and/or therapeutic protocols are working, the master for how you observe them to be working or not. It's also OK to look for another therapist if the first one doesn't work out; there are plenty of them out there.

✦ **One Day at a Time.** Encourage your slave not to obsess about the future. That's your job. Help them to get through today, and then tomorrow. If a therapist asks them about a "five-year plan", which is a tool to get possibly suicidal patients OK with imagining a future, the slave can say, "Home with my partner. I know I'll be doing that at least." Because you've told them so.

✦ **Enough With the Pessimism.** Understand that any one of these may work one day, and not work the next. The problem is that depressed people stop believing in something's efficacy after one failure. It is the job of the master to realistically assess whether something works at least part of the time, and keep reminding them of that— and keep making them do it. If the master is seeing improvement, tell them, even if they don't believe it. This flexibility is a good attitude to have with regard to making protocols to contain the chaos of depression, such as ones we've suggested above. Go into them with an experimental mindset, but be willing to alter or discard them if they don't work. Remember that this is a work in progress. Roll with the punches and keep fine-tuning it.

✦ **Risk Assessment.** This is a master's job every day of the relationship anyway, but it's especially precarious with a "broken toy". The hardest part will be knowing how hard to push them on any given day. On day one, pushing them through it works; on day two what looks like the same situation will make them crumble when pushed. This takes time and practice. You will make mistakes. So long as you are loving as well as firm, there's no excuse not to keep trying. Of course, you may want to die when you push too hard and they crumble. Figure out how to mop them up first, just in case. Apologize, then move on. They will think you are the worst master in the world at that moment. Don't let it throw you. The next time, you can err on the side of backing off, but don't let that go on for more than a week.

While it's still in recent memory, push again, gently. One can't master the skill if one can't practice it. Keep demanding those honest status reports! You can't do this without maximum information. That's why transparency is necessary.

✦ **Suicide and Self-Harm.** Knowing that your body is not your own to harm or destroy, and that your life is not your own to take, can be very useful in preventing self-harm and suicide. We both felt better with an agreement of "I will decide whether you live or die. You don't get to die unless I've decided it's for the best, and I will be very difficult to convince of that." (Though not impossible—Joshua needed to know that I would actually consider it under very extreme circumstances if his quality of life was gone and it was absolutely clear that nothing could be done.) The elimination of self-harm as a personal choice, and of suicide as an easy option, can be powerful for both master and slave as a visceral affirmation of ownership, as well as being a safety issue. It's also something that therapists generally approve of—"I promised my partner that I won't do this, and that's effective in stopping me." I would also add a very controversial point: Don't be afraid to force a deregulated slave to do what they have to do, especially when we're talking about self-harm behavior. Consent becomes a very slippery issue when your slave is screaming and holding a knife to themselves. I'd rather not let them make that choice in that moment, personally, but that's my decision and it may not be yours.

We're lucky—we've managed to stabilize the situation. Some people I know aren't so lucky, because modern mental health techniques cannot help everyone. I'd also caution submissives with mental problems who are looking for a dominant: Having a dominant, or a D/s relationship, will not make your mental health problems go away. If you have any illusions about it fixing you, stomp on them now. In fact, in such a psychologically intimate, heavily scrutinized, and cathartically intense relationship will probably bring everything right up into the open and onto the table, right quick. It's best to get what help you can first, so that you can come to a new dominant with those pages of your Owner's Manual filled in with plain English. They can't take charge of you without that information, and you owe it to them if this is what you want.

Managing Strong Emotions
pais

This is a companion essay to my piece on working with a slave who is dealing with PTSD, but the information in this essay is intended to be useful to anybody struggling with unwanted thoughts, behaviors, or emotions.

Thoughts, emotions, physical sensations, and behavior are interconnected. They can be mutually reinforcing: feel lousy, spend all day in bed, think "I'm so worthless; I can't even get out of bed." Lather, rinse, repeat. And, when you're already upset, it's much easier to look for things that are going to keep you feeling upset.

Alternatively, if you are able to change thoughts, physical sensations, or behaviors, it can lead to cascading changes. That is, if you change what you're thinking it will lead to different behavior and emotions; if you change your behavior it can lead to different emotions and thoughts. Relaxing your body and slowing your heart down will send messages to your brain to stop pumping out adrenaline. Emotions in and of themselves can be difficult or impossible to change—most people cannot simply will themselves to feel happy. So managing emotions is largely a matter of managing what you think and what you do.

The first step is to take basic care of yourself. Owners, make sure your property is getting enough sleep and exercise and eating healthy foods. I recommend reducing or eliminating illicit substances and limiting alcohol and even cigarettes and caffeine. (However, if these are your primary coping techniques, you probably want to have a plan ready for other coping strategies! Long-term reducing these types of substances is key; in the short term of course it can make things more difficult. I am absolutely including marijuana in the list of substances to avoid if there are underlying emotional problems. Research shows that marijuana use, for example, is linked with more rapid and more frequent mood cycles for individuals with bipolar disorder.) If necessary, seek professional medical help. Get a physical check-up and visit the dentist. Manage any pain issues.

The second step is to be aware of what you want to change. Journaling or logging emotional responses is a good way to notice patterns that may be keeping you from getting what you want out of life. Some people have a hard time noticing or identifying emotions; it might be easier in those cases to keep a journal of a problem situations (talking back, zoning out, intrusive thoughts, etc.) and then try to reconstruct what the emotion was that led to the acting out. Again, emotions are often fueled by behaviors and thoughts. Is there a particular chore or task that tends to lead to more challenges? Do you find yourself experiencing intrusive or negative thoughts that drag you down emotionally?

This process is also helpful when it feels like the problem emotion or behavior comes out of nowhere with no warning, · and goes from zero to sixty immediately. Once it's full-blown, it's much harder to get a grip on it. With practice, the warning signs can become more obvious, and the time between when you first notice the warning signs and when the problem is out of control becomes longer. The longer that time is, the more chance you have of changing the thoughts and behaviors that feed into the problem emotion, getting a handle on the emotion, and preventing any negative behaviors that tend to arise from the emotion.

Journaling is also used to get a handle on patterns of thinking. If you can identify a particular type of thought that tends to lead to spiraling emotional and behavioral problems, logging every time you think it is a good idea. These types of thoughts are usually black-and-white, all-or-nothing types of thoughts about "who I am", "how the world is" or "how people are": "I'm totally worthless." "Life sucks" (with the understood "always".) "Everyone is out to get me."

This is a place where owners can be very helpful. Assigning the journal; specifying a problem behavior or emotion on which to focus; noticing episodes that should be logged and reminding the s-type to do it; identifying patterns—there are many ways the owner can be part of the process. Journaling can be helpful when it's once a day, going back over the day and trying to remember events to journal, but might be even more helpful if you journal as soon as you are able to notice the emotion or behavior so that your answers are more fresh in your mind.

For most people, the quicker and easier it is to do, the more likely it's a habit that will take hold and be successful. So just a quick note of the thought, emotion or behavior might be best. Once the habit is in place, or from the get-go if it seems more productive to include more information, some factors that might be useful to include in a log entry, depending on what you think will be helpful for you, might be:

+ What time of day did this occur?

+ What was the setting?

+ What previous factors were in place—tired, hungry, upset about something else going on?

+ Any identifiable trigger event?

+ What thoughts were noticeable before/at the beginning of the episode?

+ What emotions were noticeable? How intense were they?

+ What were your behavioral urges? What did you want to do about the thoughts and emotions?

+ What did you do? How did you react?

+ Was this reaction useful/helpful, or did it lead to further issues?

+ If there were benefits to this reaction, but overall or in the long run this reaction is unwanted, what were the benefits, and how can you get them in some other way?

That last point is actually quite important and fairly complicated. Very, very often behaviors/thoughts/emotions that we find primarily unpleasant or counter-productive actually provide us with some rewards we may not always have full awareness of. Attention, either positive or negative, is a common one. One classic common scenario is the slave who acts up because getting spanked is fun! The coping strategies that we use may be tangible; perhaps when you find yourself feeling/acting/thinking in a certain way, you have a cigarette or binge-eat, or perhaps when things get out of hand you get a break from doing your chores. This might be the hardest part of changing a behavior: figuring out what the reward is and eliminating it. Eliminating it. Not most of the time, but all of the time, because for most people bad habits are hard to break and easy to slip back into—and intermittently rewarding bad behavior makes it all the easier to slip back into, and all the harder to stop because you never know when that reward might be coming!

Which means you need to have other responses ready to cope with those behaviors/thoughts/emotions, because those ways we have of coping and feeling better that are harmful in the long run, are also currently working. They are providing some results that are perceived on some level as pleasant, desirable, perhaps even necessary. So eliminating those benefits is probably not the first thing you want to do. Work on building up other coping strategies first, as follows.

You might discover a self-reinforcing, many-step pattern of emotions, thoughts, and behaviors building on each other, perhaps with no clear "beginning" of the pattern. However, there might be a place where it looks easiest to break the pattern, or it might be a simple one-two-three chain of thought leading to emotion leading to behavior. In any case, whether it's obvious what needs to change, or whether you simply have to pick a place to try to intervene, either without the journaling process or as a result of it, then you can identify options for dealing with it, choose what options to try, and practice those options for some period of time. Generally, I would give any coping technique at least two weeks of regular practice, preferably at least once a day, before deciding that it's not working. The way you respond to emotions now is like a habit, and habits take time to change. Re-evaluate what's working and what's not, and keep trying.

Here is a list of some general coping strategies. Most of them work well with a variety of different emotions such as anxiety, anger, panic, and depression, but no coping strategy is going to work for every single person or in every situation. Again, owners can help by helping s-types identify which techniques might be most useful and monitoring how it's going, as well as supporting, encouraging, and reminding the s-type to use techniques. It can be useful at this point to add to the log whether and what coping technique was tried, and how successful it was. Practicing them in lower-intensity situations first can lead to better results with more intense situations later. Once you have learned which techniques are more effective for you and you can use them with confidence, you might find that your emotional responses seem more manageable even before you use the technique, just because you know you have tools in your toolbox.

+ **Journal.** Yes, even just noticing and writing down the emotion can help take the edge off. (Furthermore, for many people, noticing how frequently you behave a certain way or think a certain thought automatically causes that behavior or thought to decrease.)

+ **Ground yourself.** Get fully present in the moment and in your physical body. Breathe deliberately and notice your breathing. Push your feet down into the floor or your rear end down into your chair or both. Use all of your senses—eat a bite of something strong like a mint or lemon drop; splash cold water on your face; pull a blanket around your shoulders and pull down so it puts pressure on your shoulders; use a pleasantly scented hand lotion; look at or imagine something that makes you feel better; listen intently to whatever you can hear or put music on. Pay full attention to whatever you're doing and how you're doing it, and be careful to watch from inside your body. Avoid imagining that you're watching yourself from above or outside. Stay focused on physical sensations. This is useful for anger and also especially for anxiety, panic, and dissociating.

+ **When you're in a good space, notice the little things that make you happy**—maybe put a list of them in your journal—and then turn to those things and be kind to yourself when you're having a rough time. This is a technique that can take a little moderation, and again an owner can be helpful here. Allowing or reminding the slave to have a piece of chocolate while providing gentle or firm support to avoid the entire chocolate cake, for example, can be helpful. Not only things that feel good, but activities that help you feel good about yourself, are key here. Notice the things that you're good at and enjoy, and spend some time doing that.

✦ **Think replacement thoughts.** Often people teach "thought-stopping" or "pushing the thought away/putting it in a box". Those techniques work too, but personally I prefer having a list of several positive thoughts prepared. When a negative thought or emotion starts, just start running through your list of replacement thoughts, or pick one that resonates and repeat that to yourself. It doesn't leave room for the non-helpful thought and you're reinforcing the positive thought, even if in the moment it doesn't feel that convincing. Positive thoughts might be "I will get through this," "I'm in control of myself," "I can handle this situation." They might be "I've survived worse than this" or "Things can only get better from here." The Serenity Prayer, the mantra "What doesn't kill me makes me stronger", or other prayers or mantras can work (perhaps one assigned by your M-type). A happy memory can help, especially if you are able to visualize it in detail, or even an imaginary scenario of a peaceful, calm, safe place. Even single, positive words, such as "peace" or "serenity", repeated on in-breaths and/or out-breaths, can make a huge difference. Sometimes, particularly if the problem is anger, it can be motivating to think about what you stand to lose if you're not able to change the behavior or emotion, but I would use that technique with caution so as not to spiral into shame, guilt, or self-blame.

✦ **Distract yourself.** Get busy with an activity you enjoy, physical exercise, or helping somebody else by volunteering. Count ceiling tiles or everything you can see that is blue. Ask your M-type for instructions or chores to do!

✦ **Wait through it.** Emotions are complicated and involve both physical body reactions and chemical changes in the brain. Our brains can be conditioned to think that once an emotion begins—sometimes before we're even aware of it—the inevitable outcome is going to be a full-scale panic attack, angry outburst, or what have you. The goal here is to teach your body that if you can just sit and observe what's going on, the emotion will wax and wane all on its own. Your body just can't sustain an emotion at full peak for that long unless it's being reinforced by other stimuli. So find a safe place to wait it out. Notice any changes going on in your body without catastrophizing them—"I'm breathing faster. Luckily, it is not likely that I will die from hyperventilating because I would pass out first and then I will stop panicking and my breath will slow down automatically. My heart seems to be speeding up. I know that I am not having a heart attack because I have had panic attacks before and survived them. Let me see if my observation is correct by taking my pulse for two minutes and seeing if the second minute is in fact faster than the first minute." Eventually, the brain can be reconditioned to notice those first warning signs not as a harbinger of doom but as the start of a time-limited process that will pass. This technique may take a long time at first, but the goal is for it to take less time with practice.

✦ **Deepen your spirituality**, whatever that means to you. Pray. Nurture your connection to nature or the universe or a higher power. Find a place to volunteer for a humanitarian or environmental cause.

✦ **Do the opposite of what you have an urge to do.** This can be very challenging and in the short (or even medium) term increase the unpleasant emotions, but it is a proven long-term strategy, particularly for anxiety and depression. If you're depressed or anxious and you want to stay in your bed or your house, get out and do things to the full extent that you can. Challenge yourself to interact with others and socialize. If you're angry and you feel like taking on the world—or one person in particular—stay away from any potential conflicts. Take some time for yourself. If you feel guilty or ashamed, determine what is leading to those feelings, and if it's objectively a reasonable thing to be doing, keep doing it!

✦ **Process the underlying problem.** For me, I find it more useful to ask, "Why am I having this pattern of problems?" rather than "Why do I feel so lousy today?"

It's always possible to find a reason why I feel lousy today. Then I have something negative to dwell on and think about to reinforce the emotion, and it's almost always somebody else's fault, so there's nothing I can do except maybe try to give the other person a guilt trip or start a fight. Those are not effective ways for me to change the emotion. But if there's a long-term pattern, then I can say, "Every week when we have social plans over the weekend I end up having a meltdown on Monday or Tuesday. I think I may have a need for more personal time with my M-type. What can I change, or ask Master to change, so that need can be met? If that need cannot be met, how can I manage the emotions that I know are going to come up?"

✦ **Keep journaling.** Notice which patterns are changing and which are not. Make changes in your coping strategies accordingly.

A few more pieces of advice for owners: reward your slave tons for trying any coping skill that you've agreed might be helpful, even if it doesn't seem to be working. Find out from your slave what is rewarding for him or her—and keep asking, in case your slave starts getting burned out on any particular reward. In fact, having several options of rewards so the slave doesn't know what reward might be coming next can be a useful technique. (Unpredictable rewards, like slot machines, can be addictive!) Reward for your slave for journaling. Reward your slave for noticing, "Hey, I might need to use a coping skill now." Reward, reward, reward. Over time, as your slave gains skills, you can stop rewarding for the more basic steps (such as noticing it would be a good time to use a coping skill) and only reward for more advanced behaviors (actually using the coping skill, or using the coping skill with success). Minimize punishment, which can quickly decrease the unwanted thought or behavior but which is likely to cause new problems since the underlying causes or patterns aren't being adjusted and no new coping skills are being learned— and remember that the punishment in some cases might actually be a reward, if your slave simply needs more attention and interaction!

It Can Only Get Better: An Interview with John and Dan

Note: John and Dan, like many of the other couples in this book, graciously agreed to be interviewed for its pages. John is the master and Dan is the slave in this relationship.

Dan:

I'm closing on thirty, and gay. How did I become the slave in this relationship? It was a long process of waiting out John's hesitance until he finally claimed me. We started out as best friends. I had a huge crush on him, but he was only into girls at that point, so it was hopeless! I had a big list of all the qualities I wanted in a master, and I tried to find them elsewhere but it didn't work, and after some years I just decided, "My best friend actually has all these qualities, and I can't seem to find anyone better than him, so I'll just wait. I don't care, I give up." I had a six-month period of celibacy, where I thought to myself, "I'll just serve my best friend. He doesn't even need to know about it, but I'll just dedicate my life to being a really good best friend to him."

So we were best friends and roommates for about five years until he finally came out as bisexual, and I said, "Hooray! Now you like boys! You should be my Daddy!" and he accepted. Well, actually it was a little more complicated than that; there was a lot of pleading involved. I waited two whole weeks before asking, and it seemed like a really long time to me. But he came around eventually.

It was his first power exchange relationship, but I had previously been involved with some power exchange relationships that didn't work out. Nearly all of my relationships have been power dynamics, except for one egalitarian relationship with a girl very early on, which didn't work out because it was egalitarian and it was with a girl.

I've been diagnosed with Major Depressive Disorder and PTSD from childhood sexual abuse and hate-crime bashing. When I was young I was sent to therapy for conduct disorders and some other problems. I've been doing better for the past few years, although I do still have nightmares and triggers, and depressive episodes when I walk around in a brain fog for a week thinking, "Everything is horrible and I want to kill myself."

John:

We've had a really hard time finding a good therapist for Dan, due to financial issues, and the fact that he's now working days and we can't find a free care therapist who works evenings. So right now he is unfortunately without therapy until our financial problems get better. So we're doing the best we can.

I'm the same age as Dan, and I'd been best friends with him for years. For some reason I have a tendency to end up dating people who have mental illnesses. I don't have any trauma or mental illnesses of my own, so I don't know why I keep ending up with people who do. I'm totally not a therapist type, either. I also had years of egalitarian relationships before I got into this relationship with Dan. It was really hard to adapt to being an authority figure to him, because we'd been buddies for all those years, so the shift in the relationship was difficult. It was very exciting at first, but it was difficult to find the confidence to be in charge all the time. That was my biggest challenge, and probably still is.

Since he was my best friend, I already knew about his mental problems. He was actively suicidal when we were first becoming friends; he tried to kill himself at least once in college. I knew that he was having a really hard time with things, but there were parts that I didn't even see until we got into an intimate relationship. Once we were together, I had a front-row seat to his problems—when he would have a nightmare and wake up screaming, I'd be right there instead of down the hall. Since this was my first power exchange relationship, learning to manage Dan's mental illnesses seemed like just part of the job to me. When we were just friends, I really wanted to help him and take care of him more than was possible at the time. Now I can really do it, which is nice.

Dan:

I don't talk about this stuff with a lot of people. Since he was my best friend, I had to say something—"Yeah, I tried to kill myself, and I have these cuts that I can't really hide,"—but I couldn't really talk about the trauma stuff until I felt safe enough to come out about it. I also had to come to terms with that myself, so that I could accept that the problem could be treated. When I became John's slave, he told me immediately, "You need to go get a therapist." I'm scared shitless of doctors, and if I had my way I'd never see one, so John goes with me as a support for my medical appointments. If he can't be there because he's at work, he convinces me to go anyway—"convinces" as in "Here's your appointment time, you're going," and then coaching me on the phone, "Are you walking out the door? You'd better be walking out the door now."

John:

I try to actively manage his health, but I don't take a hardline stance on it. I'm more of a coach. In other areas of his life I'm more authoritarian, but when it comes to his mental health I have to handle him gently. I can't push him hard because he'll freak out. I do it through hand-holding and directing, and I learned that the hard way.

Dan:

There were some early attempts to control my behavior that went very badly, with screaming in public and that sort of thing. Once I got so triggered that I elbowed him in the stomach. That's because I get triggered when people approach me from behind and touch me. But that was more a matter of him adapting to my triggers. For example, I had developed an eating disorder where I starved myself and binged. So we had the bright idea that John would be more in charge of my diet and what I was eating, but this led to a terrible scene (and not in the kinky sense) in a mall food court. He told me that I couldn't eat the unhealthy thing that I desperately wanted to eat, and I began to cry, "You think I'm a horrible failure!" and it was embarrassing for both of us.

John:

We've learned that for the food issue, as well as for several other issues, that it's best to have advance planning so that Dan has concrete expectations and doesn't have to be triggered in the moment. Instead of "You can't eat that!" in the moment, it's "Here's your meal plan, Danny." While he can ask for treats not on the meal plan, there is an expectation that the answer with probably be no, so it doesn't put him into a situation where he will be triggered.

Dan actually works in the mental health field, taking care of children with trauma issues, and yet it wasn't until after we got together that he realized that all his triggers were due to his own trauma history. I'd ask him, "So as a professional, what would you do with a client who had this problem?" And he'd deny that he had a problem. It was very frustrating. He had convinced himself that his trauma history didn't affect his life, even though he had nightmares and was phobic of so many things. That was the sort of thing that happened to the clients at his job, not him. Crazy people had trauma histories, not him. But once he accepted the fact that he actually had a trauma history, he figured out that the tools could be applied to himself. "Hey, I learned this technique at work that could help people with PTSD; maybe that will help me!"

Dan:

Having concrete structures in place has been much more helpful than having to confront issues in the moment. It's better to head them off with good management, rather than his giving me orders on an ongoing basis. He would give me an order when I was faced with a trigger, and I would freak out because I couldn't handle the pressure in that situation. Pre-emptive structure is the way to go. For example, with medical appointments, there is an expectation that I will go to the appointments. John did a lot of legwork to find me doctors that I wasn't terrified of, and he went with me to appointments and talked me through them. This involved him switching my PCP, finding a therapist that we both liked, who is gay and fine with the power exchange. We'd be in a therapy session and he'd say, "What does your owner think of this?" Finding a kink-aware professional is so important, because it's really hard to be in therapy when you're hiding your life from your therapist.

Another example is bedtime—I have trouble sleeping on my own because I have nightmares, so I have a particular bedtime routine that he has set up. I make sure that he has tissues and water beside the bed, which is service, and then I do my hygiene protocol in a specific order. The ritual aspect of it makes it so much easier to transfer my headspace into going to sleep.

When I was working my last job, it was very stressful and was driving me crazy, and John told me to quit. I said, "But it has such good benefits and it has aspects that make me look successful and I'll never find another one that pays as much..." and he said, "I don't care. This job is not working. It's driving you crazy. You need to quit and find a job that has these other criteria." I went into that change kicking and screaming, but I'm much happier now.

"You may not kill yourself" is more than just a protocol, it's a direct order. I'm not allowed to go cutting myself up, and I can't take any drugs unless he's approved them beforehand, so that kind of eliminates the whole OD thing if I have to call him every time I want an aspirin. It may sound silly, but it really helps. Earlier this year my foster sister overdosed and died, the same week that I was starting a new job. The depression got bad enough for me that I was waiting for the train and standing there staring at the tracks thinking, "I could just jump in front of it and it would be all over." But then I couldn't make myself move because all I could think of next was, "Well, if I did that, John would be mad." So it's very useful!

John:

We had to come up with protocols that would work when he was so bad off that he had a hard time getting out of bed. At first, I would say, "Oh, you're really sad, so I'll let you stay in bed and not worry about anything. Just relax!" And this would upset him, because he couldn't be useful, and I was taking away his jobs, and he would cry, "Oh, you think I'm worthless!" It actually helps him to have concrete tasks to get up and do, and I had to learn that.

Dan:

I don't like feeling like I'm pathetic. He doesn't give me difficult tasks on those days, because it's difficult enough to get out of bed and brush my teeth, when I'm that bad off. I can't neglect basic hygiene, I need to eat, and I have to put on clothes. So on those days, my tasks are to be clothed, clean, and fed, and to take my meds. Sometimes I'll beat myself up a little about the fact that I can only do these pathetic things, but it's so much better than it was before, when there wasn't any sort of protocols at all and John would just tell me to stay in bed until I felt better. I'd think, "You've given up on me! You can't trust me to do anything! What do I do now?" Even busywork is better than nothing. He'll tell me to clean out his email inbox, and I'll say, "OK, I can delete things, I can handle this." I can do some dishes, even if I'm an hour on the same dish. I can do *something*.

I think that it's impossible to tell s-types that they shouldn't have any issues before looking for a partner, but I think it's important that you know where your issues lie. Some of my earlier power exchange relationships ended in total disaster because I wasn't totally conscious of what was an issue or not. I just reacted to them as an authority figure, sometimes in a bad way, without thinking about it. If you don't have that basic level of self-awareness, it's going to crash and burn. You need to be able to explain yourself to the dominant, instead of sending them blindly into a mine field. At the very least, they need to know that it's a mine field, and they've consented to it, and not just been blindsided by your crazy. I'd also say that the dominant should not have any issues of their own that clash with the sub's issues, although that has been a problem for us.

John:

Yes. My family of origin has a lot of anger management issues, and they don't believe in therapy, and in general they have a style that is loud and expressive … and rude, really rude. I'm far more polite and considerate than any of them, but when I'm annoyed or frustrated, I have a tone of voice that makes him think that I hate him and I'm going to hit him.

Dan:

Of course, I know intellectually that he's not going to do that. He's never done that. We don't ever use physical punishments, because that would trigger me too much. When he's in a bad mood, he just walks away, and tells me that I am to stay right there and not come follow him, so that I won't argue with him and make him say something he'll regret. He's also learned to figure out when his tone is frightening me, and he'll tell me that it's not about me, it's just something else that's frustrating him. If he does have a problem with me, he tells me right away. So I am now all right with "I'm yelling, but it's OK." He's also worked on his own anger issues, so there's no throwing of things now. If I was someone who didn't have a trauma history, it wouldn't be a big deal.

I trust John because I had five years to watch him, and in all that time he never lied to me once. In fact, I never saw him lie to anyone once. He has a very firm moral code and I have never seen him shake from it in the past ten years. I don't know anyone else of whom I can say that. As long as I am fine with that moral framework, I am safe. I have a hard time trusting people, but I'm not trusting him so much as I am trusting his moral code, and the fact that he stays within it. I can't imagine him changing, after all these years, short of some sort of horrible psychotic break.

John:

For me, I came to trust with Dan because he was willing to open up to me and let me see the things that he doesn't let anyone else see. It made him vulnerable, and then he was stuck, because once I know something I can't un-know it, so it was a permanent bond. And he's good at doing what he says he will do, unless he's totally nonfunctional, in which case he tells me. We have really good communication about his condition at any time, and if he's in a bad mental state he won't promise to do something he can't do; he will say that he can't do anything right now.

We don't have a punishment context because it doesn't make sense for most things. I didn't want to be seen as some blind authority who just gives orders and expects obedience. I see us as a team, and this is our mutual goal, and we're working toward that. But we have done punishment, especially in the beginning when things were rocky, for a catharsis for him. It was more like saying ten Hail Marys when you've done something wrong, an atonement for him. They were more like, "Write a list of everything that you did wrong and read it to me," or "Why did you do this wrong? Write me an essay on it." He hates writing essays, but it really helped me to understand what was going on with him in the moment. It was one of my big early successes in mastery, but I don't feel like we need it anymore because we've got things working more smoothly now.

Dan: It helped a lot because I'd do something that would be entirely opaque to him, and he would ask me, "What the fuck were you thinking? Write me this essay on what the fuck you were thinking!" And now he knows me well enough that when I do something totally stupid, he'll say, "Did you just do this stupid thing because of this other stupid thing?" and I'll look down at my shoes and say, "Yeah." It was a venue for self-awareness for me as well. I'd start the essay saying "Fuck you! I hate this!" and then halfway through I would start thinking, "Well, hmmm, maybe he's right. I did do that wrong. In fact, I did that wrong because of this over here ... Gee, why haven't I ever realized that I do this thing?"

It didn't help that I went through a really mean testing period in the beginning, where I would say, "Well, if I say this really hurtful thing to you, are you going to lose it now? How about now? How about this other hurtful thing? Oh, you didn't lose it. Hmmmm." Fortunately we're over that now, but I needed to test him to see where the explosion point was, where I would be in danger. But he never got to that point, and after a while I realized that if I act like a complete bitch, he will just walk out the door and say, "I'm leaving because you're being an obnoxious bitch. I'll come back when you're ready to be a mature adult toward me." He was never a horrible abusive person to me, because he's just not a horrible abusive person.

John:

I read a lot about his sort of issues, but I really think that talking to professionals who work in that field was very useful, and I'd recommend it to anyone who is facing managing someone with mental illnesses. I think it's also useful to talk to them about what it actually looks like when they are having this issue or that issue. How do they act when that happens? How does it manifest? You can also ask people who have loved ones with mental illnesses—"So I know that you've said that your partner has bipolar disorder. I'm thinking of taking on someone with bipolar disorder; what does it look like when it happens? What can you tell me about living with that?" The textbook definitions don't give you an idea of what it's like to interact with it, and what's the best way to react to it. Also, it's a good sign if the sub has other people to support them. It can be really hard if they're all alone with no one, because you might need a break from being the support system occasionally, or you might want to focus on other aspects of the relationship.

I also talk to my own therapist, who is also kink-aware and very supportive of my efforts to manage Dan, and she has been very helpful. Many of my friends have not been very supportive of the relationship because they feel weird about the power exchange, so that's hard. They don't understand or approve of the extent to which I take responsibility for Dan's mental health.

Dan:

One of the ways in which we are different from many power exchange couples is that many owners are really into the idea of sexual control over their property, but since I have a whole trauma history around sex with a lot of triggers—I've been a street kid trading sex for food and a place to stay—sex is an area that he consciously doesn't control. There's no sex on demand, because he feels that it would be damaging to me, so we have a more egalitarian-looking sex life. In general, we're operating from a consensual non-consent framework, so if he demanded that sex be a certain way, I would fall into my habit of not being able to say no even when it was triggering and emotionally bad for me. In other areas, I know that I have to obey, but I'm fine with telling him if I think there's going to be a problem, and leaving it up to him to decide. In the sex department, I have so much trouble even bringing it up when there's a problem that he feels that it's better for me to be able to say no with no expectation of obedience.

He tells me, "It's totally fine to stop in the middle of sex and say that it's not working because something is going wrong for you." I don't, usually, but the fact that I can stop with no penalty makes a difference. He watches me so that he can tell if I'm becoming unresponsive. We tried sexual control in the beginning, but there were too many land mines. So we went back to vanilla sex for a while until we discerned that the problem wasn't the activities, it was the context. Then we slowly added the kink back in, which was great because I'm not really turned on by vanilla sex, but it's the one area where I do have choice.

John:

Some dominants in my place might think, "How much of an authority can I be when I'm blocked so often by my slave's triggers and illness?" But for me, I've let go of the fantasy of "Well, you're a slave, so you'll be happy to do anything I tell you, because that makes you a slave, right?" Honestly, the fact that we're broke interferes just as much with our ideal relationship, as do so many other outside factors. I mean, if we had tons of money he could quit his job and see a therapist. Lots of things make life harder. I reframe Dan's mental health problems as just another one of those life circumstances that make people feel disempowered, but that we have to cope with anyway. It doesn't feel any worse than all the other things that go wrong with life.

It can be stressful, being in charge of him and his mental health. I've felt worried and hopeless by turns, but I eventually always found a way. Most of the time the decisions I make are pretty basic—"Yes, you will go to the doctor over this issue or that issue," and they seem obvious in the moment. When I think about "Am I capable of making these decisions about someone else's health?" I feel worried and incompetent, but when I'm actually faced with the questions, I find that I know what to do and I do it. I put on the master hat and I make the decision. And we're both so much older than when we started! We were so young then, and yet we muddled through. So, really, we can only get better at it, right?

Interview with Jawn's Doll

Jawn's Doll (with some help from Jawn)

(This is a two-part interview with a master/slave couple who both cope with mental illnesses. The interview with Jawn's Doll is here, while the interview for her master Jawn is in our book on dominants with mental illnesses.)

Jawn's Doll:

I'm a slave to my master Jawn. We met in October of 2007. At first I just bottomed to him, but eventually I offered myself to him as his slave, and we wrote a contract. Now he is my master and owner, and we eventually got married.

I also have generalized anxiety disorder, which means that I can get anxious about anything, anytime, and sometimes over nothing at all. When my son was born—during my first marriage with my ex-husband—he was two months premature. When you have a baby, you assume that you're going to bring them home and do "baby stuff", but when they are born with medical problems, something in your head keeps saying, "When am I bringing them home?" and the anxiety just mounts. I spent sixty days in the NICU. Thanksgiving passed, and then Christmas, and we were still in the NICU. New Year's Eve came and went, and we were still in the NICU. I had a terrible case of post-partum depression, plus the anxiety around my son's health. It left me with a huge amount of hypervigilance. On his first birthday, my sister came to sit for him for the first time so that my husband of the time could have a date with me. We went to see a movie, and it wasn't even a particularly sad movie, and by the time we got back to the car I had a complete breakdown. The whole year had turned into a major depressive episode.

So I started seeing a psychiatrist who gave me Lexapro, and that helped a lot. I was teaching, and my administrators at the time were not sympathetic. Work issues were also not going well either, so I did have periods of time when I felt suicidal, and I was very disorganized. After I'd been seeing my psychiatrist for a while, he recommended that I start seeing a psychologist for talk therapy. That was the first time that I had someone who could look at me and challenge my negative ideas and thought patterns that I'd built up in my head. For example, being anxious and worried all the time, and constantly trying to prepare for every single contingency, that's so totally normal, right? My therapist could tell me, "No, that's not normal," and challenge me to look at myself and figure out healthy coping mechanisms. I've actually had some really great therapists in the past—I'm lucky in that way.

I came to realize that my coping mechanisms are not exactly the best. For example, when everything gets to be too much for me, I just decide to cut and run, and that was how I ended up in Las Vegas, which was really far away from all my support systems. However, running away from everything that's piling up on top of you, that never actually works. So after a while I came back to New England again, and that's where I met Jawn.

Early November is my son's birthday, and I tend to get depressed all over again at that time of year. It's my trigger point, and I know that it's going to come around. But after I met Jawn and became close to him, I found out that he understood more about my situation than I could have known—and didn't exactly sympathize.

Jawn:

I had a son who was also born prematurely, and he lived for about four hours. I got to hold him before he died, and I also have a "mourning date", in April. And I had to say, when my doll went on about how heartbreaking it was that her son was born prematurely and she had to be in the NICU for such a long time, "Well, he's alive, what are you bitching about? You can go touch him any time you want." I did kind of feel like it was petty of me, because it certainly isn't my doll's fault that my son died—she was only in third grade at the time!—but I wanted our relationship to be based on honesty, so I told her straight out that I wasn't going to be able to hear about this particular problem of hers without having it trigger bad feelings in me.

Jawn's Doll:

That actually gave me some perspective on the matter! Part of why I appreciated and could respect Jawn when I met him was that he'd been through so many things, and really experienced life.

I told Jawn pretty early on about my anxiety. We met at the end of October, and my trigger point was at the beginning of November, and so right after we started dating I started getting crazy on him. I actually started dating him while I was in the process of finding a new therapist, having just moved back to New England from Las Vegas. The first agreement we made was to have total honesty and openness between us, and since that was such an important part of my life ... well, even if I wanted to hide it from him, that would have been way too difficult. Especially since I am a terrible liar and I don't have a poker face.

If there's one thing that I have learned from this relationship with Jawn, it is that is it so much easier just to be completely honest about everything. If you're trying build a web of hiding, especially something that is such a part of you, you'll lose. They will find out. My son was also recently diagnosed with ADD, and as part of getting him diagnosed, I discovered that I also have all the same symptoms. It's so much a part of me that I can't hide it. If you're going to be a sub or a slave and give all those rights over to somebody, you have to give them all the information about what they're getting, as quickly as possible.

Jawn:

Let me also say that it's important to find a master who is educable about the subject of their slave's disorders. You don't want someone who will just tell them that they're just lazy, who will be closed-minded about their problems. I've done a certain amount of study about her disorders—not to a level where I can regurgitate facts about drugs on demand, but I've learned enough to understand that her anxiety is not mistrust of me. It's generalized anxiety, which means that it doesn't have to be based on anything rational. It could be about anything, at any time. I've had panic attacks at occasional points in my life, so I can empathize about the idea of just having sudden panic attacks for no reason at all. I can imagine how debilitating that is, and I know better than to blame her for that.

Jawn's Doll:

I have such talent in the matter that if you give me any situation, I can tell you exactly what you should be worrying about! I actually stopped teaching because I was having such bad panic attacks just walking into the school building that my psychiatrist suggest that I quit. I do take medication. It was a mutual decision, but it's really his standing orders. In our contract, it states that I will follow the advice of competent medical authorities. If it seems like a therapist isn't any good, he might have me change to another one, but we aren't going to just throw out the idea of treatment. He wants me to have competent medical care at all times.

I've tried off-and-on coping without medication; when I tried to quit this last time, I told him that I was feeling scattered and having trouble focusing on anything, and he said, "OK, so you're going to go make an appointment with your therapist right now, right?" My master is really good about making sure that I get any treatment that I might need outside of our relationship. Since he's retired military, we have really good insurance, so we're lucky in that way.

As a slave, I live under a lot of rules and very narrow choices, which is absolutely perfect for me and my anxiety. If you give me unlimited choices and tell me that I can do anything I want, I will talk myself out of every single choice, and then totally freak out. Having a narrow limited focus really helps that! Jawn's also really skilled at nudging me outside of my comfort zone. I believe that you have to get outside of your comfort zone in order to learn, but I can only stay outside it for so long before I get too overstressed. And he'll nudge me out—or pull me out, or push me out, or kick me out—but he's always there with me, and I always have him as a support.

Jawn:

One of the things I've learned through dealing with my own issues is that when you have a plan and something goes wrong, you should just take a breath and move on. This is what I try to teach her: it's gone. Don't dwell on what you could have done. Let it go and move on. I tell her, over and over: Don't chase the bus! The bus is gone, you find another bus or go home.

Jawn's Doll:

Sometimes he'll pick me up from work and I can't stop obsessing about something that happened there, and he'll say,

"Do we need to pull the car over so that you can let that go?" and I'll realize that I can stop bitching now. He's a really great reality check for me, and he keeps me from wallowing. I mean, I trusted him enough that I signed a contract! He owns me now, he has total control over everything, and I don't have to worry too much about what to do, because my job is to do what I'm told. Sometimes I overextend myself; I'll make a plan where I'm going to do this and this and this, and he'll say, "No. Just do the one thing," And I'll say, "But there are all these other things..." and he'll say again, "No. Just do the one thing well, not three things half-assed." And I'll realize that he's right. I have the Superwoman mentality that I can do everything, and I continually set myself up to fail. He has a much more realistic view of my skills and abilities, and he'll tell me right out if I'm going to overdo it and fall into a hole. So I make the schedules, and he tells me if they are realistic. I'll come up with a brilliant plan and present it to him, and he'll adjust it if it needs it.

Jawn:

If I were to give advice to masters who are looking at a sub who has various mental problems, I think the important thing is not to take on someone who thinks you're going to fix them. I can't fix a slave's mental illness. I can help them to compensate, but I can't fix them. I'd want to see that they have taken real steps to solve their problems before I'd take them on. If someone is going to a therapist or doctor, that's a great sign. I support that. But be wary of someone who wants you to fix them, or who is blowing off their problems—"Oh, I'll just wait it out, I'll come out of it eventually." That's a person who doesn't have a realistic idea of how this works. I'm OK with someone who's not totally well, but I want them to at least be fully aware of their problems and trying to fix themselves. I don't want to have to argue with them about needing to get help. I want someone who knows that they need to be fixed, and who has started that process.

And do we have to say the final piece of clichéd advice: communicate, communicate, communicate? But it's more than that. You need to find out how the other communicates, and then learn their language. Just because we're talking at each other doesn't mean that we're communicating. I tell her: Don't be brave and hold back. Tell it all to me.

Jawn's Doll:

Sometimes he'll ask me how I'm doing, and I'll say, "Fine." And he'll ask, "Do you mean ordinary fine or I-don't-want-to-talk-about-it fine?" One of the ways in which I communicate is that I talk a lot, and I've discovered that's not necessarily the best way to communicate with Jawn. He gets tired of what he calls "too much signal-to-noise ratio", and he'll say, "I want signal, not noise." He's training me to be more succinct. He'll ask me a question that he thinks is a yes-or-no question, and I'll try to explain further, and he'll stop me and tell me to just answer yes or no, and then I can explain. It's gotten to the point where we'll be riding in the car and this will happen, and he'll just look at me, and my body language will be such that he'll just ask, "Yes or no?" And I'll have to pick, but I'll keep the anxious body pose, and then he'll say, "And what?" But it's always a choice; he can have that information or not. That's an adaptation we both learned to make, and that's what this is about—making adaptations, but always keeping to the original spirit of the master/slave relationship.

Tuning In and Taking Control

vixen

I'm a thirty-seven-year-old woman with a B.A. in emergency management, and a certificate in fire science. I work for the government assisting with disaster relief. I have two sons, one of whom has severe emotional and mental issues. That's the outward self I show to the world. Underneath, I'm a slave.

I have always been a shy and quiet person, especially around men, as I don't generally feel comfortable around them. I have a history of clinical depression, anxiety, some PTSD, and I have a few Borderline Personality Disorder traits. My mother had placed me in hypnotherapy when I was a teenager, but that only lasted a couple of months before I refused treatment, as I didn't think it was helping my situation. I didn't actively seek medical help until I met my Master and came to live with him. After that, I was placed in therapy once a week, and put on medication. Today I'm on Geodon and Celexa, and Amitriptyline for my insomnia.

I started in the lifestyle very young, because I met a wonderful Dominant named Darren. He drew out the submissive in me, which was not too difficult considering that I was intimidated by all men. I was a part of a large household, with three other submissives besides myself. It meant that I really had to work on my jealousy issues. I didn't really fight that much with Darren; as there were other submissives in the household, it was not one on one. I had what time I was given with him. If things had been different and more intimate, the unstable side of me would probably have reared its ugly head.

I stayed with Darren until he passed away in a car accident when I was nineteen. I was just devastated, and I left the lifestyle for quite a long time, returning only in an online capacity when I was twenty-five. I traveled through Gorean sites such as Active Worlds and Voodoo Chat. I did have a Dominant that I saw casually for about a year, but that abruptly ended when he found his own submissive and wanted to devote his time to her exclusively. I was owned online by quite a few men, and at the time, that was all I was willing to engage in. When I moved to Washington State, I had a Dominant that I saw a couple of times but he was very abusive. I didn't handle humiliation well, nor did I like being beat harshly with a cane, so I left that relationship rather early.

I met my current Master online through a good friend of mine that I now call my sister. I took a leap and went to visit his household … and, well, I've been with that household ever since. My current Master taught me that I was a slave, not just a submissive. I'd always wanted someone to have complete control over me. One of the things I love the most is being able to come home from a long day at work and release all the baggage of having to be the dominant manager. I can do it well at my job, but it is truly just a mask. It isn't me at all.

I've now been with my current Master for about six years, and we have been together exclusively for about four years now. Our relationship is very simple: he is my Master and I am his slave. He controls, as well as owns, everything in my life, and I am to obey his every wish. He is the calm and collected one, and I need that. He rarely even raises his voice, while I am the emotional one that needs a firm hand to stay on track. Quite a few D/s and M/s couples have envied our relationship, but they haven't seen the battles and tears we went through to make it work.

My Master was willing to put the time and energy into molding me to be what he wanted me to be. I came with a hell of a lot of baggage, and I was a mood-swinging emotional wreck. Did we fight? Well, I know I yelled a lot in the beginning, but as I said, he rarely raises his voice. Actually, I think I have infuriated him twice to the point of his hands shaking. although he never lashed out. That was very scary, but by the Gods he stuck with me and pulled me through that turmoil. He was the one who got me on meds and into therapy, and now I'm much more stable. We rarely fight or argue now. I know the rules laid before me and I follow them or face the consequences.

I knew I was depressed and possibly had PTSD, but I didn't understand the extent of my mental problems. I was also heavily addicted to Vicodin and Flexeril due to complications of my back pain (spina bifida occulta). The first step was getting me off the narcotics. I went cold turkey, and that was rough. At the time everyone thought I had borderline personality disorder, and we all read up on that. We still own all the books we bought regarding the illness. When I finally received my other diagnoses, we read some more and we all adapted accordingly.

My Master observes me quite a bit, all the time. He is very in tune with how I react to situations, and plans accordingly for any repercussions I may throw his way. On a day-to-day basis, I will usually get emotional and snippy if I haven't slept well because I forgot my night meds, or if my cycle is about to start. He can tell when my mood has shifted, and he'll call me out on it to see what's wrong with me. I had never before been with a man that knew whether I was in pain or if there was something eating at me before I even recognized it! It's amazing how in tune he is to me.

We consider our relationship to be Total Power Exchange. I did hand everything over to him, eventually, but it went in stages. (I think the last thing I handed over was my bank account, and that took some time. I just realized that his decisions were always better than mine, because I have a tendency to be self-destructive which continues even to this day.) This means that he handles all the medical decisions for both of us, although I am a part of that decision and am encouraged to put in my two cents. The only time we argued over a medical decision was when he took away the Vicodin and Flexeril and had me go cold turkey. My Master always makes sure I take my meds every day—including vitamins— and monitors how I'm feeling. I've been pretty stable on this cocktail for a while, and I haven't needed to have it adjusted. In the beginning, when the doctors were trying different drugs, he was very much involved, even to the point of going to my appointments to discuss my behavior with the medication and giving his opinion as to whether it was beneficial or not.

I feel very lucky, and I probably have a one-in-a-million Master, but I am sure there are some other emotionally-tuned-in Dominants out there. If you're a submissive with mental illnesses, my advice would be that you need to carefully select someone that is willing to go the distance with your illness, and sometimes that's hard to find. Help educate them about to what is wrong and how to handle it;

buy them books if you don't already have them. Get into therapy. Bring your Dominant too! There are many psychologists out there who are well-versed in BDSM relationships. Be open about it. They can help the two of you get through the chaos.

For the dominants? Patience. Patience. Patience. It's a long hard road, but if you're willing to stick it out and stabilize your s-type, you may have yourself a wonderful creature. However, that always comes with hard work whether they have issues or don't have issues.

Moody Doesn't Even Begin to Cover It

emmie

I am a thirty-nine-year-old woman of West Indian, Native American, and African American ancestry, which combines to give me a rich brown complexion with reddish/gold undertones, comb-breaking thick hair with curls the size of pen springs, and the height of your average middle school boy. I was blessed with more bum than bust, making dress shopping a form of torture. Some people think I'm quiet, those people don't actually know me. I love talking to people in small groups or one on one, but large groups make me want to run away or hide. I have manic depression, hereafter referred to as bipolar. I am not sensitive to saying I *have* bipolar versus I *am* bipolar, so I switch between the two; others feel differently which is cool by me.

I am living in my first and only M/s relationship; my master introduced me to this way of life, and to the public scene. We have been together for seven years now. I am his slave, and for me that means first and foremost that I am obedient. There is nothing in my life that I maintain control over; he may delegate something to me that he has no desire to actively deal with (such as shopping for cleaning supplies), but he can withdraw that delegation at any time. There is also no time that he is not in control of me, whether I'm in his line of sight or not. He may tell you that he isn't a micromanager, he wouldn't be lying exactly, but let's just say the statement that is misleading. He takes great enjoyment in orchestrating every aspect of my life; he is just subtle about it.

I came to my diagnosis in a roundabout way. When I was 20 I married my college sweetheart and immediately fell pregnant. We decided I would stay at home with the child after a look at the cost of daycare versus my limited earning potential made it clear that staying home was far cheaper. By the time we split a few years later, we had had a second child. I have never been good at working at a regular job, so when I married I'd had one part-time job for a year at a fast food place. I didn't get another job until my youngest son was two (I was twenty-six) and it lasted a whopping four months. My next job lasted six months, the next one six weeks, the one after that three months. The pattern continued for five years with me being unable to maintain employment for an entire year; in fact the longest I managed was eleven months at my final job.

The funny thing is that I never got fired. I got sick. In every job I did extremely well, so well that often I received promotions and/or extra duties assigned to me. I was able to get jobs that I wasn't actually qualified to do—really, nearly anything, since starting out I'd had no experience, no training, not even a degree to fall back on. I simply interviewed well. I'm intelligent and engaging and when I'm up (manic/hypomanic) I can be an unstoppable force. However the adage "what goes up must come down" was written in reference to bipolars, I'm sure; and come down I did. I didn't realize what was going on at the time, but I would come crashing down and my symptoms would manifest physically. I went to numerous doctors who couldn't diagnose me with anything specific, but they saw that I was indeed having problems. I was fainting; my anxiety was through the roof; I was shaky; at times I had inexplicable rashes, weird weight loss and weight gain, digestive issues, and phantom pain. Even my blood work would come back suspect, then normal, then suspect in a completely different way. After a while the stress of each job would become too much for me and I would quit. There would be a recuperation period, then I'd seek employment and the cycle would start again. In five years I managed to go through 14 jobs.

I was at the last job and things were going south for me health-wise, as they were apt to do, when I met my master. Being bipolar himself, he witnessed several of my strange physical episodes, nursed me through a couple of bad flues, and observed me for a couple of months. Then he told me I needed to see a psychiatrist. I thought he was being a bit alarmist, but he insisted I was a poster child for bipolar disorder, so an appointment was made and I went. After reams of paperwork and an intensive interview, the psychiatrist agreed with my master and tacked on an anxiety disorder and PTSD for fun. I was not amused, to put it mildly. My master was a great support, as was the rest of the family (we were in a poly quad at that time of our relationship), but I still ended up leaving work several months after getting a promotion due to not being able to handle the stress, combined with excessive sleepiness from one of the first medications I took.

The first year we were together was tumultuous. I was severely depressed for most of it, with bouts of paranoia and uncontrolled anxiety, while working with the psychiatrist to find a med cocktail that would work. The second year brought some stabilization on my end in terms of the depression, but the anxiety was enough that he ordered me into therapy to learn better coping skills and have an impartial listener for my rants about the growing discord at home. He even attended several therapy sessions with me, allowing my therapist to facilitate my ability to say what was on my mind. At no time was any of this handled in such a way that it was outside of our dynamic. The idea that you have to deal with each other as equals in certain circumstances is patently false. If it is not your desire to do so, you should not feel pressured that there is no other way to successfully deal with difficult issues, such as the challenges that being mentally "interesting" can bring to an M/s dynamic.

My master very much controls my treatment; from the time he first sent me to for evaluation, to when he had me quit my job, he has shown that at every step he is in charge of how things would be dealt with. He has in the past gone into my psychiatric check-ups and given his observations on my state of mind and behavior. He tells me what he thinks are the best and worst drugs I am currently on, and when it is time to consider a change. He has had me "voluntarily" sign myself into an inpatient program when I was highly unstable. He has also insisted that I educate myself extensively on bipolar medication, treatments, history, and symptoms.

I count myself fortunate to have a master who has an intimate understanding of what I go through. He doesn't take every bad mood as a personal indictment and doesn't hover thinking that every time I'm remotely sad that clinical depression has returned or that every time I'm joyful mania is right around the corner. He is also the person that I can ask if something is real or a hallucination, and he won't look at me askance when I ask; sometimes it's hard to tell, and verification without judgment is appreciated.

In the time we've been together my need for anti-anxiety medication has lessened directly due to our dynamic. I'm not saying M/s is a cure for bipolar disorder or anxiety: what I am saying is the structure of our life together is soothing for me. He allows me to have a small enough world that I don't feel continuously overwhelmed. Within the safe bubble he provides, he makes sure that I get enough socialization to offset my inclination to become a total hermit.

Another accommodation that was made in our dynamic isn't obvious because it's accepted in our community that female s-types often don't spend much time interacting with male dominants. He keeps me out of trouble, protecting me from myself, by restricting such interaction. One of the things he did early on was curtail my flirting. At the time I thought he was being mean and possibly jealous; I found out later that he recognized both my inclination towards hypersexuality and my lack of ability to say no to dominant men. That could be a dangerous combination, particularly in the BDSM scene, so he created a safe space for me. It's an area where he knows my limitations and doesn't expect me to do what I have extreme difficulty with, so he handles it before it becomes an issue.

I am terribly absent-minded, more so now than when we first got together—it's an unfortunate side effect of many medications. He has adapted to this simply by being more patient and reminding me to write things down or put them in my phone. He doesn't blow up when I forget to do something he said, or when I mishear him. We had a few tense times until he instituted the "what I said versus what I heard" method of getting to the bottom of things. It quickly clears up where the miscommunication was, and no one is to blame, which keeps either of us from going on the defensive.

I don't hold an outside job, nor will I in the foreseeable future. I also won't be attending school. My master came to the decision that working was causing me undue stress that exacerbated my symptoms, and structured academia simply isn't my strong point. It also suits his controlling nature quite nicely, since having a stay-at-home slave provides him with service available to him at the drop of a hat. After I'd been out of the workforce for a couple of years, he directed me to apply for federal disability, which was granted with unseemly haste. I found it both validating and insulting at the time, especially since getting disability for bipolar is notoriously difficult. My not working is simply a part of our dynamic, so intrinsic at this point that it's unimaginable that I would go back to work.

Most slaves and submissives who aren't partnered and just starting out will likely not be as lucky as I was to partner with someone who was not only accepting of bipolar but also immensely knowledgeable on the subject through personal experience and research. It is an unfortunate reality that bipolar, in particular, has a terrible rep. It seems that every other person knows someone they claim is bipolar, and it's never, "Oh, I know this great person who is bipolar, but she's sweet as pie," it's always "I know this crazy-ass bitch." The perception is that people diagnosed with bipolar disorder are dangerous, cruel, hurtful, scheming assholes who will do all manner of evil if you give them half a chance. I've had many people question and outright deny the validity of my diagnosis because I seem so nice and normal. They thought they were being complimentary, but in reality they were perpetrating a stereotype. It did let me know that if I were ever going through a difficult time, these were not people I could call on. I would recommend being very careful to ascertain any prospective dominant's attitudes towards people who are mentally "interesting" in a general way before committing to them. Once that is established, hone in on your specific diagnosis, as some (like bipolar) carry more stigma than others. Many people think medication is never appropriate, others only want to try natural remedies; still others think that going without any chemical intervention is best and feel things can be balanced through diet, exercise, and stress-relieving techniques. It is important to inform yourself and decide which path you want to take, so that you can make an informed decision when partnering with someone. You want their ideas to mesh with yours, since mental health is a very important part of life. This is particularly important for a slave in the way I define it, because you'd be turning over the decision-making responsibility for your condition to this person.

For a dominant considering a bipolar s-type, my main advice would be to educate yourself. There are some very helpful websites with forums that go into detail about the commonly used medications used for treatment and their effects, with personal stories to illustrate them. There are also bipolar 101 type-sites and books. Remembering that not all bipolar people have the same experience or handle their issues in the same way—for instance, I rarely experience rage and am generally known as being even-tempered, upbeat, and compliant. I have never done anything that completely ruined my life or the lives of those around me, and while I have hurt people, it has thankfully been on a fairly small scale. My actions have been more harmful to myself than anyone else, but someone else might have a completely different story. Don't assume you are a better narrator to someone's lived experience than they are.

In addition, don't be quick to conclude that any negative thought or action on their part is a manifestation of bipolar disorder. You can be bipolar and be a jerk; the two are not mutually exclusive, nor is being a jerk a pre-requisite. Not accepting bipolar as an excuse for bad behavior, while at the same time understanding the limits bipolar may bring to your s-type, can be a thin line to walk at times. Assume you will get it wrong at times and move on. My master is very explicit about the difference between moods and emotions. I can't do anything about my moods—they are what they are—but I can do something about my emotions to a degree, and I can certainly do something about my *expression* of my emotions. I am held to a high yet realistic standard of behavior.

The only other thing I think is essential to being either the bipolar s-type or the dominant with them is a well-developed sense of humor. Laughter doesn't solve anything, but the ability to laugh at yourself, the situations you may find yourself in, and life in general for that matter, will make even the worst times easier.

Interview with Andy and Sue

Andy:

I'm Andy, from Ottawa, Canada. We've been in a relationship for nine years. We started in the BDSM community up here, and tried to have a D/s-M/s relationship with Sue in charge and me as her property, me in service to her. We did that ... well, we struggled with that, for six years. Then we decided to try it the other way around, and it's worked very well for us for the last two and a half years.

Sue:

I'm his slave, and I'm happy to be that. We have a total power exchange relationship, so I've given up control of absolutely everything, including handing over power of attorney. Andy has complete control over my medication and my medical health. We live like this all the time, we live together, and we've been living like this for two and a half years, and we hope to be doing it a lot longer.

Can you tell us about your switch-over? Why you started where you were, and how you decided to change?

Andy:

Well, when we came into the BDSM community, I was interested in experimenting primarily as a masochist in play scenes, because I like a lot of strong sensations. I also like to look after and take care of people, so from a labels point of view, the BDSM community kept telling me, "Hey, you should be a submissive!" Even though I wasn't all that submissive in personality.

Sue:

I'm a control freak. Having bipolar disorder, it was very important for me to stay in control because I didn't feel like I had any control in my life, so I didn't have any control over my mental state, and therefore I needed to control so many aspects of my life. I was a single parent, and control was very, very important to me. And I'm also sadistic, so from a labels point of view, I got labeled as a Dominant. I didn't trust easily, and part of why I *can* be Andy's slave is that I trust him so much ... and having him submit to me for years built a lot of trust. In a way, it prepared the ground so that I could let go and trust him.

But for me, slavery was more of a self-growth thing. It was coming to terms with my own shadow self, and being comfortable with what I really wanted to do, and having to learn how to trust Andy so I could let down that guard. It was also about facing my own definition of feminism and what the meant for me, and understanding that it was about having a choice, and I could choose to serve a man if I wanted to without betraying what I believe in.

The actual switch came when I was about to go into another really dark depression. I knew it was coming, and I just woke up one morning and really wanted to go to that dark, ugly, self-loathing place for myself. So I said to Andy, "I'll submit to you, I'll be your slave because I'm not good for anything else other than being a slave." He said, "OK, let's try this for a day," and that day went on to the next day and the next day and the next day. We went to get medication for me, and I learned that I wasn't going to that dark place at all, but I was actually going to a place where I felt very loved, very safe, very connected, and very special with him. So it started out as an attempted self-abuse, absolutely; but it turned into one of the most beautiful things I have in my life.

The transition was a struggle because I like control so much, but I know now that this is what I really want in my heart. Kink is about what turns me on, and this is about what makes my heart sing. I still struggle with old habits and old thought processes, and all kinds of old crap that gets in the way. I also struggle between what I want and what I thought I believed in, and coming to terms with that, so there's a lot of mental self-conditioning going on, with Andy's help and a lot of training. It's difficult, but it's good.

Andy:

The other part of the story is that I travel for a living, and I'm a type-A personality; I provided advice to executives of corporations. Originally, I thought, "If I submit, that's kind of letting me turn off that part of my head, so maybe this submissive thing will work." I kept having challenges with that though. I'm the primary bread-winner in the household, and I wasn't willing to give up that financial control. My kids from my first marriage would come visit, and I didn't like anyone telling me what to do with my kids, or when they could come over. We had lots of struggles around those things.

About six months to a year before the switch, I started exploring having submissives of my own, and I was looked at bringing in someone to serve me in a hierarchy relationship, underneath Sue overall. But me starting to explore my dominance ended up with us having another one of our fights and breaking up. I thought it was really over this time, but I said, "Well, I need somebody to look after the house while I travel, so I'm willing to pay you to be my housekeeper and my land-keeper; you can stay here as long as you look after the house."

Sue:

At that point, I was willing to do it for money, but not for love.

Andy:

So in a way that kept us together, and meant neither of us walked out the door for good. We had really gotten frustrated in our relationship; we fought about the same things over and over again. About every nine months to a year we'd have a major one and break up, and then get back together. Interestingly enough, it was often right in the middle of the Master/slave Conference. We'd go to MsC broken up and come back willing to give it another try. But there was a lot of damage done over those years from trying to live the relationship with me in service and her in charge, so we were ready to just about give up the relationship at that point. We do love each other, but we love each other enough that we would let each other go if it meant being more healthy. But we're also great friends, and we love the idea of M/s, the whole concept of it. We both believe in that, so we wanted to have each other as friends just because we believe in those ideals.

So when she asked to try submitting to me, I said, "Well, I've been looking at dominating other people, I'll try this." Interestingly enough, it seemed very natural once we did switch, even after we had struggled for six years trying to do it the other way. She calls me Daddy—I'm a parent, I know how to do that. The Daddy/girl thing ... it's partly a nurturing thing, but also a role-model thing. Even with my own kids, when they were teenagers, once they got to a certain age it was less like control and more like I was guiding them. You have a little bit of control, because they live in your house and have to follow your rules, but you have very little that you can control once they get to an older teenage level. You talk to them honestly about life, and provide the appropriate information on how to make good decisions, as opposed to controlling them.

Sue:

He struggled for a while with understanding that I wasn't a kid, and he didn't have to withhold information from me. I'm doing this as an informed, consensual adult. The only thing from my parenting experience that I bring into a relationship is to pick your arguments, and don't yell. My son taught me that when he was very young. He told me not to yell at him because he just wasn't listening when I yelled. But I don't think parenting really prepared me for M/s.

Anyway, my bipolar disorder. I hate it. It's a rollercoaster ride. I was officially diagnosed when I was twenty-three. My son was around three years old at the time. I was fifteen the first time I was hospitalized. By the time I was nineteen, I had been hospitalized three times, and two days after my nineteenth birthday I moved into a six-month recovery home for drugs and alcohol. I self-medicated a lot in my teenage years.

Looking back, I can see the mania and the depression; the swings started when I was about thirteen. I've been through lots of therapy, I've tried the medication, I've tried the cocktails; I've had to resign myself to the fact that I have no control over it at all. It controls me, and there's nothing I can do about that. Andy's helped me a lot with coming to terms with my illness. I still struggle with accepting that I have such terrible limitations, because in my family illness is weakness, and so we don't show any weakness. Ever. And mental illness doesn't exist, even though a number of my family members are also bipolar and just don't admit it. My brother self-medicates; my sister is on medication, but refuses to admit she's bipolar even though she takes bipolar medication. My mother has severe anxiety.

I still struggle with that, with not being able to accept my own limitations, but I'm at a point where I'm not suicidal any more. I want to live, I want to have a fulfilled life. I enjoy my life! I'm incredibly happy so much of the time now. But the only way to make this rollercoaster to stop, in my world, is to die, so that's when I think about suicide—when I just don't want to be on this rollercoaster anymore.

The depression is just like any other standard kind of depression. Sleeping a lot, not eating, wanting to run away from the world, not wanting to have anything to do with anybody, that kind of stuff. The manic ... oh, the manic's a riot. Lots and lots of anger, raging, lots of violence, lots of irresponsible behavior, lots of compulsive behavior, and a really high sex drive. I guess the anger is the biggest thing that gets in the way. I say things that are inappropriate when I am in a rage.

If I'm manic and wasn't in this relationship, breaking the law is definitely an option for me. In fact, there is a whole list of bad ideas that are an option for me when I'm manic that Andy wouldn't approve of, so that keeps me from doing those behaviors.

Andy:

When we met and started our first power dynamic, she was coming out of a major situation. There were times when things were challenging in our relationship, and I wasn't sure if they were real issues, or if they may have come from the bipolar. It was difficult to determine, and there were times where I'm sure I said, "Is this a sign of your bipolar? Are you manic? Are you depressed?" It made it more difficult for me to feel safe to submit, and feel that trust, because there was always a concern in the back of my head. It was hard to get past that, but I kept telling myself that it wasn't her fault. During the third year of our relationship we worked on weaning her off medication, and she functioned very well without it for a few years. The fact that she could be stable without medication made it a lot easier, and took away a lot of that concern.

Sue:

But I'm back on medication now. In fact, we just went through a change of meds. Interestingly, I've come to realize that I'm on a seven to eight year cycle. About every seven years I go through a really dark spell. I'm on medication for two or three years after that, and then I'm able to come off medication and I'm somewhat stable for a while, and then it starts to spiral again. We're just starting to recognize the behaviors of the manic side. I've always focused more on the depression side of it because that's where the suicidal thoughts were coming from, so that's what scared me the most. But now I'm starting to see the manic side of things, and that scares me more.

Andy:

For people who are bipolar, some of them like to live in the manic world, because they can get lots of things done. In the business world, they can accomplish a lot by living in the manic world. The problem is, how long can they stay there before they crash? Also, there's the problem with anger. Because they're manic, they're focused, they have goals … and if you interfere with those goals, you're going to pay for it.

So does the M/s relationship make you feel safer because you're under external control? Does the relationship become your control if you have trouble controlling yourself?

Sue:

Yes. Yes, it does, and I've had to use a lot of faith to build that trust, to be able to turn over my medical care to Andy. I've always tried to control the bipolar, even though I didn't always do it well, so to turn that over to him and say, "I trust you enough to maneuver me through this time" has had its challenges. But we're doing it, and yeah, the trust is definitely there now. I feel that safety. I know Andy can steer me in the right direction. He never steers me the way I would have done it, and he usually never steers me in the direction I feel is the appropriate way to go. The end result, though, is that I'm better for it, and the method is a lot shorter than I would have taken.

Andy:

Because I travel so much, we have a family calendar system that we use online, where she has to record her meals and record her medication. She has to show me that she's done it, that she's maintaining it, because historically if she is off in her medication or doesn't eat properly, in a couple days we'll see some bad effects of that. So I watch the calendar and make sure she's updating it. Part of the communication for our relationship is that, at minimum, she texts me in the morning and texts me before she goes to bed. Then I know when she's going to bed and when she's getting up; I know what her sleep patterns are like from that. I'm tracking her self-care.

Sue:

There are other rules as well. I'm not allowed to use recreational drugs. I know it would be very, very frowned upon if I did. I'm not allowed to break the law. I'm not allowed to run off with strange men, or other things that happened in the past. When I'm spiraling out of control or I'm in a depression, I'm not allowed to talk directly to Andy about things that trouble me. I have to write it, because I get too emotional in person, and I nitpick and I spiral and it gets me all worked up. Then we end up in a situation where I have to take additional medication just to calm myself back down or it blows up into a much bigger argument than it needed to be. So anything that's troubling me, or anything that I really need to express, I can ask permission to express it verbally. Andy will ask what the topic is and then decide. But if he thinks it's too triggering, I'm to write it in my journal. We have an agreement that if I tell him I've written in my journal, he will read it within twenty-four hours. Then I know it's read. He may not respond to it immediately, he may not act on it right away, but I know that he's heard me. I also know he's heard the real issue and not just the emotional rant or the spiral that's happening at that time.

Andy:

And even sometimes when she does write in the journal, sometimes it will be a rant anyway, and she'll come back a day later and write, "It's not as big of an issue as it was previously."

Sue:

At the beginning, I actually had three journals. I had my day-to-day journal, like this is what I've done during the day, and then I had my emotional rant journal where I processed everything and I wrote it all out and I worked it all out, and then I had my "here's the issue" journal, which was the condensed version of what was really going on. That's the one that went online.

Andy:

The calendar also helps us to keep track of what's going on. We want to do more, we love to do stuff in the community, but because of my travel I can only do so much of the heavy lifting when it comes to making those things happen. So Sue ends up doing a lot of that, but we have really looked at the balance between family, commitments to the community, and other commitments, to make sure she doesn't get overloaded. She can take on the world when she gets manic, but as soon as she goes manic—and she'll let herself go manic if she's got a whole bunch of things to do so she can get through those activities—we know there's a crash coming. She can only last so long doing that.

Sue:

It's horrible, but I've also learned certain foods will trigger it, so when I need to get through specific bad times, we will see an increase in me eating those foods.

Andy:

I've started to regulate those foods. We've got a regulation on pop, and a few other things with high sugar content. She has to ask me before she has pop, so I know how many she's having a day.

What made you decide to give him control of the medical stuff?

Sue:

Well, it was part and parcel of giving up control over everything, and wanting to honor that, because that is what I said I would do. But really, I needed an objective view of it, because I've been dealing with this rollercoaster for thirty years. I'm tired. I'm done. I don't want to do it any more. I don't want to decide whether I'm on medication or not. I've lost a lot of hope, and I still don't have a lot of hope of ever having a good, stable, normal sort of life. I know that's not the healthiest of views when it comes to my health and when it comes to making decisions, so I do need to give over control to my doctor who does know better, and to Andy, who has a different view of my life than I do right now.

Andy:

The other way she's expressed it is that she's in service to me. If I'm comfortable with the ups and downs of the bipolar when she's off her medication, and living with the effect it has on our household, that's my choice. But at the same time, how do I want her to function in the household? That comes down to the control of medication—do I want her a little manic? Do I prefer her a little more on the depressed side? Because with the medication, you never get a hundred per cent. You add a little bit of this medication and it pushes the mood this way, you add a little bit of that one and go the other way. The bipolar cocktails are individual, and getting them right on is difficult. As Sue said, just changing her diet can change her mood. So she said, "Depending on how you want me to function in the house, we can adjust the medication to allow that to happen." I decided that I prefer her just slightly on the manic side than slightly depressed, so that's where we're trying to keep it for now with the med cocktail. I prefer that because it's easier to control—I can take down the manic a lot easier than I can handle the emotions of depression—and I don't want her to feel suicidal.

What do you do now when the emotions are overwhelming you and you're having trouble being rational?

Sue:

Sometimes I'm coherent enough that I can say, "I'm being irrational, here's the emotion which is not necessarily what's really happening, and here's the logical side, and I need help." I can reach out for the help that way, but sometimes I have lost control, and the emotion is in control, and I'm not coherent anymore. If it's really bad, I'm told to take my other medication and go to bed.

Andy:

Yeah, she's got some very powerful medication that will shut her down very quickly. It knocks her out. But if she can talk rationally about it, and say, "Here's where I am," we'll talk about whether adjusting the medication can help, we'll adjust our schedules, we'll adjust activities to support it and work around it as much as possible. But if she's really emotional, well … I've had an anger problem in the past, I've done a lot of work on my anger problem, but I can't handle being badgered, because that triggers my anger issues.

Sue:

And I badger him. Once I have an issue, it has to be resolved. Now. The conversation can't end until it is resolved. And "now" isn't always the best time! Especially when "crazy" is in control.

Andy:

So she has her room—we have separate bedrooms—and she is told to go to her room, because these emotional blowups mostly happen in the evening, usually after dinner. Things have escalated since the morning, and we didn't catch what was happening, and now the day's running out and this needs to be resolved before we go to bed because Sue has this policy that you don't go to bed angry. You have to resolve it right now! But then the emotions kick in, and no discussion is going to go well, so we've had to go to bed unresolved. There have been times where I've had to prove to her that OK, we're going to go to our separate rooms and sleep, but I promise that we *will* come back to this tomorrow.

Sue:

When I'm totally gripped by the emotion and I'm confrontational, I'm told to go deal with it on my own, with the understanding that we *are* going to come back to it. So it's a time out. I can go to my room, I can draw, I can throw my teddy bears against the wall, I can do what I need to do to keep myself safe. But I'm not allowed to continue badgering Andy, and I know that the next day we'll deal with it, because he's shown me that.

When I'm not confrontational, but I'm just having a very difficult time because I've swung too far in one direction, we do turn to SM for an outlet. Andy has learned to draw energy from me, which also helps stabilize me. I just feel like he's taking it all away, he's sucking all of that out of me, and I feel that safety and balance again.

Andy:

The first incident happened when I was experimenting with SM play and I thought, "Hey, what can I do with this?" I can sense that balance point, that place in her body when she's overloaded in energy, where she's storing it. I can literally take it from that spot, and that helps her.

Over the years I've become quite comfortable with being responsible for her sanity. When she first started going down this path as my slave, she was on her way down into another depressive cycle, so it was a little scary as to where we were going to go. Historically she's lost everything every time it's happened in the past. She's ended up in the hospital, lost jobs, lost her son, lost it all ... but with me in charge, she didn't make the hospital. We kept her out! But we were asking each other: Can we successfully maintain your sanity and our relationship? It was definitely scary. We spent nine years together, and we love each other, but this was really our last chance to get it right.

Sue:

It's interesting how I see Andy talking about how he feels, being responsible for my sanity, and I instantaneously think, "He's not responsible for my sanity, I am!" But the truth is that I don't have to be anymore. I guess that's part of all this, right? I don't have to be, because I know he can be. And that's scary for me—very, very scary to know that I've given that up, too. It's just giving away one more thing, one more level. Like giving over power of attorney is no big deal because I don't value my life, right? But I value having control, even though I've chosen to give it up, for my own good.

If you weren't bipolar, would you have become a slave?

Sue:

Yeah, actually, I think I would. There were a lot of other things that were really pushing me down that path, and I see that now. Even while I was trying to understand Andy's submissive experience so that I could make our relationship better, a lot of what I was learning about submissives and slaves really resonated with me as well. In my history, I've always had submissive tendencies, and it's what I hated the most about me. I've always wanted to be a housewife, and to take care of my husband. I've always wanted to be under the control of someone else, looking back. I never felt like I had that control in my life, so there were a lot of things that were pushing me there.

Another big thing that happened for me was my son's father came back into my life. I hadn't seen him since I was pregnant, and I hadn't had any communication with him, but through that whole process of him finding my son and coming back into my life, I really had to face that earlier relationship and what it meant to me, and I realized he was my first owner. I had given myself completely and utterly to him. When he left me, his memory kept that person, and I started changing an awful lot about myself so that I wouldn't be that person. I also spent a lot of years secretly waiting for him to come back. But when he did come back, I was in the relationship with Andy and I realized I didn't want him anymore. I didn't belong to him anymore; I belonged with Andy. And that made me see just how much I did trust Andy, and how far down the rabbit hole of this relationship I was.

That was a really big thing for me as well to recognize that the person who had held me captive for seventeen years no longer had any power over me, but Andy did. The bipolar just tore down my wall and made me vulnerable enough, and it basically brought me to my knees.

What is the best advice you can give to a couple that's in your position, struggling with a slave having bipolar or other various difficult-to-control mental illnesses? What do you wish someone had said to you?

Andy:

We talk in M/s about having to be aware of yourself and the other person, but as the master you have to be even more aware. You have to watch the patterns. Bipolar is very much about patterns. Watch the whole drug cocktail thing closely; see what works and what doesn't. What are the patterns? What are the triggers for the different behaviors? Be very aware of those patterns. Scrutinize your property very closely. I'd say that this advice works even when the dominant has the mental illness. They have to know themselves. A lot of people who are struggling with bipolar don't really look at that closely enough.

I'd say that's good advice even when it's the dominant with bipolar. Sue did a lot of analysis on herself, and understood herself really well. When she was in charge, she could at least get up in the morning and say, "I'm having a bad day today and I'm going to be angry. Today's going to be an anger day." And her son and I would tread lightly. Well, actually, run and hide! But we have spent many years looking at patterns, and trying to find causes—what are the triggers for mania, what are the triggers for depression.

Sue:

My advice would be also to look for the patterns of behavior that will tell you what's going on. Become aware your own patterns so you can figure it out—am I manic? Am I depressed? Find out what it takes to self-assess. The scariest thing about mental illness is that you can no longer trust your own mind. The one thing everyone relies on to tell them what's real is suddenly failing you, and it's lying to you, and it's telling you things aren't OK when they are OK, or it's telling you you're invincible when you're really not. Recognizing the patterns of those behaviors can help you figure out when your brain is lying to you and when it's not. Then you need to learn how to express that to somebody else.

Andy:

Watch out especially for the pattern of the downward spiral. What can end up happening if you don't recognize the pattern is that you react to something they've done, and then how you react to it makes it worse. Then the downward spiral starts, and the relationship just starts crawling down the spiral. But one of you has to break the spiral, and the sooner it happens, the easier it is to deal with. Somebody just has to say, "This is where we're going." Somebody has to recognize. Somebody has to call it.

Sue:

Somebody has to have the balls to stand up to crazy. Somebody has to have the balls to say, "Crazy, you're not in control anymore, I am, and this is what we're going to do." And they need the strength to fight for that path.

Andy:

When you love the other person and they do something awful, you can run off and take that personally rather than saying, "Wait a minute. Is this the crazy and not you?"

Sue:

But at the same time, don't attribute everything to the crazy. That's the most frustrating thing in the world. Like if I'm telling you, "No, this is a serious issue to me," don't look at me and just say, "Oh, you're depressed."

Andy:

Right. You need to take the time to talk about it, and that's one of the reasons some M/s couples talk about "Porch Time", taking a designated time per week. But we can't do that. We can't say, "We're going to take Sunday afternoon at two o'clock every week and talk about our problems. Not just because I might be in Cincinnati, but because if we did that, by the time we got to Sunday afternoon at two o'clock, we're in big trouble. We usually try to deal with things by the end of the next day, if we can.

Sue:

It's important to remove emotion from communication. Having to write about it is really beneficial, because it makes me remove the emotion. Also, when Andy is reading that on the screen or in the book, he's reading the words of the emotion but not getting the impact in his face, so he has some time to react and then figure out what his response is going to be. It's a useful delay factor in which he can distinguish between, "Is this the crazy? Does this fit with the patterns?"

Andy:

As you were saying this, I was just thinking that was one of the problems with our relationship when it went in the other direction. Sue is a person who likes to talk things out and resolve it all immediately. Because she was in control, the method of handling problem situations was in her control, so we would just spiral until I got angry and the relationship would explode. What helped was me being able to say, "Stop. Not now. Not tonight, tomorrow."

Sue:

As mean as it sounds to say he sends me off to be on my own when I am in that state, it is the safest thing for me, for him, and for our relationship. It is in keeping with the fundamental truth of what our relationship is built on.

Andy:

There's really only two ways to handle that situation. One is to give her a time-out, and the other would be literally for me to tie her down or do something physical to restrain her.

Sue:

I'd like to see you try that, at that point! My emotions are very powerful when I'm there. Sometimes he needs to tell me to go to my room more than once, but I do fight with myself to obey him, even in that state. The more experience that we had with him doing it this way, and the more trust I have gained in him, the fewer times he has to give the order.

Andy:

The first time, I had to lock myself in my bedroom and tell her, "Go away. I'm not talking about this with you tonight. We'll deal with it later." And she was banging on the door! But since then, it's settled down. She started going to her room and being upset in her room.

Sue:

We were making a new pattern, a healthier one. And I'll try to remember this conversation the next time I'm in the throes of those emotions! "Oh, yeah. I said that I obey." And I really hope this interview will help people. I went to one workshop about M/s, and we were told that if you have any mental illness, don't do M/s ... and I thought that did a real disservice to any hope of getting better, of understanding how it can work.

Andy:

But it is another sign of why the choice of partners is so important in this type of relationship. The partner needs to understand it all very well, and be willing to get in there with you. Choose carefully, because you don't know what mountains you are going to get to climb together.

Trial by Fire: Trauma

PTSD Strategies for Slaves
pais

This essay is about working with a slave who has symptoms of PTSD. I am both a slave and a licensed clinician, but please bear that in mind that you may hear conflicting information or advice from other sources. And please understand that *reading this essay is not a substitute for seeking advice from a professional in person.* Much of what's in this essay is my *opinion*, and may not apply to you or your situation. The rest is material that, were this a paper for a scholarly journal, would be heavily footnoted. My goal is absolutely not to take credit for work that is not my own.

On the other hand, I have been aware of submissive tendencies in myself literally as long as I can remember. I have been involved in various BDSM communities in real life since 1999; I have worked as a professional submissive; and in addition to several years as a slave to my master, I have been in about eight years' worth of more-or-less D/s relationships. In my work life, I have spent years working with women and children impacted by domestic violence, and my coursework and training was largely geared towards doing trauma work in that setting. For the last few years I have been working professionally with adolescents, many or most of whom have trauma histories. So, with that background, here are some things I believe about slavery and about mental health.

First, our society (and perhaps all human societies) is quick to pathologize whatever isn't "normal", and often seems to have a very rigid and narrow conception as to what "normal" is. Our society (or at least parts of it) is quick to label all kinds of actions and feelings as symptoms of disorders or conditions or addictions that need to be "cured". We are quick to view any deviation in a negative light, rather than as a valid alternative. We see the natural human state of interdependence as unhealthy "enmeshment" or "co-dependence". We idolize a kind of bland emotional strength rather than celebrating the full range of human responses, and for some people their first response to any unpleasant emotional sensation is to attempt to medicate it away.

This is not to say that I disapprove of medication—far from it. In many situations, I think medication is an extremely vital tool for helping individuals lead the lives they want to lead. However, I want to start from a place of accepting that as human beings we are capable of experiencing not just low-key feelings, but intense peaks. Rage, anguish, despair, terror, guilt—these are all as much a part of a healthy set of emotional responses as joy and contentment. There is nothing wrong with having these feelings in and of themselves. Masochism, sadism, an intense desire to control others, an intense desire to surrender and/or serve—these are also valid human paths, regardless of what our society teaches us about being "strong and independent" or "kind and respectful". All of these are healthy and appropriate in the right context.

However ... if these desires and emotions and patterns of behavior are getting the way of you (or your slave) leading the life you want to lead, being successful in your chosen career or maintaining relationships that fulfill you, there is nothing shameful or wrong about seeking out professional help. Because of the way our society is set up, most people do not have a support network of friends, spiritual advisors, mentors or what-have-you who will be completely accepting, completely confidential, and completely dedicated to your well-being. Developing a relationship with a counselor or therapist who can provide those qualities—regardless of their preferred "treatment modality"—can be beneficial no matter what your struggle.

Now, in some ways, the same thing goes for M/s. It seems that various individuals and communities get ideas about what "normal" M/s relationships "should" look like. Where is the line between M/s and abuse? How does a real true slave^{TM} behave? What are the ethics of the Real True Master^{TM}? There are plenty of opinions out there about how communication should work, or how much control or service is required for a relationship to qualify as M/s, etc. Of course, I have my own opinions, and they are going to color this essay. It is not at all my intention to come across as judgmental or exclusionary, even when I choose to use the label M/s to refer to one subset of relationships that may or may not include relationships other participants call M/s. Primarily, I am concerned with individuals getting their needs met. However, this essay is aimed at individuals who are participating in M/s relationships that are fairly all-encompassing. In other words, if an individual considers her or himself an owner or master but the property retains control over health care and/or therapy decisions, when and whether to discuss certain issues, how much time and when to spend time together, this essay may be less helpful.

OK, on to the point. If you are having problems in your M/s relationship, how can you tell if the problems may be linked to the slave's PTSD, and how can you handle them if they are?

The name of the disorder gives the first clue: post-traumatic stress disorder is a condition that occurs after and as a result of trauma. If your slave has experienced trauma and now has certain emotional and behavioral symptoms, he or she may be suffering from PTSD. For the purpose of this essay, we will call trauma an *overwhelming experience of being in danger and helpless.*

+ First, *overwhelming*: By definition, trauma is an experience which the individual is unable to live through, process, and integrate into his or her understanding of the world using his or her normal coping mechanisms.

+ Second, *experience*: This could be a one-shot event, such as being under-anesthetized and waking up during a medical procedure, or a long period of time, such as growing up in an unsafe neighborhood, but what is less important than *what* actually happened is *how* it was perceived and interpreted on both conscious and unconscious levels. That is, it matters less whether the individual really was helpless or in danger from an objective viewpoint; what matters is that he or she *felt* helpless and in danger, or *believed* profoundly and viscerally that he or she was helpless and in danger. Some individuals are certainly more prone to PTSD, for reasons that are not fully understood. This might be part of that vulnerability: a greater likelihood to *interpret* events as threatening or dangerous, for whatever reason (genetics, physical factors in the environment from pre-natal on up, or social/emotional environmental factors).

✦ Third, *danger.* Perhaps on a subconscious level, the experience challenged the individual's belief that he or she would emerge on the other side whole and unscathed, the same person as before, either physically or emotionally. Even if the individual was not aware of this process, in some deep place he or she registered the experience as threatening to damage them in some drastic way, which included their experiences of both their physical body and their psyche. (This is how loss of a loved one, emotional abuse, hate crimes, and even just hearing about somebody else's trauma can be traumatic, even if the individual is not afraid of physical harm. It harms by inflicting damage to a person's self-image, or their understanding of themselves within the social or physical environment.)

✦ Finally, *helpless*: The experience was out of the individual's control. He or she felt (or was) powerless or ineffective. Here our own physiological responses can get in our way. The fight-or-flight mechanism is more accurately called a fight, flight or freeze response. Our brains automatically evaluate the level of threat. If it appears to be one that we would be able to escape or overcome with force, we are flooded with adrenaline. If our brain assesses the threat to be unavoidable and beyond our strength, we become paralyzed, no matter how much we may want to try to run or fight back. This experience of paralysis often adds to the trauma, increasing feelings of helplessness, shame, and guilt.

As a result of the trauma, a great deal of the individual's energy, which is already compromised by the long-term physiological effects of trauma, is channeled into repeatedly attempting, and failing, to integrate the experience into the person's worldview and self-view—the understanding he or she has about the way people interact, the safety and/or fairness of the universe, and his or her own efficacy, worth, spirituality, and even identity. This struggle for integrated meaning is challenging enough if the trauma consists of a single event that occurred when the individual already had formed strong, mature "schemas" or attitudes about life and self. It is far more problematic if the trauma occurred over a long period of time, repeatedly deforming these attitudes, and potentially devastating if it occurred over a long period of time when the individual was a child, so that the attitudes are formed initially with the experience of trauma as a core component. (Clinicians' and researchers' understandings of the differences in aftereffects of long-term versus unique and adult versus childhood trauma are growing, and it is likely that as a result the diagnosis of PTSD will be split into two or more separate disorders fairly soon.) Unpleasant or unsafe events are also more likely to be experienced as traumatic if they are result of directed human malice rather than impersonal forces. Thus, a rape is more likely to be traumatic, or to have more long-term and intense aftereffects, than a car crash. The key word here is "likely". Certain non-malicious, force-of-nature experiences such as being buried by an avalanche or earthquake are also extremely likely to result in more severe symptoms.

Typically, there are three types of symptoms evident when someone is struggling with PTSD. The more "psychiatric" symptoms are the "avoidant" symptoms and the "re-experiencing" symptoms. Roughly, avoidant symptoms might look like:

✦ not wanting to talk about the trauma

✦ not remembering the trauma fully

✦ being able to talk about the trauma, but without experiencing the emotions that go along with it (laughing while telling the story, or looking completely blank and "flat")

✦ avoiding the place the trauma happened, or other physical reminders (people, vehicles, etc; this can eventually progress to not wanting to leave the house at all)

✦ dissociation—which might look like "zoning out", or a feeling of being disconnected, or the experience of "losing time" (in extreme cases, this is part of what used to be called Multiple Personality Disorder and is now Dissociative Identity Disorder)

✦ some symptoms that look like depression: detachment from others, feelings of hopelessness, loss of interest in prior hobbies, etc.

Re-experiencing symptoms might include:

✦ flashbacks, nightmares and other sudden "intrusive thoughts"

✦ obsessive rumination about the trauma

✦ putting one's self in dangerous situations

✦ wanting to re-enact the trauma

✦ intense emotional or physiological responses when confronted with reminders of the trauma

However, although trauma has a huge effect on our thoughts and emotions, trauma is clearly not simply a mental phenomenon. Our physical bodies also react to the stimuli of perceptions, emotions and interpretations that comprise the overall traumatic experience. Trauma seems to have a profound effect on the system that sets off the famous "fight or flight" response. As a result, the physiological symptoms include:

✦ hypervigilance—constant, obsessive awareness of one's surroundings

✦ sleep problems, primarily difficulty falling or staying asleep

✦ difficulty managing emotions, particularly anger

✦ problems with focus

✦ exaggerated startle response—jumpiness, flinching at sudden noises or movement, etc.

Here is a generalized picture of PTSD, putting the three sets of symptoms together:

First, your system is full of chemicals that amplify your reactions to normal events going on around you, every moment. Second, your understanding of these events is colored by your experience, making them seem more threatening and making your responses and emotions even more unpredictably intense. At the same time, your brain is still trying to integrate that experience, so you have flashbacks or intrusive thoughts as you struggle to understand how current events fit together with past events, as perhaps seemingly unrelated, perhaps tiny reminders are all around, dialing up the intensity still more. However, your body cannot cope with this intensity. Your cognitive functioning begins to shut down. (This is actually a physical process—the neurons in the frontal lobe fire at a hugely reduced rate in response to chemical changes in the brain.) You become either "emotionally dysregulated"—exhibiting a sudden intense spike of emotion such as panic or anger which may cause you to act in unsafe ways, and over which you literally have no conscious control—or you dissociate, becoming largely unresponsive to what's going on around you, and later wonder why it's suddenly an hour later and you have no idea what happened during that period.

Now you've got these really scary reactions and emotional states you don't fully understand. Rather than chugging along with normal peaks and valleys, your emotional state is all over the place, swinging from uncontrollable, utterly overwhelming intensity to emotional deadness. You already know how terribly unsafe it is to lose control. In addition, you're having trouble sleeping, so you're even less in control of your emotions and unable to keep things in perspective. Finally, you feel like you can't relate to your friends anymore and, really, what's the point of even trying? Life is short and bleak. You don't trust people with little things but are careless about trusting people in big ways (because maybe you don't even deserve to be safe or protected or treated well, after all), so you repeatedly find yourself in sticky situations. You snap at people, and your friends start losing their patience with you. Maybe people are starting to tell you that you're paranoid, or you're just afraid they're going to tell you that. Maybe your loved ones are telling you to "just get over it," leaving you feeling guilty and even more isolated. Alternatively, maybe you've shut out thoughts about the trauma so effectively that you can't understand why people keep asking you what's wrong.

Now, this picture certainly doesn't apply to everybody who's experienced trauma, or even everybody with PTSD. In order to be officially diagnosed with PTSD, a person needs to have only a certain number of each type of symptom, not all of them. Hopefully this essay can also be helpful to slaves who may have what is called "features" of the disorder—fewer than the minimum symptoms for meeting the official diagnostic criteria. These features, on their own, can be debilitating to greater or lesser degree, and at the very least are extremely unpleasant to endure. Even if the experience doesn't seem as severe as full-blown PTSD, you may still improve your slave's quality of life by addressing his or her trauma history. You may want to reassure your slave that he or she deserves this quality of life no less than someone who seems more profoundly traumatized.

This is also not to say that PTSD symptomology is the only possible outcome from trauma, but discussing all the possible effects of trauma is clearly beyond the scope of this essay. This is not to invalidate or minimize the very diverse experience of individuals who have experienced trauma—on the contrary. There are other very serious mental health conditions (for example, Dissociative Identity Disorder or the personality disorders) which also seem to be linked to long-term and/or childhood experiences of trauma. If your slave has been impacted by trauma but these symptoms don't describe the problem, a mental health clinician can assess whether your slave may be dealing with one of these other conditions, and help you figure out what you need to do to address them.

A word about triggers: This term gets used *all the time* to mean "something that really bothers or upset me". That is *not* how I'm using it. For the purpose of this essay, a "trigger" is an event or thought that sends the individual straight out of control, whether it be rage, panic attack, blackout, etc. In general, if there is not a) intense sudden change of emotion, b) intense sudden change of behavior, *and* c) an objective experience of being out of control or lack of awareness of what's going on or what has just happened, I am not calling it a trigger. This is not something that "feels intolerable". This is something that *is* intolerable and the person who is triggered *cannot* control his or her response. That said, yes, some people may claim to be triggered when in fact they are exaggerating their reactions. In that case, as a clinician, my response is to assume they are doing the best they can (I try to assume that about everybody) and that this behavior is the only way or the best way they have of asking for help for whatever else may be going on with them. But "whatever else may be going on" is probably some kind of emotional regulation problem—quite possibly not being able to tell within themselves whether an emotion is tolerable or intolerable, or feeling unable to control tolerable emotions and thus afraid that at any moment a tolerable emotion will become intolerable, both of which are common for survivors of trauma. Therefore, some of the emotional regulation skills discussed below are perfect for them too, and it doesn't really matter except in keeping an open mind as to what skills are likely to be most useful for any particular individual.

OK, so now we've got a pretty good idea of what we're dealing with. Now what?

1. Consider finding a clinician.

One possible helpful step is to find a good clinician. In fact, I highly recommend this, but as a clinician myself I'm possibly biased (oh, just maybe a little bit). By "good", I mean one who is a good match for the individual struggling to deal with the symptoms. For starters, it may be beneficial to look for someone who has experience working with survivors of trauma. Look for some kind of trauma certification, or ask if they use a "trauma framework". EMDR (Eye Movement Desensitization and Reprocessing) is a technique with proven results, although not necessarily the only technique that works, and certification in EMDR does not necessarily make a good clinician, either. More important is the relationship the client can build with the therapist: the rapport your slave feels, and the level to which he or she feels able to trust and be honest with the therapist. Owners may want to be more involved in the therapeutic process than many clinicians may be comfortable with or used to; a good match for you means a therapist who is willing to work with you the way you want to work.

2. Consider medication.

Medication can also be a helpful tool. It is easier to live life, let alone process difficult material, when well-rested and not chemically primed for a panic attack! Medication can only treat the physiological symptoms, however, so don't expect it to be a magic pill that is going to fix everything.

3. Establish safety within reason.

People cannot begin to process trauma while they are still in a traumatic situation. Really. *For would-be slaves reading this essay: if you are in an abusive relationship, call a domestic violence agency (yes, after leaving is the most dangerous time, and yes, there are often good reasons to stay—but if there are also good reasons to leave, talk to somebody who can help you plan the best way to keep yourself safe.)*

This does not mean locking your slave in the house with a shotgun to repel all intruders. Normal life has some risks. If you experienced a traumatic car accident, you may want to use public transportation for a while, but eventually you're probably going to want to start driving again, because *driving* in itself is not traumatic—the *crash* was traumatic. Establish safety means *drive carefully and avoid further crashes.* The park where your slave was raped is not traumatic, unless she is so triggered that she experiences her uncontrolled emotional response as traumatic. If she can handle it, it's OK to go to the park. Find the balance that works for your slave.

Some specific behaviors for the owner:

✦ Find out, through asking and observing, what is triggering for your slave. At this point in the process, try to avoid those triggers. If your slave still cringes every time his alcoholic mother calls him, think about ways to support him in letting her know he needs some space to heal, and set up a schedule of phone calls so they don't suddenly happen out of the blue—or talk with him about cutting off contact altogether, if you think that might be what's healthiest for him. (This is emphatically not to suggest you unilaterally isolate your slave from negative relationships.) Don't push your slave to talk about the trauma yet—just the triggers.

✦ Try to keep any activity that you think might even possibly maybe be triggering within a specific framework, whether that means "Friday night is play time and is the only time we'll do these things" or "I will tell you immediately before I hurt you and I will tell you when we're done."

✦ Try to specify the extent of types of play you'll do, and don't try to do a lot of boundary pushing yet. Breath play, bondage, certain positions, noises, smells—any sensory input can be a trigger, and it may be as surprising to your slave as it is to you if what seemed like a potentially fun new activity becomes a huge scene—and not in a good way.

✦ Decide whether corporal punishment is a method that works for you and your slave at all, or whether it's better to correct your slave by talking through the problem.

✦ Be trustworthy. Keep your word. To the extent that you can, be predictable.

✦ This should go without saying, or at least fit into the above point, but: Don't make idle threats. Don't threaten to remove the collar or end the relationship for behavior that displeases you unless you really want to end the relationship. For that matter, don't bother trying to help your slave work through PTSD unless you're committed to see the process through.

✦ Respect your slave. Listen to what your slave says and read body language. Show with your actions that your slave is a valued and valuable person to you.

In general, people with trauma backgrounds are better at spotting danger than at looking for safety. Coach your slave to make a serious effort to look for safety. Have your slave look for trustworthy people, and encourage relationships with people who seem safe to you and who your slave agrees feel safe. Look for places that might feel a little calmer or more relaxing—that means, yes, go out *looking*. Take him/her places and ask about how it feels. The library? A particular quiet coffee shop? Help your slave look for and establish all the safety you can.

✦ Maintain structure. In general, familiarity feels safer. This doesn't mean you have to be rigid or micro-manage, but some predictability of routine might be helpful.

✦ Determine what level of control helps your slave feel safe. This varies from person to person. Remember, lack of control and feelings of helplessness are a huge part of what makes an event traumatic. For some people, though, that feeling of lack of control actually feels safer, protected, and cherished. The key is that the person who does have the control must be somebody who understands and is willing and able to meet the slave's needs. Sometimes your slave may need to feel that your needs come first, but if you're trying to work through trauma, I believe the slave must have the foundation of knowing that his or her needs are also valid and important, and that you are looking out not only for his or her best interest, but also his or her happiness and comfort. This might be difficult for some slaves to handle, but in the long run it is very important. On the other hand, your slave may tell you (or you may believe), that he or she needs a little *more* power in the relationship in order to feel safe. Can you negotiate a reduction in the power exchange, perhaps temporarily? (We'll come back to this later)

4. Get control of out-of-control emotions.

Piece of cake, right?

OK, maybe not. This is somewhere a good owner can really help a lot, because it is a complicated, multi-step process. Since it's a vital skill for a lot of people, not just those with PTSD, and because it's also related somewhat to getting control of uncontrollable thoughts and behaviors (which seem of even broader interest in the context of D/s and M/s), I wrote a separate essay about this, which you'll find next in this book. Before becoming a social worker, I spent a year in direct care using an Applied Behavioral Analysis model; I've also studied and used Cognitive Behavioral Therapy and Dialectical Behavioral Therapy. So I have a fair amount to say about modifying thoughts, emotions, and behaviors, much of it based on direct personal experience, although again I'm certainly not the be-all and end-all of behavioral training.

5. Process the Trauma

Once the individual is feeling reasonably safe and secure, and is able to maintain physical safety and return quickly to emotional stability when triggered, it's time to process the trauma. There are many ways of doing this, and it's where I have the least experience. Most of the trauma processing I have done was relatively minimal and went pretty smoothly; however, it can be a very tricky time. If safety and emotional control have not been established, there is a huge likelihood that "decompensation" will occur. This is the fancy clinical term for "everything falling to shit". All the symptoms may intensify; new symptoms and even whole new mental health disorders may develop. Scared yet? Maybe you should head back up to #1: Find a therapist!

Here are some points to think about if the owner does want to do the processing:

+ First of all, go slow. Start processing with the least traumatic event or aspect of an event. Work your way up over the course of time to more difficult memories.

+ If something seems too difficult to process, don't. Trust your gut, and your slave's gut. Work up to it. We have "defense mechanisms" for a reason. We don't plow through them until we've got something to take their place. Hopefully the work you've done on helping your slave get in control of emotions will have helped them develop some coping skills. If your slave still doesn't feel ready, have them practice their coping skills some more.

+ Don't expect to necessarily process something fully the first time. It may require repetition. At the same time, you may find that processing one memory releases the pain and trauma from other memories as well, so that they require less processing.

+ This applies to both the owner and the slave: Take care during the whole time. Be gentle with yourself. Keep tabs on how your functioning is impacted in other areas—

sleep, job, relationships. Keep remembering your grounding and coping skills. Owners should have someone else to lean on—and discuss with your slave how you're going to handle their confidential information when you need to turn to somebody else for support. Remember what I said above about being traumatized just by hearing about somebody else's trauma? It really does happen. Know your limits, and don't try to push past them for the sake of the work. The work will happen.

+ The goal is to integrate. It does no good simply to narrate events. Have your slave go slowly. Coach him or her to describe physical sensations and to feel the emotions throughout the retelling.

+ Keep asking, "What happened next?" Don't get stuck in the trauma. You survived. How? Who helped you? How did you get out of the situation? How did you get to where you are now, safe and healing?

+ Expect to recover emotions possibly long-buried. Most common are fear, sadness, anger, and guilt/shame. Accept these emotions, and *show* your slave that you accept him or her and all these emotions. Remember they all have their purpose. Fear teaches us to take care of ourselves. Give your slave permission to mourn losses—of innocence, time living with unresolved trauma, the person he or she might have been, or the choices he or she might have made. Let your slave rage against the unfairness or against the person or people who caused her or his suffering, and explore the guilt and shame so that your slave can find self-forgiveness. None of these emotions are wrong. Believe that, and help your slave believe it.

+ Remember that trauma is not simply a mental/emotional phenomenon. Trauma affects us in physical ways. The body remembers trauma. Often this may be the case because the trauma was something physical that happened to the body. Triggers are often physical cues such as body positioning, and the body reacts by cringing or startling to triggers without necessarily any conscious awareness. Therefore, the body has to overcome the trauma as well. Just talking about the trauma is not going to help. Include physical movement such as tai chi, qi gong, yoga, self-defense classes, etc. EMDR seems to work by helping the two sides of the brain integrate the trauma together by moving your eyes back and forth. Some research seems to imply that other repeated cross-body movement has a similar therapeutic effect. One of the physical effects of childhood trauma is actually a reduction in the size of the structure that links the two hemispheres of the brain.

✦ Do not expect your slave to be "fixed" or "cured". Trauma changes us irrevocably and we cannot turn back time, but just because we are different than we otherwise would have been does not mean we are sick or ruined. We are just different. We have learned, we have grown, we have (hopefully) become wiser and stronger.

✦ Finally, trauma recovery has a great deal to do with developmental stages. Trauma processed and dealt with for one stage may need to be processed again at later major life milestones and transitional stages, times when our identity and our place in the world are shifting. In other words, trauma processed as a teenager may need to be dealt with upon hitting the leaving-home-becoming-an-adult stage. Trauma processed as a free person may need to be re-covered on entering a stage of slavery.

6. Assess what further work needs to be done.

This is especially important when trauma began in early childhood and/or lasted over a long period of time. There are certain "developmental tasks" that we all have to master (no pun intended.) They build on each other, and if earlier tasks are not mastered, later stages of development will be askew even if no trauma takes place during those periods. Even if trauma occurred as an adult, some of those earlier-mastered developmental tasks may become more difficult again. This might lead to problems in areas such as:

Trust. For example:

+ Difficulty trusting people, even those who have demonstrated trustworthiness

+ Continuing to trust, or even feeling greater trust for, people who have demonstrated untrustworthiness

+ Trusting complete strangers, which can lead to placing one's self in dangerous situations—the classic "walking in the park at night" symptom

Self-esteem. For example:

+ Excessive feelings of shame, guilt, and doubt

+ Doubting one's self-efficacy or competence; feeling incapable

+ Craving positive reinforcement, constantly hungry for attention and praise

+ Difficulty initiating or following through on tasks

+ Constantly second-guessing oneself

+ Doubt about identity or role in life, feelings of lack of purpose or place

Intimacy. For example:

+ Extreme independence, emotional distance

+ Extreme dependence, not feeling sufficient or comfortable when alone

+ Difficulty empathizing with others

+ Seeing people in black and white terms, either all-good or all-bad

+ Difficulty maintaining attachment once the "new" has worn off

The way to work on any of these issues is to start by becoming aware of them. Notice specific interactions, and the positive and negative effects your slave's thoughts, emotions, words and behaviors may have on relationships, job performance, and overall well-being. Decide if there are specific emotions, thoughts, verbal patterns, relational patterns, behaviors, etc. that you want to change, and encourage mindfulness in those areas.

Surfacing the Inner Pain

Lisa

I'm a forty-eight-year-old female sub who has been diagnosed with borderline personality disorder, PTSD, major depressive disorder, major anxiety disorder, dissociative identity disorder, and agoraphobia, in December of 2005.

Prior to that date, well I knew I had issues, but really didn't have a name for them. I am the product of two very self-centered, lousy parents. My father was an abusive alcoholic, and my mother ... well, I guess I can't blame her too much, as she was fighting for her own life through most of my formative years. The abuse was very serious; at one point, Dad tried to blow Mom's brains out with a rifle. He missed, but the echo of that single shot is still heard today. At some point in those early years my personality splintered, leaving me with me and two others inhabiting my body. I have very little memory of my early childhood, and what little I do have is horrific. My brain has effectively locked those memories away, and though there are suspicions of physical and sexual abuse, I can't access the memories to prove it.

I learned very early to ignore my feelings, needs, and wants, and for God's sake don't cry in public! Those lessons, are still with me today, and are actually part of the root of my "brain glitches". In my teen years, I started cutting. Life—including the wonderful hormones of being a teenager—overwhelmed me, and I learned that the kiss of a blade and watching the blood well up and drip made me feel better. I was lucky; I never cut deep enough to need hospitalization (hmm, maybe that wasn't so lucky, come to think of it), or leave scars. Somehow I managed to get that craving under control as an adult—that is, until I was pregnant with a baby I didn't really want and my then-second-husband triggered some seriously bad memories. We divorced shortly after the baby was born in 2003.

Life overwhelmed me again in the fall of 2005. Between working nights, not sleeping, and having some issues with Child Protective Services, I reached for a blade after some 30 years without cutting. Once again, I was lucky, but this time, it was because of a wonderful angel in Texas that I had never met in person. She did the research, found the names, addresses and phone numbers of all of the mental-health-type places in my area, sent them to me, and then asked me every day if I had made that call yet. I finally couldn't take the nagging any more and called. I credit her with saving my life.

The first psychiatrist I saw, started me on Celexa, and I will say for the record that I slept pretty much the first two weeks of taking it. Oh, I went to work, but I often fell asleep while working. Once the fog lifted, I was able to think clearly for the first time in my life. About eight weeks in, I was experiencing some pretty serious cotton-mouth from the medication, so he switched me to Lexapro. His associate added Wellbutrin to the mix, with really good results. I have been with the same therapist for the entire time I've been in therapy, and we have made wonderful progress, not counting the bumps in the road. Today I am on 20mg. of Lexapro and 450mg. of Wellbutrin. When I need help sleeping, I take up to 100mg. of Trazodone. For the most part, I am stable, although I still have the craving to cut, and have some seriously bad days.

I first discovered BDSM from reading Victorian Era erotica. It intrigued me and, yes, aroused me to a degree that I didn't think was possible. I was in my thirties, more or less. At this point in my journey, I believe I was raised to be submissive by osmosis. My mother was submissive; she never fought back when dad was beating on her. She always did as he ordered. I have no doubt that those early lessons stuck with me into my adult life.

I actually let my submissive side out in real life in February of 2006. I had met my first Master online, and since he was within a twenty-minute drive of me, we met in person, and began a three-year-long relationship, with me as a secondary in a poly family. He passed on in November of 2008, leaving me a broken, lost, and frightened submissive. I met Daddy the following March, and we have been together ever since.

Relationships are a difficult topic for me. My life has been plagued by stormy relationships that never really last. My parents' relationship was terrifying to watch, and my mother abandoned my sisters and myself when I was seven, leaving us with an abusive alcoholic. I married the first time at the age of seventeen; I was pregnant with his child, and the only logical response was to marry him and hope for the best. My first husband was physically, verbally and mentally abusive, and ultimately raped me in my own bed before we divorced nine years later. I was married again less than two years after that divorce, and in retrospect, that was a big mistake. Although we were together for eleven years, my second husband was also mentally abusive to me, and physically abusive to my sons from my first marriage. In both cases, we fought, a lot, and I lived in fear that the next fight would be the one where either I got killed or I killed him.

When I finally got into a power exchange relationship in 2006, Master T understood my mental health issues better than I did, and he helped me learn how to deal with them at least as much as my therapist had. In fact, I actually told my therapist about my relationship, and what I was learning from the power exchange and BDSM aspect of it. BDSM and D/s have both kept me safe and sane.

Daddy and I have been together for three years, and I've been collared to him for one year. While he doesn't always understand my glitches, he does know when I need to have a session so I can bring the inner pain to the surface. He has learned how to push me past the point where I can control my response to the pain, and make me cry. I can't make myself cry; I was taught way too early that crying was forbidden.

The movie *Secretary* (while fictional) actually asks and answers one of my biggest issues for me. When the female lead was asked why she cuts herself, she responds that she doesn't know. The male lead then says, "...Is it that sometimes the inner pain has to come to the surface, and seeing it tells you that you are real, and watching it heal is soothing?" (Or something to that effect.) This is more true for me than not, and explains why the safe pain of an SM session can short-circuit the need to cut.

Honesty is important. When I first began talking to Master T, I disclosed my mental health issues within the first few conversations. It was the same with Daddy. I told them because I knew better than to hide it from them. I can only control my problems for so long, before they come out, and other people get hurt. Master T had already dealt with more than one submissive who had mental health issues, so he didn't have any problems. Daddy had to study, read, and ask questions in order to understand, and even now several years later, things trigger me that he couldn't possibly understand until after the fact.

Working is a challenge for me. I have trouble working and playing well with others. I don't really like most people, and can't handle large groups of loud people at all. Like my personal relationships, my work relationships are stormy at best. I've had six jobs since 2005, one of which lasted just eight weeks before I was fired. Work and I have a hard time getting along. Leaving my house on a bad day is all but impossible; I get overwhelmed really easily, and have to walk away to some quiet corner to get myself back in control. To cope and compensate, I attend group therapy and Dialectical Behavioral Therapy, and use the coping skills I learn there as much as possible. It doesn't always help, but occasionally I can short-circuit the meltdown before it goes too far. I am currently in a job-training program run by Community Mental Health, where I am learning how to work and play well with others. My people skills still suck, but I am better now than I used to be.

I handle most of my own medical decisions, but he is supportive of what I need in managing my conditions. He reminds me to take my meds, and talks to me when I am overwhelmed in order to help me deal. The only arguments we have over my medical decisions are when I fail to get my prescriptions refilled in a timely manner. Me, off my meds, is a bad thing.

What do I recommend to a submissive with these issues? That's easy. Take your medication like you are supposed to, and attend all therapy sessions. Don't scoff at treatment. Take your time in trusting a dominant, and be as open and as honest as you possibly can with them from the beginning. Your safety and well-being should be their number-one priority, and if it isn't, they aren't the dominant for you. If you feel comfortable enough with your therapist, by all means tell them about your chosen lifestyle. It can be a terrifying thought, but once you have it out in the open, you don't have to choose your words carefully, and that helps the therapy work better for you.

For dominants: Learn everything you possibly can about your submissive's issues. Get them to tell you as much of their life story as they can, and be on the lookout for things that could become triggers down the road. That way you aren't blindsided by something that causes your otherwise happy, submissive to come unglued. Be patient with your special submissive; life can be hard enough for us without having to do battle with an impatient dominant. Also, if you feel that you just can't handle the mental health issues, please don't pretend to try. It is far kinder for us if you can just be honest in the beginning.

M/s as Healing
Judy L.

My name is Judy L., and I am clean and sober in a recovery fellowship for alcoholics for twenty-one years now. During most of that time, I was in a vanilla marriage for ten years before being collared by my Husband for our tenth anniversary. I also have Bipolar disorder and PTSD from traumatic abuse by my birth-mom, as well as being molested by the friend of a neighbor at thirteen. I found Wicca as a religion around 1979 and was very active in online sharing, but it seems to be my path to walk alone.

Where to start? I don't know. I do know that when I first met my late Master, we tried exploring BDSM—not as a full M/s 24/7 thing, but hoping to get there from where we were. It all started when during a hot and heavy encounter, Master—who referred to His Deity as His Master—asked me if I "surrendered to Him". At the time, I thought that He meant my sexual surrender for that encounter. I had no idea that this "surrender" thing meant more than that. He, on the other hand, thought I had agreed to be His slave—He had ADD and "lesdyxia" (dyslexia) Himself, and from watching my medical treatments, he felt that my conditions were being misdiagnosed and maltreated. He felt that he could better help me if I was entirely surrendered to Him.

I had no idea what He was talking about. Church leaders in the Mormon Church He was ordained in, as well as the sacred and somewhat secretive temple sealing, include a vow of obedience, so He did feel that he had the right to expect this from me. While He had had BDSM experience with His second wife (a bottom but never a sub or slave), he had wanted something like this for twenty-five years.

However, there was my own past; at first I loved the play, but when I was punished, I could only think of it in terms of abuse. I'd been made legally (though not completely) blind from abuse by my first ex, so I took His reprimands as more abuse. I had a lot of baggage. Not surprisingly, I flipped out. I mean really freaked out. He blamed Himself for hurrying things too quickly and not clearly communicating what I was agreeing to. In the meantime, the therapy I was getting was telling me I should be more independent, set up boundaries, etc. At that time "incest survivors" were treated with intense encouragement to feel the feelings that many of us had supposedly numbed out and repressed with abuse. The problem was that many of us were encouraged to "remember"—often via strongly suggestive hypnotism—abuse that did not occur. I kept being told that my father must have also abused me and I just didn't remember it, and many counselors who claimed to specialize in this field, as well as a famous/infamous book on the subject basically implied that all males were perps. It didn't look at moms who used the buckle end of a belt on a child, or told her she was named Judith after St. Jude the Patron of Hopeless cases, so she was a hopeless case, as my bio-mom did at the time.

Many of these insisted it had to be male abuse, and that one had to wallow in unpleasant and harmful feelings, especially anger. This therapy was not conducive to my desires for BDSM, and I was quite confused. More recently, I've learned that many pros in this field now believe that most abuse and trauma sufferers with PTSD actually do remember the trauma that caused them to get said diagnosis and condition, but back then memory repression and exploration via hypnosis was very in.

My husband blamed himself for going too fast and not communicating clearly, as well as not understanding my mental health challenges; however, as we were going through a period in which I resisted, it was hell on earth for both of us. He wanted to fix me, and I wanted ... well, I didn't know what I wanted. I pushed him away and then wanted Him back. At one point, despite His heart condition, I kicked Him out of the house and got a restraining order on Him. Finally, my diagnosis was changed from depression to PTSD and Bipolar Disorder, and at that point Master began to study my diagnoses. With His background—he had two PhDs—He became quite compassionate and understanding once He realized that my problems were as much biochemical and trauma-related as anything else. Our marriage, still vanilla, got better. Why He put up with me I don't know—He only said that He clearly saw potential in me.

During this time He had suffered a heart attack, and we also learned that he had heart disease causing irritability due to fatigue and lack of oxygen to His brain. After we went through a period with proper diagnosis and a better understanding of each other's condition, as well as marriage counseling, our vanilla marriage improved immensely. The counseling was through His faith, which emphasized women submitting to husbands as to their Deity, so the Church counseling actually prepared the way for better understanding of possible D/s. While I was dealing with my abuse issues, Master had stopped all play because it sent me into flashbacks of the abuse—even the play I had once enjoyed at the start. But I got a new therapist who was more focused on helping me learn to live life on life's terms today rather than wallowing in the mire of abuse memories, as well as a psychiatrist who came up with the right diagnosis and started me on better meds. As a result of this we were reunited in a vanilla marriage, but things were still rocky and we didn't know why.

In 2003 I landed in the hospital with kidney failure from a bad reaction to my meds. It was my body reacting atypically to the medicine; it could not have been predicted and was nobody's fault really. In fact, only two weeks before, I'd had the routine blood tests and had "normal" apparent levels of the medication, but it skyrocketed overnight. Master's insistence that I go to the hospital literally saved my life—and my kidneys.

Master, still playing the role of my vanilla husband, was also a certified hypnotherapist and started using hypnosis skills to help me. It was those skills that enabled him to take charge and put me in the hospital. The doctors lowered the dose and the level of the meds, and overnight my personality and our marriage changed. (This was just before our tenth anniversary.) Master had been very patient with me once He had understood what my problems were, but we still had our days in hell—not whole months any more, but days. But once the meds were adjusted, I was a whole different person.

Then, right around our tenth anniversary, CBS had an episode of the TV program *CSI*, involving one Fem-Dom named Lady Heather. In the dialogue the head Crime Scene Investigator made the remark that the Dom was responsible, but the sub was in control due to safe words. Well, it was like in those cartoons; a light bulb went on over my head. I suddenly understood everything Master had tried to get through to me of what He wanted during the early days of marriage, and the bit of BDSM play we'd undertaken, as well as why He thought He had the right to physically punish me—that He thought I had agreed when I said I "surrendered". All of it became clear, perhaps because I was thinking with some clarity for the first time in my life.

I literally crawled on my knees to Him in His study and told Him I was sorry I hadn't understood for so long, and that I wanted to give Him me for a tenth anniversary gift. He was so pleased He took me to Wal-Mart the next morning and bought me a dog collar—I guess He was worried my mood would change. The only witness to that collaring was a high-school-age kid working the counter. Said kid turned beet-red and had a hard-on, so he clearly knew what was going on. Master had a calling for being a bit of what some Native American tribes would call a Sacred Clown, so He played it to the hilt. When the young guy gave Master His change, he was stuttering.

It was a simple event, but it changed the dynamics of our marriage. He made me another collar for lifestyle events, crocheted by His hand out of 25-lb teal-and-beige fishing line with a hook for a leash and a fastener crocheted in. Those He got at the plumbing store, believe it or not! I still have it and it is a great consolation. For the next four years we "lived happily ever after" as far as our marriage was concerned. Master took it very slowly—slower than I wanted, but it was a very wise way to approach it and He was right to do so. That's the first word of advice—if you are dealing with a slave who has trauma issues, go very slowly. Don't rush, even if they want you to.

Master had actually been impotent since His heart attack about seven years before that, and the only sex was via toys of various types, but it didn't matter to the whole dynamic of our marriage once it changed to 24/7 M/s. I can't say we lived "happily ever after" in every way, but the challenges—some huge ones too—were now Him and me against the world, so to speak. For the first time in my life I was happy, content and satisfied. Master was a gentle Dom and chose to control me by hypnosis, praise and pleasure. We played with ageplay sometimes too—I think He wanted me to have the happy childhood I'd never known. It worked well for us, despite nay-saying mental health pros who thought it would bring me back to my abusive childhood.

Who would have thought BDSM could be non-sexual for the Owner and still be greatly enjoyed by Him? Although I did find other ways besides intercourse to give Him some pleasure, as He gave me the toys and greatly enjoyed mine. We had four and a half wonderful years together, and the structure and discipline went far to help me in my mental health. My dear Owner was very protective of me; he would not share His "toy", nor would He allow any type of outside play for either of us. He felt that I was not mature or secure enough to handle Him playing with others, and also the faith He was ordained in would forbid it—and He Himself recognized that physically, financially, and emotionally He did not have the resources for any kind of polyamorous arrangement, even temporarily. I know He would have liked it, but it wasn't meant to be.

As His sicknesses caught up to Him, our non-vanilla social life was no longer possible. But somehow, even when He went into hospital and then cardio-pulmonary rehab, and back to the hospital when massive infectious long-term pneumonia caught up to Him, I did not have the collapse I would have feared due to my mental health history. I was strengthened by the M/s dynamic, structure, and discipline. I was able to advocate for Him until He died, plan a funeral in the faith He'd been ordained in, and a military burial for a Veteran, with full honors. I've been able to survive, and get financial help and other agency help for my own disabilities, which went downhill quickly when He died.

Most of all, to my amazement, although it's been hard as hell, I've kept my commitment to not harm myself ever again—part of the terms of our M/s—and I have not ended up in a psychiatric hospital. He is still my Master, even in death, and His word still stands. I've also kept my oath not to serve another, as by His faith we are believed to be sealed in marriage for all eternity, not just "as long as you both shall live" or "until death do you part". I've been able to get a dual widow's pension and get by okay, get agency help for my physical disabilities, and get help from the church as well. I've become stronger. They say whatever does not kill one makes one stronger, and this has been my case. I'm not as deliriously overjoyed and on a pink cloud as when I was first collared, nor as happy as I definitely was during the remainder of the period I was collared. But I am satisfied with my life and making the best of it to honor His memory, with gratitude for the time I had with Him, as well as the patience He had to bring out the best in me. He helped me to see myself as a Very Big Beautiful Woman, instead of "fat and ugly and useless" as I used to call myself until He strongly forbade it.

To satisfy my very eclectic Wiccan side, besides having a funeral service in our Church and the military burial, I had a memorial tree planted in the state where we had spent our honeymoon. This satisfied my Pagan soul and seemed fitting as He had grown up in the country, had been exposed to Native American values by an uncle by marriage who had adopted Him into His tribe, and used to like to skip school and roam the woods. Before our vanilla marriage, I had told Him just how sick I could get and begged Him to call off the marriage. He wouldn't, nor would He let me out of it. During the difficult years of my mental health obstacles, He was as patient with me as anyone could have been. I am glad He saw the potential for me to become a valued and clearly treasured possession—I don't know how He could see that before I did, but He always knew me better than I knew myself. He also believed He had to Master Himself in service to His faith and Deity before He could Master another, and this built up my trust in Him. He had my total respect and admiration and gratitude—as He still does, as I believe He is watching over me from whatever the next life is. He taught me to be grateful—to live with the death sentence every human being has from the day of their birth as one "living with dying", not "dying from death". Through His eyes, I became something more than my mental health issues and physical disabilities: a Zen-like paradox, having more dignity as a slave than before.

Despite my illness—which may yet rear its ugly head, I know M/s hasn't cured me completely, I still need to take meds and take care of myself—I have known happiness that I think few people in this world know, I let Him be the Potter's apprentice, as He might put it, and I let me be the clay. He used to tell me many times that I was a goddess in the making, but I am quite sure He was and is the instrument of the Divine that continues to do that making. I might add that this was foreshadowed on our honeymoon, where this city girl saw her first rainbow when He pointed it out to me—a double one—and by the butterflies, symbol of change, that surrounded our honeymoon cabin. I'm glad I didn't know how hard it would be to find happiness or I would have probably run for the hills, but I am glad He wouldn't let me.

The former therapist who was the first professional to try to teach me to live life on life's terms instead of wallowing in bad memories (and nightmares of memories that did not happen) thought that I should write a book about all my recovery and experiences for others. Well, this essay is the closest I've come—and I do this a bit in her honor too, as she got me to a place where I was well enough to accept the accountability of being a collared slave.

Epilogue:

Since I first wrote this essay, it's been six and a half years since Master died. I've had some really horrendous times with deeply grieving Him, and I'd say I still do. I especially get down in the dumps and outright clinically depressed on days like the anniversary of our marriage, or when our marriage was sealed and blessed by the Church He was ordained in, or on His birthday, or Valentine's Day, or the day that we got engaged. Those specific dates trigger a deep sadness for me. I usually do a little rite where I light a candle in His memory, and that helps. The most amazing thing, though, is that I've never had to return to any type of psych hospitalization through it all—that's the anchor that our M/s has given me. I live a life where I'm pretty satisfied with the way things are, most of the time; and sometimes I am even content.

One thing that helps me stay on an even keel is to count my blessings. I know so many people in this world—in and out of the lifestyle—who have never had a happy, permanent relationship. I had the privilege of having the last four and a half years of our marriage being the best years of my life. There is a song—I don't remember who sings it, but it goes like this: "I wouldn't have missed it for the world, wouldn't have missed loving You." And that is honestly how I feel. It was worth it to me—all of it—to have that time with Him.

Since His death, I am in a wheelchair, as well as having severe vision limitations. I don't leave the small city apartment that I live in, except for medical appointments. I like to joke and say that Master has me more in bondage now than He ever did when He was alive. I've been in the hospital at least eight times with diabetes-related cellulitis infection in my legs, once for surgery, once for MRSA, once for cancer and once for pneumonia; however, He is still my anchor and I got through it all—even fighting with the state's Medicaid program to get appropriate treatment for the Cancer for several months. I've been blessed with two Dom/Owners who act as my protectors. One is a moderator for the online site known as Fetlife—she was especially helpful when I was going through the cancer and the fight with the state over it—and also a Dom/Owner and His slave/wife who act as my protectors, both in advising me and even helping in material ways. They are my Guardian Angels!

I've kept my promise to my late Love of my Life and Lord of my Heart to remain celibate; not to even play or date. This He asked me because of my prior lousy track-record with abusive men. He also asked it of me because He wanted to continue to provide for me financially and, having had the heart attack and being disabled, He could not get health insurance. He wanted me to get His Surviving Spouse Social Security benefits, and a state pension He earned by serving in the Military during the Vietnam war era, as well as material benefits and a good deal of other help from the Church He had been ordained in, which has been very generous in all areas. If I remarried, I could not get the government benefits, and His Church is extremely strict—anything vaguely sexual outside of marriage can result in one being temporarily or permanently expelled, depending on how "repentant" the person is. I know He wants me to have a local community of real people that support me, as well as my online BDSM community.

Because I have an amazing home health assistant and dear friends, as well as the folk of His faith, my AA sponsor, my Druid mentor, and my computer, I've been able to live independently in spite of all the health issues. I even do my AA meetings, which are a large part of my staying functional and stable, online. I can get most anything else from Amazon, an online grocery store that delivers (Peapod), and a pharmacy that delivers. I have amazing doctors too—both my PCP who also has psych experience, and a series of wonderful mental health professionals, including the one I have now. I crashed and burned recently for a while in a severe depressive episode with awful insomnia and I almost did have to go to a psych facility, but it turned that conflicting meds prescribed by different doctors had caused the crisis. Once that was ascertained, one of the meds was changed and I've been on an even keel again.

I know that this is because, when Master was alive, I found for myself a firm foundation for living that worked—and that continues to work because I strive to remember what He would want me to do in each of life's challenges, and then I do it. This is making all the difference in my world, even today. I guess I'm doing well—this month I shall have, God/Dess willing, twenty-seven years clean and sober in AA. On Thanksgiving of 2013 it was twelve years since I'd needed formal psych hospitalization. Just going to my psychiatrists and doing my 12-step groups has been sufficient to keep me going. Back when I married Him, if someone had told me I'd become a widow and stay sane enough to function, I'd have laughed in their face. Yet I have! And for this I am grateful to Him and to the God/Dess of my understanding.

Rev. Judy L, Papa's owned always: still proudly wearing His Collar and Ring, rest in peace, beloved Master/Husband!

Interview with Bella
Bella (with help from her master Ki)

(Note: Bella has DID—Dissociative Identity Disorder, formerly known as Multiple Personality Disorder, so she is using the self-referential plural pronouns "we" to indicate all the "alters" in her "system". Ki also refers to Bella as "they" in this interview for the same reason.)

Bella:

I'm Bella, and I'm Ki's slave. I have depression, possibly a mini-bipolar thing according to my therapist, and DID, which we only recently discovered in the last two years. That's really late to do it. I don't recommend waiting that long. We haven't yet found the initial incident that triggered the DID. I believe that when I was two there was an incident where a man attempted to rape my mother, according to her. He couldn't rip off her dress and didn't manage to actually rape her, but my stroller tipped over and I was inconsolable for days. I'm assuming that is the triggering incident—and there was the trauma of my father dying, and other traumas throughout my life that clipped more and more people on.

I currently have a psychiatrist and a talk doctor, and they both work together. I'm on Wellbutrin and blood pressure medication because the Wellbutrin shot my blood pressure pretty high. That's working well at treating the depression. My talk doctor believes in the integrative family system where everybody has their parts—you have your angry part and your socially concerned part, and so forth. Getting those parts to talk together is very important. The parts of people with DID. are just a little more fully formed than those of other people, but she feels that everyone has facets to some extent, so we work with that as a theory.

Are you completely responsible for her medical care at this point in time?

Ki:

I'm completely responsible for everything now. Medical care, money... her ass is mine and everything attached to it.

Bella:

If it wasn't for her, I would not have found therapy. I was very much against it. She didn't give me a direct order to get into therapy, because that would not have gone over well and would not have made therapy productive for me. Instead, there was a very subtle campaign on her part to walk me around to the idea of therapy perhaps being a good thing. It took a few months for me to actually find a therapist, too. I finally went , but I did not tell the therapist I had D.I.D. I just told them that I had depression and was going through a divorce. About three-quarters of the way through the initial interview and she asked me, "You talk about 'we' a lot; do you have other people in your head?" I owned up and said, "Yes?" and she promptly said, "I don't feel like I'm competent to take your case." Crap! She was supposed to try to find me somebody else, but after three months of back-and-forth emailing with her, she obviously was not going to do that, which led to more depression and "Well, why bother trying? I'm obviously too damaged."

But I've since found my current therapist, who recommended medication for the depression because first the chemicals needed to be fixed. So I have a psych and I have a therapist now, and it's actually extraordinarily helpful, and I've become an advocate to other people that it might not be a bad idea to try some therapy. My therapist knew a little bit about BDSM, and I gave her some more information about BDSM versus self-harm, and as long as it is productive, she is good with it. The fact that we are in an apparently lesbian BDSM power dynamic relationship, she's fine with that.

Ki:

It was more persuasion than an outright order. It was several steps of subliminal programming. Until the back of her brain could accept it, the front of her brain could not comfortably manage it. So I just planted a little seed and let it grow, then another little seed and let it grow. It took several months but I knew that if I just said, "You're going to go to therapy," it wasn't going to do any good because she would have just done it without involving herself, and if you're not involved, it ain't gonna happen.

Bella:

Later on, as our pieces and parts started really falling into place and I had names, I made a spreadsheet of who and what and when and why. I found out that not all of us are submissive, and not all of us necessarily wanted to be in a Master/slave relationship. We had always naturally been drawn to being on the right-hand side of the slash, but also trying to accept the fact of the people inside us that didn't want to be on the right-hand side of the slash. "But that's who we are! What do you mean that's not who we are?" We had a lot of internal discussion as to how that was all going to work. It did create some issues, because if we had switched out and were not one of the right-hand-side-of-the-slash people, and had not communicated that yet because we didn't know how to, she would make an order and we'd say, "Fuck you," and that obviously did not go over really well.

So we had to start finding ways to communicate that, yes, you're looking at the body of this short blonde woman, but the person you are used to dealing with is not currently in, and the person currently in charge is a six-foot-tall black man who is not submissive at all, and really takes offense at being told to do anything. We've worked out ways so that we present a consistent front if we are out in public, because our issues are ours, and nobody else should have to deal with that, but it did create some problems initially with our personal relationships, because we were wonky.

We do all get along with Ki now, though. We communicate differently, and we don't always realize that we've made a switch, but often times Ki will notice it before we do, and she will call us out and say, "Hey, Cassie," or, "Hey, Mal," or whoever popped out. For example, Beth is easy to find. Beth is six years old, and she is one of the most defined personalities when she comes out. Often times Ki will spot it first, and will understand that the normal communication styles are not what's needed in the situation if I'm a little six-year-old versus a six-foot-tall angry black man versus Bella.

Ki:

The first thing I did was to implant a compulsion in them, and to this day, they get pissed at me for it. They don't deny the need for it, they don't deny the use of it, but they still get pissed that I did it, and that I did it without them knowing it. I implanted the compulsion to write down everything emotional. It doesn't matter who it is or what they're feeling, they have a compulsion to write, and it goes in a journal that I have absolute access to. It also doesn't matter what they write in their journal, because they aren't going to get in no trouble for it, ever. There will not be repercussions, there will not be punishment, but I have to know. They have to be literally more emotionally transparent than most M/s slaves, because when I see the slightest bit of glitch, I've got to start catching it right then and there. That's because one little glitch may snowball in four months to them being checked into a hospital, so I'm real careful.

So our protocols are around them writing and me reading. For instance, Mal is a 13-year-old pissant, just bound and determined to yell at everybody. She'll get on that journal and say, "Goddamnit, I hate that I have to write, I don't like writing," and then she'll write what she's pissed about, and say, "I still don't like writing!" But it's OK, I know who did it, I know that she's pissed, but it still got written. I still know what's going on with more than just my girl. Because it is ultimately me who is responsible for their system. There are other people in my own system who help me with that, but we had to designate one person who was ultimately responsible for their system. When push comes to shove, even if I have to go up against Trey, Trey and I will butt heads, but I'll win.

Bella:

Trey is the six-foot-tall black man. The others don't feel slave-like, but everybody sees how this influence has helped dramatically. Especially when we've talked in therapy, and talked about what we've done, what coping skills we've learned, what Ki's done specifically to help us, whether we knew it or not at the time. Sometimes we were being led in a certain direction very quietly, because we would have fought it tooth and nail if we'd noticed anything. That trust has been built, and all of us believe that Ki has our best interests at heart. We also believe that Ki's not going to try and order the six-year-old to do things that are inappropriate just because one of us is her slave. So there's a respect in the relationships between them that all manages to work well together.

Ki:

There are a number of other rules as well, designed to help them manage. First, there's the A-word. Appropriate. If Mal the thirteen-year-old wants to come out, is it appropriate for her to throw a tantrum in the middle of dinner? If she just wants to throw a tantrum, that's fine—she can throw it when it's just her and me in the bedroom, not when it's going to affect the kids who live in this house. Are they being appropriate in their clothing choices or their purchasing? Because eventually it comes back around. Their system does not have consistent communication with each other yet, so I am sometimes their communication between one another. She'll look at me and say, "Do we have milk?" and I'll tell them either yes or no, because Beth may have decided that she wanted to drink the last of the milk, but nobody told Mandy, who was the one out shopping. So are their actions appropriate? Have you looked forward at what may come from this action? That goes right along with being an appropriate, well-behaved slave; it's just that all of them have to follow these protocols at this point. I'll help them, I'll support them through it.

The one other rule is: I told them that I loved all of them, and they were under the impression that when she was angry and hateful and going through her divorce, and struggling as a mother, struggling in her soul, that I only loved her when she was good, but no, I love all of you. When the system started making itself known to each of the others, that became crucial. It becomes almost a rule and a protocol, because I have to keep reminding them. Sometimes it's the only thing that gets through that head, knowing that they are all accepted here.

In M/s, we often talk about the difference between compromising with the slave and compromising with reality. For something like this, there's a lot of reality to compromise with. How do you keep that from making it feel like, "Who the hell is in control of this relationship anyway?" How do you keep it from undermining the sense of being in charge when there are all these other things that you can't control or can only barely control?

Ki:

The first thing is that you have to understand that reality is going to be reality. It's going to take precedence. So you put in a lot of little tiny acts of submission. She asks me if her food is an acceptable selection, and asks permission to start eating. Most of her people do, actually! Trey just doesn't come out for food, but even Beth will look at me and ask if she's allowed to have the jellybeans. Mal won't necessarily ask permission, but she'll stop and sigh dramatically and say, "Is this *acceptable*? Is this *appropriate*?" It's a little bit of protocol that gets dropped in all day, throughout the day, and it helps a lot. They have to write in their journal—that's not only part of their mental healing, it's part of their slavery. It's a service to me, and they know damn well I'll be checking it. They also keep a food diary, and they know damn well I will be checking that too, and I will come down on them if it's not maintained. It's little things like letting me know when they are going to walk away and go talk to someone in a public place. It's letting me know what's happened during their day, like a debriefing at the end of the day—not for their emotional stuff, but the details—"This is what happened at work" or "This is who I spoke to" or "I have this problem with this situation." Those are the little things that keep the Master/slave relationship alive through all the other shit. It keeps it going through her being in charge at work, through her being in charge in front of the kids.

I left the kids, ultimately, in her care. They're her kids; she has the final say about them. Now she and I have gone some rounds over that, because if they'd been my kids from birth, they would not behave the way that they do. She pointed out that they weren't raised that way, so I can't expect them to behave like my own kids did at this age. But while the kids are in her charge, I make sure that she is on the ball about taking care of them. I don't let her slide, and if she's doing something way out in left field, I pull her in. Sometimes I've had to look at the kids and say, "Your mom's having a hard time. I'm in charge for right now." And that's reality.

We've also established safewords, and I don't mean for BDSM. Safewords are for any time. She's having a fit? She's being irrational? I can look at her and call a safeword, and she will go to her room and take some time, and I will go to my room and take some time. Those got established because I ordered it. You can make orders to cope with the reality of things. They can become protocols that adjust for reality, and make it easier.

How do you cope with issues like—as you mentioned—other people spending your money? What about when that affects the whole household?

Bella:

We've done fairly well with that. We had a lot of good coping mechanisms already in place—our therapist is very confused by how well we've done by ourselves. We have what we call "filters". We have a "mom" filter who deals with the children no matter who's running things in here, so that the children have a consistent mother figure. We didn't have a huge problem with overspending—we didn't have a situation of not being able to pay our rent because we'd bought something else. That didn't happen because we didn't have that option. We had to maintain a home for the children, because we were mostly a single mother while they were little. We had to do things for our own survival. At base, DID is a survival coping mechanism, so we did what we needed to do to survive. At most we would find a twenty or thirty dollar difference because somebody went to the thrift store, and we'd find a bag full of stuff and not know where it came from. Now we know to ask, "Who bought this? Who wanted this? Who thought this was a good idea?" For years, though, we would find things and assume that we were just really forgetful. But we didn't run into a lot of things that really damaged reality.

Once we became a mother, it was no longer an option to suicide out or really screw up our lives, because we were now responsible for two humans. We made 'em, now we gotta deal with it for at least eighteen years and possibly longer. We are responsible for making them into decent people. We can't be living on the street because we screwed up our money; that's not an option. So we had very strict guidelines about it, no matter who was here.

What advice would you have for masters who are facing down a sub with these issues? Who are saying, "I want to do this, but I have no idea what I'm doing, and it's scary!"

Ki:

Oh, it's really scary. It is beyond scary. Number one: Sign yourself up for an abnormal psych class. Preferably in a college! Number two, get to some support groups. You want to get to some support groups for the condition itself, and support groups for the partners, because you have to know both sides. You have to know what's going through their head, and you have to know how to deal with it. That will give a lot of insight. And study ... and study. And flexibility—in dealing with any mental illness you have to have flexibility. Learn a little bit of NLP (Neuro-Linguistic Programming). Learn a lot about body language. Learn at least something about nonverbal communication—gestures, microexpressions, intonation—because those can suddenly become your only clue as to what is actually going on, especially with DID, mood disorders, bipolar, borderline, where they just can't communicate effectively. They get frustrated, and all they can do is sit here and clamp down and rock back and forth, thump on their chest or their head, but their face and body will still tell you what's going on under that. Get to learn those methods of communication, because that's what's going to lead you to be able to bring them up out of that state, and to keep them out of the hospital. The last thing you will need is more patience than you will ever know exists ... and then you will find some more.

What's your advice for being able to know when they are out of their depth?

Ki:

If you're already in the relationship, the moment you think that you're out of your depth, start looking for outside help. The moment you think you've got all the answers ... get some outside help for yourself. What happens is that you get so in the groove, in control, that you stop thinking that outside influences might be assistive. Then you get so far down in that groove it becomes a canyon, and that may not be the help they need to get out of their problems. You've made a road that is not going to be a solution. So if you absolutely think that you are the be-all and end-all, you go get some outside help. If you are questioning, "Oh my god, I might be out of my depth!" go check the support groups. Get some extra ideas. The minute you are no longer creative, go get some outside help, because you need to be creative in dealing with a lot of this. You have to develop six different methods of possibly stopping their fall when they go down—on the fly. Nope, it's too late, you didn't do it in time! And, healer, heal thyself—get your own ass into therapy. Get your own ass a life coach—somebody that understands and can help, who can give you some ideas that you can follow.

Do you have any advice for the slaves who want a master to fix them, or at least make things better?

Bella:

My first advice would be that they can't fix you. Nobody can fix anybody. They can help you, but they can't do it for you. A hammer will fix a nail that needs to go in, but the hammer can't do it on its own. The master-person isn't going to fix it, and if that's what you're looking for, you're looking for the wrong thing. If you're trying to find someone, and you're being open and honest and saying, "Yes, I've got these three other people in here," and you try and it fails, don't blame them. If they come to you and they honestly say, "I thought I could handle this but I can't, I can't wrap my head around it," don't then blast them on the Internet, and don't feel bad for yourself for failing in some fashion. Understand that not everybody can cope with it. There's a reason that not everybody is a hospice nurse—not everybody can deal with death like that, and that's OK. So if you try and work on a relationship and it just doesn't work, that's not your fault, it's not their fault, it's just not a good fit. Keep trying, keep journaling to find out what it is that you need and want—not that you just want somebody to fix you, but more like understanding "I need this structure. I need help with these things. Maybe I need financial help because I'm bad with my money—because people I don't know keep spending it from inside!" Be up front with that and say, "This is something I'm going to need—are you OK with helping with that? Is that something you can do in your role as the left side of the slash, as the master-type person?"

Don't try to match up with somebody just because they're hot. "I think they could do it, because they look like they should be able to!" If you don't come clean with what you need, or you don't even know what you need, they can't give it to you. Be honest with yourself and do a lot of introspection, a lot of looking inside. Get your people talking to each other and find out what they all want. If you have people in there who are not on the same side of the slash that you are, are they OK with letting you be in a submissive position in the relationship? How can they deal with it? What would they like out of it? Do they need their own relationship where they are a top for somebody? Do they need their own vanilla relationship? Maybe you're looking at "monogamous body, poly people"!

Tips for Helping Self-Esteem in Your S-Type
Raven Kaldera

(The original version of this essay was first posted on Fetlife. A small handful of people objected to it on the grounds that if the master was a shit and walked off in the middle of it, the s-type might be even worse. However, over seven hundred s-types and their masters loved it, and my omega boy—on whose damaged self-esteem I honed these techniques—begged me to include it in this book. While it is not specific to a single problem, most damage to self-esteem comes from some sort of trauma, so it is being placed here.)

One of the many negative myths generated about power dynamic relationships is that the subordinate partner is there because they have terrible self-esteem ... because why else would anyone willingly choose to be in a subordinate position? This type of circular reasoning is, of course, false as a general rule. However, that does not change the fact that a certain percentage of s-types do struggle with low self-esteem, just like a certain percentage of egalitarian people—and, for that matter, a certain percentage of dominant types as well. Low self-esteem is the psychological equivalent of the common cold in our society. So, given that, some dominant/master-types are going to end up with s-types whose self-esteem is not so great. And, because so often We Want To Fix Things, of course we want to fix that, too.

The vast majority of M-types do not want a "worthless worm", regardless of the porn. We want competent human beings who are proud to be in our service. This may make an s-type with low self-esteem feel that they aren't even worthy of offering themselves, and they may gravitate to the few who do want "worthless worms" because "obviously those dominants who want strong, competent people wouldn't want me." This doesn't have to be the case, though. And if that new s-type who is sitting adoringly at your feet turns out to have somewhat damaged self-worth, is there something that can be done about it?

This is a list of techniques that have had good results for me. Obviously not every technique is going to work for every s-type; they're all different people. But if any of these help anyone, it will be worth writing them down.

1) Find their strengths.

First, find areas in which they can excel, and push them toward excellence in those areas. One of the things that builds self-esteem, even in an s-type, is "mastery experiences". By this I mean being able to achieve something they didn't think they could achieve. This is a technique much lauded by masters of disabled slaves—find an area that is not trashed by their disability, and push them to excel in that area. (Even when my disabled boy is so bad off he can't get out of bed, he can still work on giving me accurate and honest self-assessments, being cooperative when I tell him ways to take care of himself, and having a good, cheerful, smiling attitude when I come up to check on him.) It's important to stress the difference between perfection and excellence. Perfection is irrelevant. Excellence is achievable—and stress also that it is your standard, not theirs, which decides what is excellent. You can also tell them that failure is not a bad thing—one master says that his slaves are either good, or they are learning, and never anything else.

2) Believe in them.

When you push them toward excellence in these areas, look them in the eye and tell them that you believe in them. You believe that they can do this thing. You will be there to help them do it, if they need help, but you have a rock-solid belief in their ability to pull it off if they put their minds to it. (Start with something you really are quite realistically sure they can do—it's not good to set them up for failure on the first few times you try this.) After this has worked a few times, they will internalize your belief in them. To paraphrase one slave who mentioned this: "I believe what he believes, and he believes in me."

3) Mandatory affirmations.

An exercise I really like: Order them to tell you three good things about themselves. Even small things. Don't let them leave until it's done, and done right. Next time, three other good things about themselves. Do not accept anything phrased in a self-deprecating manner. Make them say it again, more proudly, or at least more matter-of-factly, if necessary. A variation of this works well for depressed s-types—"Tell me three good things about your life!" or "Tell me three good things about me."

4) Consider neurochemical issues.

In that vein, get them checked for neurochemical problems. Depression or other issues of bad brain soup can set up a fog of negativity that nothing can penetrate. If they need medical help, see that they get it, or you're battering yourself against something bigger than you. If they need therapy, see that they get it. Be patient and understand that it's going to take longer if they are constantly being sabotaged by their own brain chemistry—even when you're medicated, the medication doesn't always work, and years of bad brain soup can set up patterns that take a long time to change.

5) Eroticize the challenge.

A somewhat dangerous tool, but one that can work with an s-type who is strongly sexual and finds it easy to eroticize weird things: If there are specific and unchangeable qualities that are the pivot-points of their self-esteem issues, see if there are ways that these qualities can be played with during sex or scenes which eroticize something about them. Perhaps it's eroticizing that quality, perhaps it's eroticizing embarrassment around that quality, perhaps it's eroticizing the master's use of that quality. This does not mean something as clumsy as yelling triggering insults during sex (unless you've both negotiated experimenting with that). This needs to be done very much as a team, perhaps trying it out with sexy storytelling first before enacting it. However, it can totally turn around an s-type's attitude toward a specific obstacle. "Hey, that obstacle's kind of hot, or weirdly desirable, y'know?" "Wow, I never thought of that!" Again, this won't work for all obstacles or all s-types, but it is a legitimate tool for the right s-type in the right situation.

6) Prevent negative self-talk.

Set up a discipline of stopping internal negative self-talk. Have mantras that they can say when that voice starts. One of the best ways to slowly silence that voice entirely over time is to just never let it speak. Perhaps a good starting mantra could be, "Master/mistress says that I am worthy, and I trust him/her," said to cut off every time the nasty voice starts up in the head. Ask them, at the end of the day, how many times they used that mantra to cut the voice off. Praise them for doing it, even if they only remembered to do it after fifteen minutes of writhing under their own self-torment. Eventually it will become not just a discipline but a habit.

The next two suggestions are more controversial, because they rely on the existence of a healthy, fulfilling power dynamic relationship that is going to be around for more than a year or so. I've found these to be the most important—and most effective—tools in my box when it comes to healing an s-type's self-esteem, but don't use them if you don't intend to stick around, or if this is not a serious and committed relationship for you.

7) What Would Master Say?

Work hard on getting your s-type to internalize your judgment as being the voice they should follow, even when you're not there. Every s-type has a "master puppet" in their head, which may or may not have traits and qualities that are based on that of a realistic human being. That aside, however, your job is to slowly replace that puppet with a puppet that looks like you, and speaks in your voice, and gives them the advice you would give them. This is a long, slow process and won't happen overnight, but it is crucial. You want to give them the equivalent of an automatic "WWMS"—What Would Master Say—bracelet. Once you've done that, you can reinforce the fact that *you say they are worthy, and it's your opinion that matters.* They can't argue with that opinion without owning the fact that their internal voice is more important and valid to them than you are. If this isn't working yet, you need to work more on that internal master puppet, through other means.

8) Make them proud of their service.

Assuming that this is a long-term committed relationship, it can help to tie their self-esteem to how well they please you. Both my boys have large parts of their self-esteem tied to being my good boy. Being proud to be your good s-type, and proud to be in your service, can slowly spread over time to other areas of their life. Really. I promise. But to make this work effectively, you need to show your pleasure. Not just pats on the head and "Good girl" or "Good boy", but "Wow, this is awesome!" "Well, look at you!" "Have I mentioned lately how great it is to have a slave who can make baklava?" and so forth. Pleasing you needs to be a top priority for them. Encourage this. Then, eventually, they will value pleasing you more than valuing their internal negative voice ... and because they know that it would please you for them to work on their self-esteem, they will be more motivated to do it.

One objection to the idea of "outsourcing" self-esteem is that it's just plain bad to base it on external sources, even if those external sources are good people who aren't going anywhere. People who object to this usually go on about how there are better tools and methods out there. However, those other tools and methods don't work for everyone. For some s-types, the only thing that *will* work is these latter two options, and even the other techniques on this list may be ineffective until you've done that. Also, these techniques can be used as training wheels—the s-type may need them for some time, perhaps even years, but they may eventually be able to be weaned off them if necessary.

My omega boy, Brandon, was one of those people. The child of an emotionally abusive narcissistic-personality-disorder father and a codependent mother, he'd had years of therapy, a year of DBT and was in the middle of CBT when I got him ... and his self-esteem was so non-existent he couldn't take a compliment without wanting to throw up. As he puts it himself:

> I find that for me, it helps my boundaries
> when my Master takes for himself the things that
> I otherwise give too freely. For instance, I'm a

very submissive person, but we established that my submission is his now, so I feel more driven to find ways to say "no" to people who aren't appropriate to submit to, even when I can't find a way to say it that doesn't make me cringe. This extends to the boundaries I (don't) keep around who gets to decide my self-worth, especially if that person is not even around anymore, or if that person is myself. So it helps me when he takes an attitude of, "OK, you externalize your self-image anyway. Since you keep giving that away to everyone else, I'm taking it now. It belongs to me, since you cannot be trusted with it yet."

Yes, in some cases this would be an unhealthy option, and it could also set one up for one heck of a potential downfall. However, at the most basic level I know that if I ever had to leave him, I trust in his honor and his word that he would not just toss me out the door to be a wreck elsewhere. I have repeatedly seen his ability to be civil and do the right thing in situations where no one would have blamed him for throwing up his hands, cussing everyone out, and storming off; and I have full faith he would show it again in this situation. And even if he were to be hit by a truck and die tomorrow, the work he has done on me has made me stronger than when I first came to him. I would remember his faith in me, and he would still be the person whose memory I would depend on if I became self-denigrating.

But even with that aside, I know what I have been doing on my own hasn't been working. Loving friends I've had for almost all of my life, years and years of various types of therapy, taking actual steps in improving myself and my situation ... if none of these have helped, I'm not going to turn down the one thing that has been actually shown to work, and that is outsourcing my self-esteem to my Master. Hopefully I will be able to pick up more of the slack as time goes on, but the other option of staying stuck in the morass of low self-worth became a non-option when I signed up with him, and the very fact I can see improvement is proof enough for me. Certainly it's not the method of choice for everyone, but hey, that's one of the joys of everybody being different and all that jazz, right?

Holding an s-type's self-worth in your hands is a delicate and terrible thing. You can crush it with a word, with the wrong phrase, with one callous day ... and yet, if you do the work right, you can slowly shape them sturdy enough that your off day doesn't faze them at all. And the result is truly a beautiful thing.

On the Borderline:
Personality
Disorders

When Your Bottom Has Borderline Personality Disorder

Del Tashlin

✦ Know what BPD is and what the major markers for it are.

✦ Make sure your bottom is in some form of active acknowledgement and frequent self-reflection about how the disorder affects their relationships.

✦ **Impulsive behavior:** Borderlines suffer from perpetual boredom, and frequently make strange requests in order to spice things up. Frequently they will ask for sex or play at strange times, and/or will be impatient with negotiations. It helps to have a set standard of play, knowing what their limits and turn-ons are, so you can keep negotiations short and focused. Be prepared to be asked for play when it seems like it's out of left field—they may be using it as a coping mechanism.

✦ **Abandonment:** BPD people are terrified of being abandoned, and this feeling can be invoked in a shorter amount of time than one would expect. Best practice is to not blindfold your bottom and stay within line of sight. Keeping physical contact with them, especially when changing toys or taking a break can be incredibly comforting. If they are blindfolded, talk to them firmly when there's no physical contact. Particularly be aware of this feeling when the scene is over; make sure someone is with them at all times when they are coming down from emotional intensity. You may want to make plans to have someone else clean up after you, so you can keep your focus and attention on your partner.

✦ **Idealization/Devaluation:** Some weeks, you'll be the best Top they've ever played with and you can do no wrong. Then something minor happens—you wrap a strike, you hit them the wrong way, you take them to an uncomfortable mental place—and you're the worst Top that has ever lived and every scene you've ever had, even if you remember them fondly and they were fulfilling and moving, were horribly planned and went awry. It's normal for a Borderline to struggle with this dichotomy even when they're aware that it's faulty brain wiring and not the truth. Have a strong sense of self, and let your own memory be your guide. Be gentle but firm about reminding your partner about good scenes you've had when they're being negative, and about mistakes you've made when they're feeling positive.

✦ **Instability in Identity:** A common Borderline fantasy is to be a Top's molding clay—they want to be whatever it is you want them to be. D/s and M/s relationships are particularly attractive to them, because of the perceived freedom of following clear, concise orders as definition of role. However, you're playing with a chameleon. Be unsurprised if they identify as a switch and go through periods where they will want to be the Top, or to Top others, and be less interested in play where they're the bottom. They will probably shift social groups too; this week they'll be keenly interested in Daddy/boy play and find an identity that fits them within that dynamic—a few weeks later they'll go to an ageplay munch and be all about their little. Borderlines have developed a sense of fluid identity as a coping mechanism for trauma—it's well-honed and hard to turn off.

✦ **Black and White Thinking:** As with idealization/devaluation, this also holds true for other aspects of play. They may identify as the biggest cane slut ever, and then you have one scene where they have a bad experience and they will change their tune to never liking canes—not now, not in the past—and will bend and flex stories to make them out to where they fit the new paradigm. If you have a bad experience in a dungeon, even one you know and love, it will be some time before they'll come around to seeing things as balanced again. Gentle, firm reminders of good times had doing X activity or in Y place or with Z person help tremendously—but be ready for some resistance at first. It's easier for Borderlines to classify the world this way, and once things start getting gray they become uncomfortable.

+ **Problems with Emotional Regulation:** Along the same line as Black/White thinking, Borderlines tend to lack subtlety of emotion—when they're mad, they're angrier than they've ever been in their whole life; when they're happy, they're euphoric. It can be refreshing to be with someone who is so easy to read—it also means that when they're turned on, they're incredibly emotive about it. It becomes a problem when things go awry, or when you push them to uncomfortable places in your play. Be aware that bright fuses burn fast—the body physically has a hard time holding emotional responses of deep intensity for very long. This means that they'll be tired and grouchy before long, or recalcitrant and weak. This can become a real problem in longer term relationships—when they feel like they're in love, it's the deepest, most passionate feeling they've ever had (even if it's the sixth or one hundred and sixth time it's happened to them); when they're feeling unsure of the relationship, all they can remember or conceive is the bad stuff.

+ **Self-Harm Behavior:** This is probably the biggest concern I would have as a Top playing with a Borderline. An earmark of BPD is self-harm—cutting or scratching the skin, pulling out the hair, biting the self, picking wounds so they do not heal, or other forms of intentionally hurting oneself. BDSM can either be a godsend—as a focused activity where the impulses to self-injure are being met in a safer atmosphere under controlled conditions—or a nightmare, where the maladaptive behavior is encouraged. I personally make it a rule that I do not play with Borderlines who are actively self-harming—I look for recent marks, admissions of behavior, or other signs—or have not yet begun addressing their habitual self-harm in more positive ways. It is encouraged to know your bottom's preferred modality of self-harm and stay away from it during play, as it could possibly trigger further episodes later, when you're not around.

When Your Submissive Has Borderline Personality Disorder

Del Tashlin

+ Find and participate in a support group for partners of people with BPD. It is a challenging experience, especially when your partner is currently symptomatic. Learn all you can about the disorder, and what the markers are.

+ Find and maintain a strong sense of who you are and what you believe in. It sounds unrelated, but people with BPD, especially ones in power dynamics, will actively rewrite history to fit their current perception of a person, place, or thing. This is not meant to be deceptive or manipulative; it's actually a coping mechanism so they can see the same person as benevolent/good and abusive/bad. This will no doubt come into play in a D/s or M/s relationship. Know that when they rebel and say they hate you, it feels very real and very immediate to them, and that they can only remember times when you were mean to them or misused their trust/submission. Gently remind them of good times when you were benevolent and trustworthy, while still listening to what they are saying and dealing with the trigger that caused the switch.

+ Emerging research is saying that the majority of people diagnosed with BPD are survivors of abuse, either parental or peer, and that the markers are actually maladaptive coping mechanisms. Encourage your submissive to be actively engaging in recognizing the ties (if any) between their desires as a submissive and their healing process as a survivor.

+ One of the most difficult aspects of having BPD is that few medications do much to treat it. Be patient with your sub and listen when they tell you a drug isn't working if they've been taking it for longer than a week. This often translates into frustration with the entire therapeutic process—seeing a counselor, going to peer groups, etc. If it is within your power dynamic, encourage/demand your submissive to be actively pursuing some sort of therapy until the therapist releases them. BPD can and does go into remission; but people with BPD who say they are in remission still struggle with symptoms from time to time. It's usually better to err on the side of caution and ask them to be engaged in some form of process if they're actively symptomatic to the point where it's interfering with your relationship.

✦ Authority is both intoxicating and frightening to a submissive with BPD. Take your role seriously; do what you can to be worthy of the role. Own your mistakes, and actively encourage feet of clay. Be aware that they will go out of their comfort zones to keep you happy—including losing their identity in the process. Remind them about aspects of themselves that you particularly like or are attracted to, to help them keep a handle on who they are and what makes them special.

✦ Be prepared for your relationship to grow and change in short, traumatic spurts. Borderlines like to play with roles and identity, and may want a few months off from the collar if that's where they're headed. Personal experience has found that having a power agreement with a lot of freedom gives the Borderline permission to explore new identities while maintaining their position as a submissive or slave.

✦ Self-Injury: It happens. It is not a gauge of how "successful" you are as a Master, Mistress or Owner as to whether your submissive engages in this behavior or not. SI tends to be a marker of deeper issues, and it may be useful for you to write into your agreement that incidents of SI are always met with discussion and wound care first, behavioral correction later. For most, it is an incredibly private and deeply embarrassing behavior, so it is a sign of intimacy and trust if they feel comfortable discussing it with you. Rarely do bouts of SI indicate actual plans of suicide, but if you see evidence of both it's time for professional intervention.

✦ BPD people suffer from impulsivity, usually in areas that are self-destructive. They may find it useful in power exchanges if you become the Master of those domains. If they tend to max out their credit cards as a coping mechanism, make it so that all credit card charges that aren't living-expense related must obtain permission. If you are in a swinging or poly relationship, and sex impulsivity is an issue, make it an agreement that you must meet and approve all of sex partners of your sub. This is one of the most healing, helpful ways a Master can support a submissive dealing with these issues.

Having a Slave With BPD

LyonSlayr

I happen to own a slave who has what's known as Borderline Personality Disorder. A major part of the effect is high anxiety and depression. Even though I am a trained counselor, there are many new skills I've had to learn in order to support her and keep our dynamic strong at the same time.

The most helpful thing I've learned is that the disorder is not "her". It's an ailment she suffers from. Making that distinction helps Me to be more aware of when it's the disorder and when she's up to her usual shenanigans. I've developed almost a sixth sense around it. I need to be very intuitive on a day-to-day basis.

When she's in a state of anxiety, I stay calm and speak to her very clearly. I try not to engage in too much conversation that may aggravate the anxiety. I also communicate My boundaries very clearly, as I need to keep in mind where I end and where she begins. I sometimes need to remind Myself that I'm not the one with the disorder. It helps to remember that she is suffering and would change it if she could. The one thing I avoid is engaging in the chaos that anxiety can bring. It's important to stay very consistent with this attitude, which is difficult because being with someone with BPD can be very draining. I make sure to look after Myself and stay in a relative state of calm in all areas of My life.

There are times when the whole thing just pisses Me off. It's natural given the circumstances. It used to take Me by surprise and I would lose My cool out of sheer frustration. After living with her for almost two years, I seldom act out My frustration, which has turned out to be a key to handling her. She needs to know that she's safe and I don't hate her. We keep the topic on the table and talk about it regularly but calmly. I don't want her to be afraid to approach Me and tell Me when she's having a bad time. That way, most days, we're on the same page.

Pain can sometimes be useful for us. When she is in a very high state and can't seem to calm down, I will use pain in a more violent manner than I would in a play scene. We call them "therapy beatings". Pain can give her relief as it provides a focus outside of the anxiety. It's akin to cutting, which is often practiced by those with BPD, but it's much safer because I control it. It pulls her out of chaos. One of the other effects that can come with depression and anxiety is what's known as "shutdown" or "flat affect"; a numb, disconnected feeling. Pain opens the door to feeling something, anything. She doesn't enjoy the feelings from the pain, and will fight tooth and nail because I won't bind her at times like these. The sheer pain and violence of the experience tends to ground her afterwards. She will often present to Me afterwards and thank Me for helping her.

Why do I go through this with her? I will tell you that I came into to kink in the 1980s, and I have yet to meet a better slave. She faces her disorder head on and knows that she needs to maintain outside support. She wants nothing more than to be the best slave she can be to keep Me proud to be her Master and Owner.

Dialectical Behavior Therapy as a Tool of Mastery
Jonathan Carvey

I have had two slaves in my time, both with Borderline Personality Disorder. My first slave was killed in an accident some years ago, and somehow I ended up with a second one who echoed my first one. During the decade I spent with my first slave, I worked out a number of techniques to help her to control her raging emotions. When my second BPD slave came to me, she had just started a round of Dialectical Behavior Therapy classes. When she described them to me, I realized that I had already figured out a large percentage of the DBT exercises through trial and error with my first slave, and had integrated them into her training and everyday management. I looked further into DBT, and found more useful tools to work in with my second slave.

When I described this at a large BDSM event, I was met with a number of stares from masters. "You've got one too?" they said. "How do you cope?" I was amazed at how many BPD people had ended up slaves—certainly not all or even most of them, but a much larger percentage than you might find at, say, a scuba divers' convention. They asked me to write down my experiences with using DBT for BPD slaves, and that is what I'm doing here and now.

What Is BPD?

Before I begin, however, a little background is necessary. Borderline Personality Disorder is a condition where the sufferer has a great deal of difficulty regulating and controlling their emotions. The feelings of a BPD person are huge and overwhelming, and tend to err on the side of fear (usually of abandonment), panic (sometimes to the point of paranoia), rage (often impulsively without much ability to control the actions), and depression. They think in black and white; anything is either all good or all bad, and people and things can go from white to black the instant that they show themselves to be imperfect. They may self-harm or engage in self-destructive behavior, and about ten per cent commit suicide. They lack theory of mind, in that they find it very difficult to imagine or understand how the inside of someone else's head might be different from theirs—this disorder does make people fairly self-involved—and as such they project their own thoughts and feelings onto everyone else, usually unconsciously. They may "rewrite the past" mentally and insist that their version is correct, especially when it makes them out to be the victim. They can be very manipulative, as manipulation of the truth and the emotions of others is a favorite fallback when they are panicked over losing someone's goodwill. (If you would like to learn more about Borderline Personality Disorder, please refer to the books at the end of this article.) It's recently been discovered that BPD people have differences in their brains, that this is more of a neurological problem than a chemical one. (See *Overcoming Borderline Personality Disorder: A Family Guide for Healing and Change* by Valerie Porr.)

With all these problems, why would anyone want to be with them? Well, if this is the person you've fallen for, and you enjoy other parts of their nature—their passion and intensity, their imagination, their charm—and you're the type of person who likes to patiently train someone to improve, this might work for you. But the most important part is that they are able to stick with it and let you do your job. If they can't make themselves obey enough to make this work, or if they keep running away, it will fail.

I want to make it very, very clear, before we go on, that I am not advocating becoming a slave (or even getting seriously into a relationship as a submissive) as a cure for BPD. It will not work. Master/slave relationships only work with people who are *naturally* dominant or submissive, who would be that way regardless of their mental health. So if you have BPD and you don't find it fulfilling to have someone else tell you what to do all the time, don't think that pretending to be a slave and finding some poor dominant to attempt to master you will work. This article is written for BPD sufferers who *are* naturally submissive—my definition being, as above, that they really enjoy being told what to do, even when they freak out and rebel against it. (I will go out on a limb, however, and say that DBT is a useful tool for anyone with BPD, be they dominant or submissive. But it only works for those who are ready to receive it.)

The following techniques are ways that a master can incorporate DBT into their training program in order to help a BPD slave. This can be done alone, or with the slave going to DBT meetings and the master adding in the protocols and home training as the group moves through each skillset. While I did it alone, I should also point out that if it's not working that way, try doing it in tandem with DBT group therapy before you give up altogether. That kind of external reinforcement can help a great deal. Your slave should also have a therapist who understands both BPD and DBT; regardless of whether you want to discuss your Master/slave relationship, you should at least appear as the supportive partner who wants to help them continue the lessons at home, as they should be doing.

(Note: My slave is female, so I use a lot of "she" and "her" in this article. I am aware that BPD is not limited to women, and may be underdiagnosed in men. Please mentally insert whatever pronouns you feel are appropriate to your own situation.)

Mindfulness

It's not easy to train a slave in mindfulness, and honestly the first step is to make sure that you have that skill yourself. If you don't, cultivate it in yourself before you try to teach it to anyone else. The steps are as follows, and while they are written for your slave, you can do it for yourself as well.

✦ **Observation.** Most importantly, observation *without judgment*. I'm a fan of old science fiction, and I had my slave read *Stranger In A Strange Land* by Robert A. Heinlein, where they have people who are trained and employed as Fair Witnesses. They describe only what they see, with no assumptions or speculations about what else those things might be. This is a good skill for a BPD person to learn, because their mind automatically jumps to all sorts of assumptions about the person or thing they are looking at, and at least half of them will be dead wrong.

+ **Description.** Putting the observation into words. This can be cultivated in a slave by periodically instructing them, "Describe that thing for me, in completely neutral language." I tell my slave, "Fair Witness mode. Describe that thing." Doing this over and over will slowly train them to let something be only what it looks to be until further investigation. They learn how to make things "neutral" and take the emotion away from them.

+ **Describing Feelings.** When you and your slave have mastered the first two, the next step is to apply that to their feelings. When they are having a freakout, have them sit down and breathe, and describe the emotion. Figure out a list of emotional intensity from one to ten, and have them observe and describe how the feeling waxes and wanes. When they've become used to this, have them consciously apply thoughts in order to make the feelings wax and wane, while you're sitting there listening to their play-by-play of what's going on. This helps them to get control over their "dial", which first means showing them that the dial is actually controllable by them. Eventually, they should be able to describe the entire emotional "story"—the trigger, their perception of the trigger, their physical sensations and what their body language did, and the action they took (or wanted very much to take). This is also a useful tool when they aren't sure what emotion they are feeling—going through this process can slap a "label" on the feeling.

+ **Describing Situations.** The next step is to apply this to emotionally-laden situations. Have them describe the situation in neutral language, and then describe their feelings about it, also in neutral language. Have them practice this skill around volunteers who will help them understand what sorts of situation-descriptions might or might not be offensive to others. This is a way to start them on the theory-of-mind concept, or the idea that everyone has a whole different mental world, and it's possible to figure out someone's mental world (and thus how to communicate with them most effectively), but only if one can get past one's own assumptions. For BPD people, this is usually the assumption that other people have wants and reactions like they do, or like the "villain" in their head does.

✦ **Right Vs. Effective.** This is very important—perhaps the most important DBT skill of all—because it brings them out of their emotions and into functionality. Being "right" is a very subjective thing when it comes to interpersonal relationships, and your BPD slave probably has their own strong subjective opinions about other people doing "right". Have a conversation with them about what's more important—having those emotions (which may be positive ones; self-righteousness is often pleasant, if otherwise useless) or actually making change in the world. Once you've sold them on the latter (which may take a while, and require a mandate from you that they are to "act as if" whether they like it or not), do "thought exercises" on a regular basis, using real-world scenarios. Have them brainstorm responses to the situation that might make change, and grade them on the basis of "what will likely be most effective". You might also have them grade the same list on the basis of "what will be most emotionally pleasant in the moment", if only to highlight the fact that the two are often very different.

✦ **Focus.** BPD people are often distracted from the task at hand by their emotions. Start small—have your slave do a low-emotional-impact activity while being completely focused on the task at hand. If they have trouble with this, you can back up a step and do a guided meditation where they focus on parts of their body, one at a time. If you are into it, this can be incorporated into a scene where sensation is applied to different parts of the body in order to help them focus on it. However, the end result of this training should be the ability to focus entirely on a task, without interruptions from the internal negative monologue. Have them say a mantra over and over again while they do the activity, or talk to them in a soothing rhythmic voice while they do it. (Practice that on other people first if you don't have that skill.) "Slavey" tasks, such as personal service, work well for this as a start; eventually you will wean them onto more mundane tasks such as dishwashing or floor-sweeping ... or their job at work, assuming they have one.

Distress Tolerance

BPD people have a lot of trouble with tolerating any kind of distress. Upsetting situations that might make the rest of us roll our eyes and plod on send them into a tailspin. I liken it to having overly sensitive skin, so that a little bump becomes crippling pain. In order to "toughen up" their emotional "skin", we work on exercises that build up their tolerance. When the emotion of the situation is getting too strong for your slave and they are losing control, remember the acronym ACCEPTS. This refers to a list of options that a DBT person can use to forcibly distract themselves from the emotion until the chemistry of it subsides. Every one of these should be a tool in the Master's toolbox for those meltdown moments. I'll go through them one by one and give you examples:

+ **Activities: Use positive activities that you enjoy.** For example, an act of dominance—grab the slave by the hair or the neck (not in a punitive way), put her on her knees and have her kiss your feet, touch her in a way that reminds her of her place. You can also order her to go engage in some activity she likes, such as a hobby or taking a walk. She will probably object and say that it won't help, because she won't believe that it can. Make her do it anyway. If you are worried about her ability to focus on it, make her do it near you and check in frequently, keeping her on task.

+ **Contribute: Help out others or your community.** You, her master, are the center of her community, and she owes you service. Put her to work serving you in some way. It is especially important for it to be a service that you can obviously enjoy, not an "invisible" service where she is to be unobtrusive. Have her make you a drink exactly the way you like it, or rub your feet.

Show her your pleasure. Give her that reward for selfless behavior.

+ **Comparisons: Compare yourself either to people that are less fortunate or to how you used to be when you were in a worse state.** It's in your best interest to point out how far she has come compared to where she used to be—assuming it's true, of course. She may not remember, because some BPD people remember things in a distorted way. Keeping a copy of journals written in the "early days" of her relationship with you, journals which enumerate problems that you two fixed together, can be a source of positivity. You can also remind her about how she felt while she was searching and alone, if that is relevant.

+ **Emotions:** Cause yourself to feel something different by provoking your sense of humor or happiness with corresponding activities. Use humor, and draw her into it, if you have that gift.

+ **Push away:** Put your situation on the back-burner for a while. Put something else temporarily first in your mind. Redirect her to do some task, ideally one which she can manage without too much trouble—this isn't the time to challenge her with something at which she might fail. It is best if this is a task with some real need, not make-work—it will challenge her to rise above her emotions and do what is necessary.

+ **Thoughts:** Force your mind to think about something else. I have a series of speak-and-response mantras for my slave to say back to me, which break the mental pattern and redirects the mental train back onto different tracks.

+ **Sensations:** Do something that has an intense feeling other than what you are feeling, like a cold shower or a spicy candy. For us, since we practice SM, a slap in the face or on the butt is a good wake-up call. SM includes plenty of strong sensations, so a scene can "reset" her mood and attitude. When she is in a bad place and I smack her, I make it clear that this is not a punishment, it's an "attitude adjustment", for real. It's done to make a quick chemical change in her head, not to tell her that she is "bad". That has to be hammered home repeatedly before you can use this. When I actually do punish her, I do things entirely different—it's very formal, she has to kneel and reiterate what she's done and why she did it, and (assuming that it is not simply a mistake, which I won't punish), tell me that she hopes this will prevent her from doing it again. It helps her to hear herself say that last part.

The "IMPROVE" List

This is a list of activities that a slave can focus on when they are having trouble in the moment. You can walk your slave through these steps at first, and then wean them onto doing it with no prompting (but still describing the process verbally to you), and then doing it by themselves.

✦ **Imagery:** Have the slave imagine a comforting or beautiful situation. If nothing comes to mind, tell them to imagine the two of you somewhere pleasant, interacting with each other in a way that the slave particularly likes.

✦ **Meaning:** Find purpose or meaning in what's going on. I like to ask, as a thought exercise, "So if there was a Higher Being who loved you, but whose job was to improve you even if you hated the idea, and they put this situation in your path to teach you something, what might that lesson be?" Direct them away from self-hating or fatalistic explanations. Encourage them to speculate on the most positive lesson possible for the circumstances.

✦ **Prayer:** Not everyone is religious, and if they aren't, they use an affirmation or personal mantra instead. It can even be hooked to you: "I am improving all the time, and I am making my master proud." If they are religious, have them pray, and pray with them.

✦ **Relaxation:** It helps if you can condition them to automatically relax when you do a specific thing, such as grab the back of their neck, or pull on the hair there, or stroke them in a specific way. This is useful for times when they can't bring themselves to relax. Of course, it does make them somewhat dependent on you, but then a BPD slave is going to form a dependency pretty quickly anyway, so you have to expect that. However, the next relaxation conditioning should be something they do themselves, first in your presence and then out of it after it's well conditioned.

✦ **One Thing In The Moment:** This is a focusing exercise, like the "Focus" one above. Have them focus on one thing, like the feel of their tongue on your boot leather or staying in one position while you do something to them. You might give them an article of clothing to carry with them, something with your scent on it that they can focus on smelling, or some small item that they can stroke. We use her tattoo, or I tell her to concentrate on opening her throat as if a cock were going down it.

✦ **Vacation:** Sometimes there's nothing like a time-out. This is especially important if you are not feeling your best, and you can't be firm and focused enough to help your slave. She will probably try to take advantage of you and run you over when you're in this state, because her subconscious wants to prove that you're not really strong and you will let her down. The best thing you can do at this point is to send her to her room. (I strongly suggest that if she lives with you, she should have her own room, but you should be able to get into it at will. If it locks, you should have the key and lock her in, and let her out later.) Being able to set that firm boundary, no matter how bad your headache, will give her comforting proof that you are still in control of the situation.

✦ **Encouragement:** Tell your slave, over and over again, that you believe they can learn these skills and improve themselves. You're working against the BPD negative world view, which comes with an assumption that nothing will ever get better (including themselves), but you're perversely aided by their tendency to chameleon with influential people. Make them tell you good things about themselves and their improvement. Order them to repeat these good things during stressful situations.

Other Techniques

Self-Soothing. This is a big part of DBT. That's the ability to find some activity that makes you feel good in the moment, like listening to music or playing video games, and it can be used to redirect the emotions when they are overwhelming. An example of how I helped my slave find a self-soothing behavior is that we got her a tattoo. She really liked the symbolism of the labyrinth, in that she felt that her interior life was twisted up and she would "spiral down" into the bad place in the middle, where the monsters were kept—rather like the original myth of the Minotaur in the center of the labyrinth, eating human flesh. I encouraged her to get a simple black line-tattoo of the classic Cretan labyrinth, and then when she was spiraling down, she could trace the labyrinth on her arm while focusing on coming out of it, bringing herself out of the dark place and up into the light. While she did this, she focused on how I was her guide, holding the lantern and walking her back up.

I first had her do it with me present and reminding her, then slowly weaned her into going off and doing it herself. That went slow because I didn't want it to be a "Master is abandoning me" thing, but a "Master is always with me" thing. I even told her that if I died tomorrow, I'd still be her guide, walking ahead of her with that lantern. While different slaves will respond to different self-soothing behaviors, this is often a useful way to train them to it—first in your presence, then going off to their private space to do it at your command, then getting to the point where they can do it without you, knowing that your will is still controlling the situation from afar.

Secondary Gains. Talk about the secondary gains to be had by not being in control of one's emotional reactions. They might include people dropping difficult requests and leaving you alone, getting attention, not being asked to take responsibility, bullying people into doing what you want, etc. This will be a hard one, because your slave will probably not want to admit (or be able to understand) that she gets secondary gains from the situation. As the mindfulness work comes along, however, she may get to a point of understanding with this.

Radical Acceptance. This is an important goal for a slave. Your slave needs to accept that she is not in control of this relationship, or of any part of her life that has been ceded to you. Have her talk about how positive this is, how it can be comforting to be helpless. Discuss other areas in the slave's life where she might benefit by just giving up, because there is nothing to be done and obsessing about it only makes things worse. Use mantras to help her get a better attitude about hard tasks. Start with the difficult things that *you* order her to do, because you at least have control over those. Have her experiment with trying different mantras and attitudes for a particular ugly task, and report back to you about how they worked.

Emotional Regulation Skills

Once your slave has the mindfulness skills to describe her emotions, the next step is to talk about what's getting in the way of changing them. Take this on a case-by-case basis. Using encouragement, see if you can get her to find a way beyond the obstacle. Keep in mind that you will have to build up hundreds, maybe thousands, of instances of her overcoming the emotional obstacles before she will believe that this technique works. You are working against years of the opposite result.

It's also useful to remind your slave to do positive things. Sometimes they get so bogged down in their emotions that they forget about the enjoyable things in life. Order them to do those things, if necessary. Make sure that you're ordering them to do activities that they actually find positive on their own time, not activities that they only enjoy when they're doing them with you.

"Opposite behavior" is another tool that they can be ordered to use. This is doing the opposite of what the irrational feeling mind wants to do. For example, being in distress and wanting to eat candy, but exercising instead;

or wanting to hit someone because they have inadvertently annoyed you, but doing a nice thing for them instead. This is a combination of "act as if" and "fake it till you make it", and it can slowly change behavioral triggers. You can definitely order your slave to do something that is the opposite of what their emotions want in the situation (and perhaps *is* what they'd want if they were reacting more rationally). They don't even have to understand it at first, except as a "Master just wants this", but eventually you start working on their attitudes while doing it, and then it becomes a useful tool for them.

PLEASE Master

Yes, this is really the next acronym in DBT! It makes me happy whenever I see or reference it. This acronym refers to keeping the slave physically healthy, which is definitely part of the master's job. The letters "PLEASE" stand for:

+ **PhysicaL Illness:** Get them treatment for it, even if they don't want it. That includes chemical illnesses like depression and bipolar and OCD.

+ **Eating Right:** Dietary control is definitely within the purview of most masters. Make sure that they eat regular balanced meals. No slave ever died from not having junk food, no matter what they say. The BPD slave may skip meals or go on hunger strikes when they are in a self-hating mood. Make them eat anyway.

+ **Avoid Mind-Altering Substances:** Their brains are wonky enough, they don't need substances to make things worse. Restrict them from recreational drugs. I allow my slave one drink during social occasions when I am present, no more than once a month.

+ **Sleep:** If they have a crazy sleep cycle, get them on a schedule. It's a master's prerogative to give a slave a firm bedtime. If there are real sleep problems, talk to their therapist (they should have one!) about sleep aids. Use those judiciously. In fact, you should probably be the one to hand them out. Above all, don't allow multiple-day-no-sleep binges.

+ **Exercise:** Another activity that can be mandated. Not only does it help overall physical health, it creates temporary positive changes in brain chemistry that can change moods.

The "Master" part of the acronym is Mastery. Set them to doing something positive where they are more or less guaranteed to succeed, at least once daily. This is a "mastery experience", where they learn that they are competent human beings. Set them up for success, but make it real. This can be service to you—have them do something you like, and that you know they are reasonably good at, and show them how pleased you are.

Giving and Getting

We'll start with Getting, which is a list acronymed "DEARMAN". You can order them to use this with you (and other knowing volunteers) until they have mastered it as a skill, and then order them to use it whenever they want something from someone else. The list of actions is:

+ **Describe** the situation. Neutrally. Don't lie or slant so much it might as well be lying.

+ **Express** why this is a problem for you, and express your feelings about it in "I" statements.

+ **Assert** yourself by clearly asking for what you want.

+ **Reinforce** your position by telling the other person what good it would do you to get this.

+ **Mindfulness,** as in don't get distracted by the other person's words, tone or body language.

+ **Appear** confident even if you don't feel confident.

+ **Negotiate** cleanly with the other person.

If your slave is doing this with you at your request, and is using this list to ask you for favors they want, there will come a time when they ask for something you don't want to give them. Make it clear from the beginning that the "reward" for using this list is not necessarily getting the thing they want, from you or anyone else. For interactions with you, the reward is your visible pleasure with them, even if you refuse the request. Reinforce that even if that thing is not happening, you are pleased with them for presenting it as they were told, and you might be more willing to grant a different request.

On the other side of things, we have the GIVE list, which can also be mandated when speaking to you or others:

+ **Gentleness:** This can also be respectful verbal protocols. This is especially useful if you've got someone who likes verbal put-downs and can be verbally vicious. Don't take "But I'm just a sarcastic person!" as an excuse. Anyone can learn when "clean" sarcasm is appropriate to the person and the situation, and that resentful, nasty sarcasm is never appropriate.

+ **Interested:** Act interested when other people are talking to you about something, even if it's boring. Have the slave practice by listening actively and positively to you talking about some hobby of yours.

+ **Validate:** I find that this is best done during relationship discussions. Have your slave periodically repeat back to you what she hears you to be saying, and validate it in some way: "I understand how you could feel that way, since I know you really dislike X..."

+ **Easy Manner:** This is the hardest one of all, I think. We do a lot of breathing together, and use a lot of humor. I encourage her to use humor to get herself into an easier mood and express that mood in the world.

The last list is acronymed FAST, and is about keeping self-respect. It can also be about being an exemplary slave, of whom the master would be proud. Talk about how a slave's behavior reflects on the master, whether we like it or not. Then encourage these things:

+ **Fairness:** Being fair both to yourself and to the other person. Reinforce that this is actually possible. Brainstorm ways to do that, if necessary in the moment. This is really "No Heroes Or Villains!" BPD slaves will want to make everyone black or white, and you want to discourage this before your hat turns black, if possible. Being "fair" to someone means seeing them in the shades of gray that really exist, and not making them into a caricature depending on whether they are helpful to or critical of your slave. Every time you see black and white thinking in your slave, call them out on it, and encourage them to reframe the situation in a more realistic and thoughtful way.

✦ **Apologies:** Don't let your slave apologize for something that was not their fault. Don't let them apologize more than once for something that *was* their fault, unless you think the apology was insincere. (In which case make them explain in detail why it was their fault.)

✦ **Stick To Your Values:** Or, in this case, the master's values. Have discussions on what those values are. Have discussions about how to stick to them even in the face of temptation. Do "temptation run-throughs" if necessary.

✦ **Truthful:** No lying! This may be a hard one to break them out of. Every slave needs to learn that both master and slave must be one hundred percent honest with each other or the relationship will not work, but for a BPD slave, this needs to be seriously beaten into their head. Reward them for telling the truth when it's painful, just like you would a child.

Having a slave with BPD is going to be a roller coaster ride, even with the best intentions. She will challenge you and push you, and you have to be one step ahead. If you're not up to the job, don't take her on. It will just go down in flames. Training a BPD slave to be a better person is like playing with fire—I liken it to fire-spinning, where you have to be constantly mindful of the flames or you'll get burned. But if you do it right, it's a beautiful dance, and afterwards the wildfire can burn in a nice, peaceful bonfire. It's an amazing thing for both parties—the transformed fire and the transformer. It's also doing a good deed in the world. Be careful, get outside help whenever you think you need it, and enjoy each other!

Resources

I Hate You—Don't Leave Me: Understanding the Borderline Personality. Jerold J. Kreisman and Hal Strauss. Perigee Trade Books, 2010.

Stop Walking On Eggshells: Taking Back Your Life When Someone You Know Has Borderline Personality Disorder. Paul Mason and Randi Kreger. New Harbinger Productions, 2010.

Borderline Personality Disorder Demystified: An Essential Guide to Understanding and Living With BPD. Robert Friedel, Da Capo Press, 2004.

The Borderline Personality Disorder Survival Guide: Everything You Need To Know About Living With BPD. Alex Chapman. New Harbinger Productions, 2007.

Understanding the Borderline Mother. Christine Ann Lawson. Jason Aronson Inc. 2002.

The Dialectical Behavior Therapy Skills Workbook. Matthew McKay, Jeffrey Wood, Jeffrey Brantley. New Harbinger Productions, 2007.

Skills Training Manual for Borderline Personality Disorder. Marsha M. Linehan. Guilford Press, 1993.

Overcoming Borderline Personality Disorder: A Family Guide for Healing and Change. Valerie Porr. Oxford University Press, 2010.

Head Glitches: Neurological Dysfunction

Care and Handling of the Autistic-Spectrum-Disorder S-Type

Raven Kaldera and Joshua Tenpenny

Raven:

I've had my slaveboy Joshua for nigh on a dozen years now. He's smart, detail-oriented, hard-working, and eager to please. He's alphabetized my pantry, designed my websites, and done a million other wonderful tasks that make my life easier. He also has Asperger's Syndrome, which is a very high-functioning form of autism. (The DSM-IV has now decided to roll Asperger's into the full Autistic Spectrum Disorder, regardless of functioning, largely because of the grey area between "Aspie" and "not-Aspie", and the difficulty in diagnosing borderline cases, but most Aspies still refer to themselves that way.) This means that he sometimes needs special handling. In order to manage him in the most effective way, I have to take his disability into account.

Unlike a simple physical condition (like a bad back or arthritic hands), this is a subtle and pervasive condition, popping up in all sorts of interesting places in his reactions, preferences, and mental obstacles. When he does something irritating or strange, one of the first questions I have to ask is, "Is this an Aspie thing I just haven't nailed down yet?" There's a fair chance that it is, and a master cannot blame their s-type for their inborn neurological wiring. Not only is that unfair, but it removes any hope of finding an effective compensatory behavior.

Autistic spectrum disorders vary widely in both range of symptoms and severity, and while the two of us hope that this article will prove useful to dominant types with ASD s-types, we also realize that we cannot hope to cover every problem or issue, nor will the ones that we discuss necessarily be relevant to every couple. Some ASD folks posit the existence of at least two different "flavors" of disorder, for example—one that is more logical and "Spocklike", with difficulty being aware of and expressing emotion; and one that is highly emotionally expressive and reactive. (For good examples of this, read *The Unwritten Rules of Social Relationships: Decoding Social Mysteries Through the Unique Perspective of Autism* by Temple Grandin and Sean Barron, who are good examples of these two different forms.) At any rate, your ASD s-type may well go through this article and find some problems that they do have, and others that they don't. They may also have problems we didn't go into, although we've not yet met one who didn't have issues with their sensory "filter" getting overloaded a lot sooner than that of a neurotypical individual. As with any disability in a slave or submissive, it's the M-type's job to find out anything they can about that disability ... and it's the s-type's job to aid them in that discovery, through both research and personal transparency.

Not every dominant is going to want to take on a submissive or slave with ASD. If you're the kind of person for whom the ability to figure out what you want and have it given to you without your asking is a signature of love or commitment to the relationship, you will probably be continually disappointed. If you are stuck on having someone whose emotional reactions are simultaneously socially normal and genuine, you may also want to think again. If you're not interested in "motoring them through" (a term for physically training ASD children often used by their parents) situations that most people would react normally to, then you might want to look elsewhere. However, if none of these obstacles (and the others I'll go into in this article) bother you in the least, then by all means go ahead. For myself, I'm happy to train my slave how to act in any situation, so long as I know he'll do what I say to the best of his ability, which he does.

Joshua:

ASD people can have a wide range of life skills, but their social/emotional development is generally rather uneven. I know that when my master got me, he was shocked by the contrast between situations I could handle gracefully and those where I was entirely clueless.

By the time they reach adulthood, many ASD folks may be very good at faking it, but in a close relationship you'll likely be able to see the holes in their understanding. For example, I had very little conception of what love, trust, or intimacy actually felt like when my master first got me. Without the power dynamic, I would not have been able to develop that understanding, because I didn't desire emotional intimacy and I didn't see what the allure of it was all about. In my previous relationships, it was either not expected of me (as in my first master) or my partner was constantly frustrated with his acts of intimacy not being reciprocated (as in my long-term egalitarian partner; I liked him fine, but didn't understand what emotional connection he expected). I wasn't connected to my family, either; I liked them, and I knew they cares about me, but for instance I never understood why the other kids at summer camp missed their families.

However, my current master was able to get into my head and pull me into those emotions. There was an early stage when I didn't quite understand what he was subtly motoring me through, but in an egalitarian partnership I would have broken it off, where here I simply followed orders and walked right into the intimacy maze because my master told me to do so, and I was invested in being obedient. I was also very self-enclosed due to a fear of vulnerability, but in a M/s relationship I was rewarded for being vulnerable, so it opened me up in ways I didn't know could happen.

This was helped by our mutual discipline of radical honesty with each other, which only could have been done successfully in a M/s setting. If I didn't have a partner who could—and would—specifically tell me how to phrase things in a more kind manner, and whose word I would absolutely follow, radical honesty would become an venue for verbal abuse, as I have a hard time understanding which words do and don't hurt people.

Overstimulation

Raven:

One of the problems that ASD shares to an extent with ADD is having a too-permeable filter. On an ordinary day, most neurotypical people automatically shut out up to 80% of their stimuli—appliance noises, electric hums, moving shadows, bright colors, the shifting of clothing on the body—but one of the prime symptoms of ASD is a filter that won't shut out enough to function for long periods in a high-stimulus environment. When the edge of overstimulation is reached, ASD people often have stronger emotional responses to it than most adults with ADD, for example—including, sometimes, freaking out. Their version of freaking out may be atypical; if you've got one of the less emotionally expressive sorts, you might not even know that they've been freaking out for several minutes until they blow up over some small thing. The more emotionally expressive sorts may freak out with unusual gestures and noises. Most have learned to leave and find a quiet place when the edge is looming, but if they are "on duty" and not free to run off when necessary, the M-type has to make that decision for them.

As an example of how we handle this, Joshua has a special hand signal that he uses when he is on duty in public and has reached his limit of stimulation. Even if he's serving in the middle of a loud party, I know that if he gives me that signal, it's time to let him go sit in a quiet place for a while, or he will soon be worse than useless. (I also trust him implicitly to never use that signal unless he is actually nearing the end of his rope; he wants very much to do a good job at whatever I ask.) The hand signal is not something that others might interpret, so I can say, "Josh, go do X," and he can go calm his mind without having to mention his issues in front of people. (He's uncomfortable with discussing his ASD problems in public in party situations, less out of humiliation and more because of the unhelpful ways that well-meaning people try to accommodate or assist him, or because he's found that people often interpret it as a negative judgment on the situation: "Your party is too loud and you are talking about things that upset me so much that I have to leave.")

Loud, confusing crowd noise is only one of the host of sensory issues that may dog an ASD individual. I've had it described to me by my slaveboy and other Aspie friends as living every day under a barrage of sensations that they must constantly struggle to block out and focus around, and while many of them have learned to do that, it eats up a lot of their resources. Certain textures can be like torture—itchy clothing tags, slimy food; each ASD person may have their own list of texture-hates. That can, in some cases or on particularly bad days, become other people's skin or even their own; my slaveboy's central nervous system is aggravated by allergic reactions (which makes the ASD symptoms worse) and there have been days when he can't stand to touch himself, much less me. On those days, sexual service is pretty much out; we've managed at best to snuggle with a smooth, soft sheet between us.

Some ASD folks can't look at certain visual patterns without mental discomfort; others become hypnotized by visual patterns. (I've lost Joshua in the grocery store, only to find him staring glazedly at a geometric arrangement of cereal boxes.) Some find certain sounds unblockable, as nerve-wracking as fingernails on a blackboard. In fact, one common symptom of this disorder is that their "startle reflex" doesn't turn off when it should. You know the physical response your body has when someone sets off a firecracker or slams something loudly behind you? Imagine that it went off a few dozen times a day, five times more intensely, and then kept going for several minutes no matter how you tried to calm yourself. I've got Aspie friends who can't ever be around recreational target gunfire for this reason.

As an example of sonic sensory issues, my slaveboy can't stand the sound of plastic bags crackling. If he is driving me on a shopping trip and the wind is blowing our plastic shopping bags in the back seat, and he asks to be allowed to stop and tamp them down … well, I can refuse him and make him keep driving and deal with it, but I'll have to understand the consequences. Does he have the resources to keep driving with that crackling noise going on? Yes. Does he have the resources to cope with crackling plastic, driving, and being anything but grouchy, distressed, and largely nonverbal? No. Will he have the resources to recover from that distressing drive immediately upon coming home? Probably not. This is why I say that I do not compromise with my slave, but sometimes I have to compromise with reality. I've learned what his nervous system can tolerate and what it can't. He's willing to push himself to that limit for me; he depends on my honor and common sense not to push him beyond it.

In terms of S/M: Some ASD folks have told me how a good beating smoothes out their central nervous system, overriding the built-up tensions, and calms them down. Others—like my slaveboy—have anomalous random responses to physical stimuli. Any stimulus, from itching to orgasms to pain—what feels good on one day can feel terrible and almost traumatizing on another, and there's no way to know until you do it, so S/M is something of a minefield. Make sure you find out which type you've got before you start playing with them.

Joshua:

For me, overstimulation is about knowing what is a drain on my mental resources. My resources are not infinite, and if I can remove some excess stimulation, I have more resources left to do my job. Previous to me really understanding this diagnosis, I would tune out many of the things I found annoying because other people didn't seem to be bothered by them. After coming to terms with my diagnosis, I became much more willing to look at that. Now I'll assess whether I can cut myself some slack with regard to avoiding stimuli, or in being OK with a less perfect final product when I am working in a difficult situation.

With our M/s relationship, we had to find a balance between my master setting up special circumstances for me to work at my best, and him inconveniencing himself in order to do so. We found through trial and error that there was only so far he was willing to go with that, and so he decides how much he's willing to let imperfect circumstances affect my productivity. I've also found that if am able to reduce most of the sources of stimulation over a long period of time, it helps me to focus better, but it also makes me more sensitive to it in the long run. Smaller things become almost as annoying as the larger things, and then if I have to deal with a chaotic outside environment, it becomes really awful. So being in a *somewhat* chaotic home environment instead of a perfect greenhouse actually keeps my tolerance up.

It also helped me understand that the overstimulation is my problem. It's not that the people who are at this party are so terrible, it's that I am having trouble coping with it. Before my diagnosis, I would blame the external people and circumstances for my distress, and I couldn't see how different my responses were from those of other people. The M/s relationship with Raven was the first time I'd had someone pay that much attention to my inner process— especially someone who had the authority to order my behavior.

After reading about Dr. Temple Grandin's squeeze machine—a mechanism based on something used to calm down cows, which she built in order to get her nervous system calmed down—I made myself a rock blanket. It's a sturdy canvas quilt of pockets, and each one holds a plastic bag of gravel. I lay it on myself when I need nervous-system calming; even all-over pressure is a classic tool that ASD people use to calm themselves down. Sometimes I have had Raven lay on top of me, which was wonderful, but he's the master and he gets bored and wanders off. Now we have a second boy who is my "little brother", and I sometimes have him lay on me for a while as he's very submissive and less likely to take off before I'm done. Still, the rock blanket is there when I need it, because I never have to worry that it is bored.

Then there's the issue of eye contact. Many ASD people have trouble with any kind of sustained eye contact—one Aspie memorably described it as: "We're having the meeting on Wednesday—Eyeballs! Eyeballs! Eyeballs!—um, uh, I think I can make it—Eyeballs! Eyeballs! Eyeballs!" and so on. The human gaze is just so neurologically overstimulating that it turns the brain off and we can't talk. I've learned ways to do it obliquely in social situations, but the kind of sustained eye contact that masters often want is just hard for us. I remember being at a M/s weekend intensive, with another ASD-spectrum slave and her master right beside us. The teachers had us all do an exercise where we held eye contact and communicated our feelings. It made the other couples all lovey-gooshy. It made me and the other slave very, very uncomfortable and kind of freaked out. Both our masters are sadists, though, and they knew how far they could push us before letting us go, as we quivered like bugs under a needle and had to shake and breathe for a while. For me, intense eye contact with my master is as mentally overwhelming as being grabbed by the throat. It can be hot, in a way, but I can't have a coherent conversation. (I don't suggest playing sadistically with your s-type's ASD triggers until you've been together a long time and you are both fine with it, though.)

Literality and Precision of Instructions

Raven:

While—again—every ASD individual is different, one frequent frustration that new ASD s-types have with masters is that the orders they give are too vague. Many masters, upon hearing this, may raise their eyebrows— "My orders aren't vague!"—but they underestimate how literally and specifically many ASD people take those orders. The classic "example joke" about the new Aspie sub is that the M-type tells them to fetch a glass of water, and they wander back empty-handed saying, "There are no clean glasses—will a mug do?" They probably stood there and agonized over whether the M-type intended them to take the time to clean a glass, thus fulfilling the order literally but taking up a lot of time, or put the water in a coffee mug which was "wrong". Some might default to the first choice, leaving the master wondering where they vanished to and how long it could take to simply get them some water, or default to the second with apprehensive tears in their eyes, genuinely fearing to be reprimanded because it wasn't an actual glass.

While this may seem oversimplified, literalities like this trip ASD people up all the time, and it isn't the least bit amusing to them. It's stressful, and ASD folks often have lower stress thresholds than neurotypical folks, because their entire environment is so often a source of constant low-level stress that the buffer gets used up quickly. On the other hand, if you've got the precise and meticulous sort of ASD s-type who loves specific instructions, you can have anything exactly the way that you want it, if you just put in the time to make things detail-oriented. One master of an ASD slave told me that her slave never made her morning coffee the way she liked it. Upon questioning him, it turned out that he wasn't sure exactly how she liked it, because while he'd seen her make coffee for herself, she seemed to do things a little differently each time and she hadn't ever described her exact method. Given this confusion, he reverted to making her coffee the way he had previously learned as the "correct" way. I suggested that if she were to take the time to figure out and write up the exact procedure for making her coffee, and hang it up right next to the coffee maker, both parties would get exactly what they wanted—correct coffee for her, and the comfort of a "correct method" for him.

This, of course, means that masters have to learn to give more precise instructions, and masters of both genders often become disgruntled when told that they have to change how they issue orders and instructions. Many of them—especially the more emotionally-oriented types with a strong sense of subtlety—will be very uncomfortable with what may feel to them as being forced into a precise "mechanical" style. However, this is the same issue that the dominant of any disabled s-type runs into: sometimes one has to compromise with the disability, or nothing will get done. (It's important, though, to discern over time what is an unchangeable side effect of the disability and what can be slowly worked on with time.) One possible aid might be getting a third party who is good at breaking down instructions into a more precise form, and having them "translate" the master's rules, perhaps into a written rulebook. At any rate, even if the master isn't normally the sort to write things down, most ASD s-types do better with a written rulebook that they can refer to, and be sure they are doing things right. Knowing that if they just do X they'll always be correct is very comforting to them.

Joshua:

It is important not to let the "clarification of instructions" not become a power struggle. You should be aware of whether they are really just trying to find out what you want, or whether they are using a search for "clarification" as a way to obstructively react to an order they disagree with. Observe them over time to figure out the difference, and don't let it become manipulative. If you as the master are feeling pressured to give them more specific instructions, watch to see if simple clarification helps their genuine confusion, or if it's starting to feel like a negotiation about how you will give them orders—in which case, shut it down.

Also, if you want to teach them how to generalize this from other situations, you can prompt them—"What do you think I would want in this situation? Based on what you've seen of me, what do you think I prefer?" If they get it right, great; if they get it wrong, just correct them and move on. If they seem to be tripping up on the basic concept that you are not them and don't want what they want, that's a bigger issue that needs to be addressed separately. If they seem clear on that basica concept, make it clear that you want them to observe how you do things and take note of your preferences. (They may need to actually write these things down.) Prompt them to extrapolate in new situations. Take time to train them to respond how you want. You want, ideally, for them to come to a place of using good critical thinking skills and showing insight into your preferences, and at the same time not using their confusion as a way to get out of things. If they have emotional baggage from a lifetime of people whose reactions were opaque (and who were not willing to work with them) and they've given up on understanding anyone but themselves, you may find resistance to this progression.

My suggestion to masters in this situation is that they ask the s-type to propose a few different methods, and then the master picks one. If you routinely just have them propose one method, because you don't really care exactly how it is done, that can be detrimental in the long term to their sense of submission. By having them suggest multiple possibilities, you make it less likely that they would feel like they were just doing what they wanted anyway, and more likely that both of you will get something you want out of the situation.

Rigidity

Raven:

For many ASD s-types, as long as they have specific rules to go by—rules about how to act, how to speak, how the relationship is to be run—they really don't care whether the rules match anything considered socially "normal", or even currently in existence outside the household. This can make them remarkably easy-going when it comes to unusual relationship styles such as polyamory or long-distance relationships, so long as they can be entirely sure what they can expect, and how they should respond. Sometimes, however, they get hung up on another chronic ASD problem: rigidity.

Because ASD folks have trouble figuring out heavily social-mandate-laden or social-emotion-laden patterns, they tend to figure out one specific way to do a specific activity that someone (perhaps their parents) have told them is Right, and they cling to that method for dear life. Changing structures can also be excruciatingly difficult for them, making it even more of a challenge to get them to learn a new way of frying bacon, or hanging laundry, or assembling your sandwich. If the instructions are specific enough and the ASD s-type is still resistant, suspect this issue.

However, part of being an s-type is that one has to adapt at least to some extent to the master's patterns. It is quite possible for an ASD person to adapt to a new way of doing things; practice and building a new "rut" works just like it does for anyone else. They may need extra support, though, and appreciation of the fact that it's extra difficult for them, and lots of patience.

Joshua:

It would not be unusual for an otherwise submissive and obedient ASD s-type to argue at length over the correct way to hang pants, perhaps even citing various expert sources to support their method or repeatedly detailing the flaws in the master's preferred method. The master may naturally think, "Why do they care? Why can't they just hang my damn pants the way I want them hung?"

One useful method for handling this might be to say, "First prove to me you can do it my way—that you are willing and able to obey me in this—and after three months, I will consider the method you suggested. Your obedience is more important to me than creased pants. Until then, no comments or suggestions about how to handle laundry." Understanding relative priorities is hard for many ASD folks, and they may need it spelled out. The time period is important, so they can attempt to put it out of their mind until then. Having a very clear definition of what, exactly, you've declared off-limits is also important. A general statement like "I don't want to hear about this again!" is likely to be interpreted too narrowly by the ASD s-type, leading them to think that only one specific aspect of the issue is off-limits.

If there are specific types of responses you find annoying, the ASD s-type may not able to effectively generalize the concept of, for instance, "Don't be such a pedantic ass about trivial shit!" You can attempt to describe exactly what you mean, but it may be more effective to pick a consistent phrase you use for that particular type of annoying behavior (such as "pedantic ass") and each time they do it, clearly point it out using the same phrasing. Interrupt them while they are doing it, and say, "That! That right there is what I mean by being a pedantic ass." Even if they are not consistently able to prevent the behavior, they should be able to learn to identify when they are doing it. There is rarely any good reason to allow them to argue about why you oughtn't find a certain behavior annoying, whether this ought to count as an instance of that annoying behavior, or what term you ought to use to describe the behavior. Just be consistent, and point it out every time you notice it.

Alternatively, some ASD s-types do very well with a "Because I'm the boss and I said so" approach. It may be easier to convince an Aspie s-type that their master, for some unknown reason, prefers their pants hung the "wrong" way, than it is to convince them that the master's way is "right". The master may not like the s-type seeing their way as "wrong", but to put it in perspective, consider that ASD people routinely fail to understand the complexity of other people's motivations. The s-type may already believe that their master, like nearly everyone else in the world, continually does things "wrong" (illogically, inefficiently, etc.) for no discernible reason, and that society in general is full of bizarre and conflicting layers of inscrutable, ridiculous rules.

An older, more experienced, or more introspective s-type may genuinely want to understand why their master wants things a certain way, but it is likely to be quite a struggle for them to understand and accept their master's priorities and worldview. It is generally best to make it clear that understanding the reasons behind an order is valuable, but being willing to obey regardless of understanding is more valuable.

Another good point to impress upon the ASD s-type is the concept of "right versus effective". If their goal is to ensure you have the flattest pants possible, then being a pedantic ass about it is not furthering their goal. What would be effective? Looking at things from another person's perspective is very challenging for many ASD folks, but it is a skill that can be learned and applied mechanically. It can be helpful if you can figure out how to explicitly state your priorities in a way that the s-type can see how, given those priorities, your choice is logically consistent. From there, they may be able to generalize surprisingly accurately, even if your priorities are very different from theirs.

Switching Gears

Raven:

Have I mentioned yet that ASD folks don't like change much? That includes hour-to-hour changes. I'm a versatile master with a lot of different needs. Sometimes I want a quiet, efficient sidekick who will follow my instructions in the moment to the letter. Sometimes I want an intelligent, problem-solving sidekick who will brainstorm effective methods for a project with me. Sometimes I want a warm, supportive partner who will talk to me about emotionally intimate things, remaining respectful and loving at all times. Sometimes I want someone to hold me when I'm wracked with pain and at the end of my own resources. Sometimes I want an eager servant who wants nothing more than to give me pleasure, and glows at my compliment or orgasm. Sometimes I want a completely surrendered slave who trembles at my touch and desperately wants to spread himself vulnerably for me.

Joshua wants very much to be able to give me every one of those things, and he has. The problems inherent in that versatility, however, are twofold. First, although by the time I got him he'd already figured out how to act out some of those roles, there were others that he had no clue about, and I had to train him very specifically. "When I do this, you do that. When I am like this, you do that. When I indicate that I want this—in one of these three ways—then you do it in this way." While I'm not ASD, I'm also not a very emotionally-oriented person—and, being a "control enthusiast" as a friend of mine put it, I can find pleasure in "programming" my slave to act in exactly the way I want, when I want it. I just have to be willing to put in the clear, precise work to do it. I also need to have a good understanding that for him, these "artificially trained" affects are not him slapping on an alien mask over his natural way of expressing; it's that he doesn't *have* a natural way of expressing them, and he might as well use one that pleases me. (He'll talk more about that further on. He's one of the less emotionally expressive sorts, in case you hadn't figured that out by now.)

Second, I have to make it very clear to him which sort of "slave role" I want from him, and for best results I need to let him know at least half an hour beforehand. For the more "intense" roles, it's best if he has an hour or thereabouts to himself, to get his head switched over to the affect and body language and emotional responses that I want from him. This takes time and effort for him; switching gears doesn't come quickly or easily. If I ask him to go into a mode of total surrender straight from coming home from work or playing an engrossing video game, he will become flustered and distressed, and be unable to give that to me. By giving him advance warning, I don't set him up for failure. This does cut down on a certain amount of spontaneity, but it's a compromise I am willing to make in order to get what I want. (If constant emotional and situational spontaneity was a very high priority for me in a M/s relationship, perhaps an Aspie slave wouldn't be the best choice. That's just a matter of being realistic about what you want before you get stuck together.)

Joshua:

I often feel like my inner pressure cooker of emotions has no vent. I can feel like I'm full of emotions—I feel my body doing something—but the things that neurotypical people do to vent and express those emotions don't work. My emotions don't make the connection. For example, let's say that I think I may be sad right now. What do "ordinary" people do when they're sad? Well, they cry. Let me try to cry. No, this isn't helping, it doesn't connect to that emotion at all. It would be as if someone neurotypical was sad and I suggested that they lick their nose to feel better. Over time I've been able to program or condition myself into having my emotions connect to some activities, but really, it's all artificial for me. So I might as well condition actions that my master likes.

Where it's especially hard for him is that my behavior and the apparent intensity of my emotions may have little to do with the intensity of my internal emotional experience, so he can't make assumptions based on my body language and affect. I will inadvertently act as if I feel strongly about something when I don't, or not have much affect when I'm actually experiencing very intense emotions. It's up to me to communicate it verbally, because I know that I'm not giving clear nonverbal signals. Any relationship that didn't have a lot of radical honesty about emotions wouldn't work for me. If a partner did the "Oh, nothing's wrong," thing, I'd never catch on. I also need my master to trust that I'm giving him truthful information about my current state, so I'm careful when I communicate that in words.

I can't speak for anyone else but me here, but for me, being deeply surrendered and having problem-solving skills are two opposing states. When I'm in a state of vulnerability and deep surrender, I panic when asked to do anything that requires more than a trivial amount of cognitive thinking. It's terrifying to follow any but the simplest and clearest of single-step orders, or established protocol that I've done so many times I could do them in my sleep. Being asked for my opinion or preferences in that state is also panic-inducing, because I lose them when I go there. It's also hard for me to keep my affect going—

you'd be surprised how much work an expressive affect is for an Aspie—and that surrendered state comes with a purity of single-minded emotion that uses up all the resources I would normally use for facial expressions and body language. If I have to solve a problem or figure out an order, I have to come out of that space and go into "work mode".

I find that state very calming and fulfilling, but I realize that perversely, it's not all that much fun for my master, unless he's only interested in a warm body to do things to. I love being in a mindless, robotic state, but it's really not his kink. We still hold out hope that we can find a mutually fulfilling activity that can be done in that state, because it's no fun for either of us if he's doing something just to humor me.

Social Skills

Raven:

Another classic hallmark of ASD is difficulty with socializing. Their neurological wiring is flawed when it comes to mentally interpreting people's clues of body language, facial expression, tone of voice, clothing choices, phrasing, etc. Understanding and utilizing those clues themselves, to communicate with others, is also not an option. Neurotypical people learn this unconsciously in childhood, because our brains are wired to do so, but ASD folks don't have the same wiring. This leaves many of them feeling as if they are aliens, attempting to figure out some telepathic language that everyone else is speaking, and expecting them to speak as well. That's why they are often referred to as "dorky", "geeky", "weird", and sometimes "creepy" from people who are put off or made uncomfortable by their unusual behavior.

Some Aspie folks, however, have applied themselves to learning this alien language well enough to more-or-less understand and use it, because it can be learned intellectually, studied like one would study Japanese or Swahili. (Of course, it would be much simpler for them if there was actual instruction available as easily as taking a class in Japanese, but society isn't quite there yet.) They "pass" as normal, if perhaps slightly stilted or reserved or "old-fashioned", and can even be charismatic. What we don't see is that it costs them a great deal of focus and energy, and they can't do it 24/7, or perhaps even 12/7. Joshua has learned, painfully, a lot of good observation and social-affect skills, and most people think that he's charming when he's out with me (or at least "charmingly dorky"), but I know what that constant consciousness of body motions, tone of voice, and word choice is costing him. I know that he can't keep it up on a round of involved public social interactions, starting in the morning and ending in the wee hours, with no breaks.

That noted, I would not set him up for failure in this way, and I always assume for periods of rest and down time for him during public event weekends. (The fact that I have a second boy now is a great relief for him; if he's in no shape to go to a public party after a whole day of loud events where he is expected to be socially smooth, I can always take the other boy.) One hallmark of many ASD folks—including high-functioning ones who are just having a hard day—is the loud, flat staccato voice with no apparent affect. When that voice starts coming out of Joshua, I know that he is "all out of charming", as he puts it, and needs to go be alone for a while.

I also accept that one of my jobs is to brief him on acceptable behavior in new or non-standard venues, and to stop him (often with coded pre-chosen verbal or gestural cues) if his behavior becomes unacceptable. On a less skillful or more overstimulated day, he might back someone into a corner while monologuing about some obsessive interest of his, not noting their desperate, fixed smile that (clearly only to someone neurotypical) longs to get away. It's my job to step in at that point and break up the interaction in some face-saving way for everyone, and then carefully go over it later so that we can figure out if there was any way he could have noticed. Sometimes there isn't, especially when he doesn't have enough resources on line to be aware of it; at that point, we talk about ways to head that state off at the pass.

Joshua:

It is incredibly embarrassing for me to misjudge social circumstances, or say something that ends up being hurtful, or corner someone to babble endlessly at them about something I genuinely but mistakenly thought they had expressed interest in. I strongly prefer both that my master cue me about my behavior, and that he do it subtly so as not to embarrass me further. It's also more practical that way, because I don't want people making excuses for my inappropriate behavior. I'd rather just behave appropriately.

The idea of formal protocol—a well-defined set of behaviors—had great appeal for me when I got into M/s. I liked the idea that I could be told exactly what to do or say, and if I misstepped, it would immediately be explained and corrected. Sadly, my master is not very interested in formal protocol (which often seems to be bottom-driven in many cases, from what I've seen). A very formal situation with strict manners, where people are not allowed to act casually and do what they like, is—once I know the rules—actually much easier for me. It's the casual socializing that is hard for me, because the wider range of acceptable behaviors makes it harder for me to guess what not to do.

Early on in our relationship, my master made a rule that I aside from a few specific friends, I was not allowed to touch women (and yes, he had to then clarify that sniffing them or sitting too close counted), especially in casual, touchy, flirtatious social situations. The problem wasn't that I was making awkwardly inappropriate attempts to flirt with women (I prefer older men sexually), but even affectionate touching from a man is a loaded minefield. It was very easy for me to misjudge what kind of physical contact was acceptable in those situations, and when I was younger I did some very inappropriate things. While those were innocent mistakes on my part, they were entirely unacceptable, so the safest course of action for me was to cope with being seen as a little uptight, as opposed to being freer with people and risking someone feeling violated because of our interaction.

Because I need to pay so much more attention to social rules (or risk being wildly inappropriate), I end up being very uncomfortable seeing my master violate social rules, even though I know that he's much more skillful at assessing that risk than I am. I also become uncomfortable when he puts me in situations where I am on the edge of risking social deviance. My fears make my social behavior limits much more conservative. Some people like to say, "I don't care what people think," but if I thought that way, I'd have no friends, no job, and no master. Me in my natural state just doesn't work in the world (although my master is OK with it to a certain extent in private with him). My master is one of those people who doesn't care, but he knows how to maneuver on that edge. I don't have the skill to find that middle ground, and even though I know he's good at it, it still makes me nervous.

Structure and Rules

Raven:

This, again, will vary depending on your ASD type. Some love and crave structure and rules, some don't. My slaveboy craves it so much that he's considered going into a monastery, except that he wasn't actually practicing the religion of the monasteries he'd gazed at longingly. (And he likes sex an awful lot, and he's queer, and ... anyway.) I wasn't structured enough for him—he longed for a micromanaging dominant who would keep him on a strict, unchanging schedule. Instead, he got me, and he copes as well as he can.

When I've spoken to ASD s-types in the past, a majority of them spoke about how they loved the narrow, structured life of slavery. Rules gave them comfort, unlike ambiguous social and life situations where they are expected to guess ... and guess wrong all too often. Many also lauded the state of having one's basic decisions made for one—what to wear, how to walk, how to keep one's hair and nails, what to say to please their partner. Figuring those things out by themselves, often on the fly, was stressful enough that they would rather give up their choices and lay the decisions on someone else. (I remember Joshua's pleasure when I got him "uniforms" and told him what situations were acceptable for which ones; it meant that he would never again have to navigate the "What clothing is appropriate for this party/work/social occasion? I have no idea!" nightmare.) If they can learn to enjoy the emotional state of surrender (or already enjoy it quite a bit, thank you very much), this love of rules and structure can make them much more obedient than many other subs or slaves.

Of course, not all masters live lives of strict discipline, and order—I certainly don't—but giving him rules and protocols makes him feel secure, not restricted. That's definitely a plus in my book, and it makes for an exceptionally obedient slave. Other masters have commented wonderingly on how absolutely obedient he is; I smile and wonder how to tell them that his well-behaved rule-following probably has a lot less to do with my power as a master than his ASD-induced love of following rules.

One of the fundamental desires of any s-type is to clearly know what is expected of them in order to do their job correctly. Vagueness and inconsistency in this area can upset any of them, but for an ASD sub or slave it is downright terrifying. It's more than a desire for them; it's a deep need, and one that a master shoots themselves in the foot by deliberately undercutting. On the positive side, though, I've found that unless they are also carrying a heavy burden of old PTSD and/or have an additional untreated neurochemical mental illness, most ASD s-types are very good at taking constructive criticism in a positive way, especially if it is given in an emotionally neutral way (and they believe they have the ability to eventually succeed at it). Once they've been assured that it is simply an assessment and not an attack, they will usually be able to calmly take it as such, and work with it. That's another very positive side effect that masters may enjoy.

Joshua:

I would love having one of those masters who wants you to put a specific number of ice cubes in his glass, and insisted the table be set with utensils carefully aligned exactly one inch from the table edge. That would make me so happy! I dreamed about having one who would put me through all sorts of formal protocol, and my challenge would be to master that discipline. Instead I have a master who is training me in how to be kind, loving, respectful, and skillful at social situations, as much as possible. It wasn't what I expected at all, but I am so much better for it. These skills are more difficult, because they are softer, but I can now teach in public as his co-presenter and hold down a career requiring a lot of people skills because of it.

Emotional Expression

Raven:

As we've mentioned, ASD folks come in a variety of abilities to notice and identify their own emotions and express those in a socially acceptable way. Some of them, when behaving naturally, tend to express them in odd physical ways—hand-flapping, jumping up and down, making strings of strange noises, etc. Usually they've been discouraged from doing this in childhood, but it may still remain their favorite—if private—form of expression. Allowing them to indulge in it when you are alone together can be a great gift—you'll be the one person with whom they can be themselves.

Others don't seem to have any natural way to express emotion. (At its most severe, this is called alexithymia, which indicates a serious inability to feel or express emotions.) Joshua had trouble figuring out what he was feeling, so we worked on his awareness of his physical reactions; usually his stomach will figure out that he is stressed well before he does, if he ever does, so checking with his body helped a lot. (I later discovered that this is a therapy technique used for mild alexithymia.) It's not that he doesn't have emotions, it's that they don't have a natural way out. Someone like this could actually be a positive project for a master who enjoys shaping and controlling their s-type, as they could train them to consciously respond a certain way when they are feeling a certain emotion. Eventually the learned behavior would become the "doorway", and then you have a slave whose emotional reactions you've custom-designed. (That's what we're working on, slowly, over time. Such projects, of course, need to be entered into with the enthusiasm of the s-type, without whose aid you will not be able to achieve anything.)

Aside from that, if you really don't care that your s-type's response to happiness is to flap, beep, or just stand there like an expressionless statue, then it really doesn't matter. As long as they can verbalize their feelings enough to keep you in the loop, then things will be all right. Transparency may be a serious discipline for them, though, if only because it requires noticing, interpreting, and articulating feelings on a regular basis.

Joshua:

It was incredibly freeing to understand my ASD diagnosis, and give myself "permission" to use ASD-type coping mechanisms in private. I'd already run through all the "normal" social expressions of those emotions, and even some of the pathological and unhealthy ones, as an attempt to make a connections between feelings and actions. I was so desperate to find behaviors that would connect meaningfully to my emotions that I intentionally tried a various self-harm behaviors, to see if that would work. (They didn't, fortunately.) However, when I finally got comfortable with my diagnosis, I tried some of the "traditional" ASD behaviors—hand-flapping, rocking, making high-pitched noises—and I was shocked by how good they felt, and how naturally they connected to my emotions. There really is some kind of neurological basis to those behaviors. Most of them are not appropriate in public, but it's great for me to have a new variety of coping behaviors (if only in private) to work with.

Self-Help and Resources

Raven:

In general, the more that your ASD s-type learns about their disorder and how it functions—which does mean learning enough about how neurotypical people work to understand the contrast—the more information they will be able to give you, and the more skillfully you'll be able to manage them. Therapy with a professional skilled in helping ASD folks may help. For both of you, I suggest talking to other ASD people, and especially other ASD s-types if you can find them. They may have coping mechanisms that neither of you have thought of.

If your new ASD s-type has given up on learning more—if they have become demoralized by their failure to figure it all out on their own, and decided that it's all just too confusing—remind them that Knowledge Is Power.

The more they know about their own mind, the minds of others, and the contrast between them, the more opportunity they will have to create compensatory mechanisms and get more of what they want out of life.

Joshua:

Unfortunately, a lot of the resources available are for parents or educators of ASD children, and many seem excessively concerned with drilling the child in "normal" behavior, without understanding the reasons behind their unusual behavior. I recall an essay by one mother who, after years of scolding her ASD son to have "quiet hands", tearfully realized that this was actually a way he expressed emotion, and that she had spent much of his childhood telling him, basically, not to do his equivalent of laughing or crying or expressing any feelings at all.

There is definitely great value in learning how to be socially appropriate, but for me to do that healthily, I had to come to it not from a place of self-hatred or hating everyone else's opaque behavior. A straight-up focus on drilling someone to be "normal" can be very demoralizing. It's important for you to look at their behaviors and decide which ones are completely inappropriate and which ones are just unusual, and while those latter ones may be slightly problematic in some situations, seriously consider whether they can be left alone as an expression of your s-type's individuality. If you don't understand your s-type well enough to see *why* they do all the weird things that they do, they will never trust you enough to allow you to train them.

Another thing to keep in mind is a point made by Temple Grandin: For many ASD people, the most fulfilling thing in their life is not their social or relationship contact, but having meaningful work in their lives. This means that if it's handled right, a M/s relationship can be a truly amazing gift for them, especially if it is less about "having a relationship" (although it is certainly that) and more about "having the best job ever". It doesn't even matter if it is work that the world values, so long as they are good at it, enjoy it and find it fulfilling, and their master is pleased by it. For me, whatever other work I may do, this is my primary job—being Raven's slaveboy—and the me-that-I-was before I met him would never have believed how terrifically fulfilling this job can be. I've got a purpose in my life, and the best master ever. How much more lucky can one boy be?

Living As An Autistic Slave
Emma

So I'm Emma, I'm in my late twenties, and I was diagnosed with classic autism a couple of years ago. As a child, I was misdiagnosed with ADD, PTSD, Bipolar, Anxiety, Agoraphobia, etc. As an adult, when correctly diagnosed, I do not have any symptoms of anything *other* than those traits related to classic autism in the stereotypical fashion, and sensory processing issues. (I'm still dyslexic, my auditory processing is fairly slow, and I jumble up speech when I talk.) I get overstimulated easily, which may look like anxiety to people who don't know me well, but it's just my brain misfiring from trying to process too much information at once. I don't have actual mood swings, but to people who don't know me well, "stimming"[1] behaviors can look like mood swings or ADD traits simply because I use it as a way to process external stimuli in my environments so I can focus and function better. I may appear anxious, confused, agitated, or excited when overstimulated and trying to keep up with verbal speech; or in new situations when I need to process everything in my environment *before* I can be social; or really pay attention to people or to what I'm supposed to be doing.

I'm anti-social and very picky about who I will be friends with, which often makes me seem agoraphobic. I actually don't have any issues doing errands, or paying bills, or going out in public, other than overstimulation; but I have to balance my plate carefully to make sure I have enough juice for every activity I need to do, so that I don't shut down from overloading my brain with too much information in any given period. That can be hard for people to understand.

---

[1] *Editor's Note:* "Stimming" is a term commonly used by people with Autistic Spectrum Disorders to refer to small behaviors designed to give positive physical stimulation and calm down the central nervous system during stressful times. Examples might be idly playing with something soft or tactilely "interesting", rubbing something, flicking something, etc.

The biggest issue is that people have a hard time reading me and understanding how I'm really feeling. This means that they tend to assume wrongly and project their own feelings or thoughts on to me. Sometimes, even when I attempt to convey or communicate my feelings, they brush me off or assume I don't know what I'm talking about. It's actually kind of irritating to tell someone I'm not anxious, I'm just trying to focus on them instead of the sound of the darn clock ticking across the room and it's bugging me ... and then they often assume that being mildly irritated at a noise that's distracting is the same as being anxious. It's not.

I find that I take a lot of words literally, so being in a relationship where someone else is in charge and helps set clear social boundaries and rules for daily living helps me function at my best. Add in the fact that I like shock value and kinky spice to my life, and words like "Owner and property" make me giggle. They fit the weirdness of who I am. I like to live outside normal terms, and it works for me.

To me, M/s means one person is in charge and makes the rules, while the other person follows the rules. Since I do best with structure and clear boundaries, this type of dynamic works well for me. I'm free to speak however I like, give my input, share my feelings, and give advice for situations. We work as a team; I just do a more supportive role to his "in charge" role. Being in an "old-fashioned" dynamic works for me.

I've been with my partner since I was twenty; about eight years now. It took him a lot of time and patience to learn my quirks (for example, learning that when I flap it doesn't mean I'm freaked out; it could mean I'm excited or happy, and it's best to ask me what I'm feeling or thinking), and that I have a variety of mannerisms that mean different things. It took him a lot of work to learn those signs, those things no one else had ever bothered to take the time or effort to learn about me. He understands when I get overstimulated. He expects me to communicate with him about how I'm feeling about new situations, or for that matter how I am feeling at any given moment of every day, so that he can make educated decisions about our plans and figure out ways to compensate. For instance, I can't stand when he leaves the car door open and it dings repeatedly. He's learned that this little thing will use up a heck of a lot of the juice I have for going out—it sucks the energy right out of me and puts me on edge before we even leave the driveway. He's learned to shut the door and not let the door ding. It's little stuff like that, things that others take for granted, which mean a lot to me and show me that he cares how well I function.

I struggle the most with organization—I have to make lists, and I can't veer from them or I get flustered and have to start over. I have mental checklists for simple everyday tasks, like bathing, eating, cooking, grocery shopping. I have routines for which I have to do everything in order to get it done; otherwise I will get flustered and overwhelmed. In addition, I don't respond physically the way some people do. I'm not into soft romantic touches; I've lost partners in the past for being "cold" or "unresponsive" to them. He's learned that I am very responsive *if* I'm touched correctly, and in the right ways. Sometimes I get physically overstimulated from touch and it has to be changed to keep my body from shutting down from too much sensation.

I'm complicated, and it's a good thing that he's patient. Due to my verbal communication issues, we write back and forth a lot—this gives me tools to communicate more effectively with him, as I have speech issues and can be hard to understand, especially when I'm flustered or thinking too hard about other things. I need time to find the words to phrase a simple sentence. Typing reduces the time it takes to communicate because it removes a step in communication—trying to process everything and then find a way to form the sounds of the words in a coherent fashion. I see and think in pictures, and speech is really difficult for me to translate back and forth. He is understanding about that, and lets me type to him; we use typing and emails as a way to skip a lot of the frustration I get with verbal communication. It wasn't his ideal, but he loves me enough to compensate for it to accommodate me.

When I came to my master, I was honest and up front about my previous diagnoses and my difficulties and struggles. Many of the ways I've changed for the better are because he researched and read up on autism (even before I was officially diagnosed, because he suspected it) and helped me change how I approached things. He even taught me that it was okay to say "I can't do this right now," and to accept help. He was fine with it; nothing I was or am has bothered him. He saw the potential of who I was, and was willing to be patient to let me blossom into the person I am today—which is a person he loves, admires, respects, cherishes, and couldn't picture not having in his life.

My writing and communication skills are a direct cause of my master's hard work and patience with getting me to communicate as well as I can. I recommend that if you have "different" wiring (like autism) that directly effects peer-to-peer relationships and communication, you need to find *something* that gives you the ability to bridge the gap and effectively communicate with people who matter to you. It can destroy a relationship if you can't remember to say simple things like "I love you," and "I appreciate you," or "I need help with..." and even "Please" and "Thank you." Basic, simple everyday forms of communication are what allows you to function with other people. If you want a functional relationship, you have to be able to do those simple things that come naturally to others. It's definitely hard work, but it's worth it.

In terms of medical decisions, we deal with most stuff as a team. Everything in our life directly effects everyone in our household, so we talk about it all and make decisions together. He lets me share honestly, bluntly, and truthfully things that I won't tell anyone else. My fears, my joys, things that excite me or make me happy—for example, that I need my video games in order to function, because it's the only thing I really use to de-stress that actually works for me. But he expects me to balance my activities; he doesn't let me forget to live in the real world or pay attention to the people who matter. He's very good at dragging me out of my bubble to be social. Avoiding people is my number one problem. That can include going out in public and not wanting to talk to the sales clerk or the doctor. He's good at pushing me to use my words, and have plans in place for handling situations that make me uncomfortable, or that I dislike.

I trust my master's judgment in these things; he's wise, capable, and won't set me up to fail. I listen (and usually take) his advice, and apply things that may work better for future situations. I think the two of us together make a good team. I suck at reading people, but he's really good at it. I flap and act weird, and he's a very steady rock that draws zero attention to us. I can be very literal, due to my lists and plans and hating surprises; he can get tunnel vision and get too focused on the end result, and I'll bring him out of it to pay attention to the little everyday things. He has the bigger vision, and I struggle more with only focusing on details and not the bigger picture. Together we balance each other out.

If you're a would-be sub or slave and you've got neurological differences, research them. Understand yourself so you can explain it to others. If you don't understand yourself, no one else can. You need to have a good grasp of who you are, in order to be functional with someone else. And then, please, pick someone who *likes* your strengths and weaknesses and quirks, and finds you funny and adorable because of who you are, and doesn't see the need to try to "make you normal". For dominants who are considering such a partner, I have only one piece of advice: Be patient.

Property With Asperger's

Grace

Just answering the questions in the survey for this book was very hard for me, because the questions have no right or wrong answer, and that is a difficult thing for my brain. In addition, I had a hard time making the thoughts in my head come out understandable in writing.

I'm a 37-year-old female, self-diagnosed two years ago with Asperger's Syndrome. I have also been diagnosed with "severe, recurrent, major depression" after multiple suicide attempts and social anxiety. Looking back, I believe much of my depression and anxiety could've been reduced had we known about the Asperger's. (I also had undiagnosed hypothyroidism which is now controlled with medication.)

I started a profile on Alt.com back in 2002, and ended up marrying the one and only person I messaged on that site. I was completely new to the lifestyle, but attracted to the "s" side of things; mainly because I hate making decisions. I see the pros and cons of every decision, and have a hard time choosing which is the right one to make. I see many things as black and white, therefore (in my head) one decision is right and the other is wrong. I consider myself a slave because I need control and direction in so many aspects of my life. General everyday tasks can easily overwhelm me, and I need someone to help me prioritize things. (To me, a submissive gives up control in some areas, but not all.)

I have only been in one power-exchange relationship— my current one. We met in 2002, and I moved from Maine to Michigan to live with him in 2003. We were married in 2004. Our relationship at its core is owner/property, even though it may not look like it to outsiders. We are not high-protocol, and we joke around with each other, but at the end of the day, he is in charge. If I forget that, he will remind me.

When we met, I did tell him about the depression, but I didn't know about the Asperger's yet. We were together for eight years before I self-diagnosed myself, with the help of my Master and other family and friends. Early on, since we didn't know how much my brain was wired differently, there was a lot of frustration on both our parts. Since then, I have done a lot of reading on Asperger's to come to terms with it myself. He first did research on depression, since that's all we thought I had, finding out what not to do or say. He's more accepting of me than I am. He listens to what I tell him about having Asperger's in order to learn how my brain works.

He is very patient and understanding of my quirks. I take things literally, and I have a hard time noticing body language, subtlety, etc. There are times when I need things explained a different way or in more minute steps than someone else might. Being told to "clean the house" is so overwhelming to me. I need specific tasks spelled out. Cooking is difficult. There are a few meals I can make, and I hardly ever venture into creating new ones. Most folks will make a plan B, or maybe C, but my brain jumps to plan D, E, and F. This can be helpful or hurtful. When traveling, I tend to remember the details and pack for all the contingencies, but that process stresses me out. In play, when he says to go get Toy X, I freeze because I'm already thinking about what is going to happen with said toy.

I can easily get into a spiral of depression, social anxiety, and self-loathing. He'll let me wallow for no more than two or three days before getting me out of the house, usually for dinner. We discuss my medical decisions together, but I can be stubborn and not want to go to the doctor even when I should (not emergency situations, but a nagging pain that won't go away for example). In that case, he will make the appointment and take me himself. Also, he will always go with me to an appointment if I ask.

If I could give advice to a master who is working with an Asperger's slave, I'd say: If there is some task/rule that just is not working out and causing frustration, make sure to reexamine things that happened in each person's past, and how it made them feel. For example, when our relationship was new, I had a hard time communicating what type of play I wanted, so I would lay a toy out on the bed. He didn't take this well, because he wanted me to verbalize my desires. I couldn't even communicate to him how difficult it was for me to communicate! I stopped being proactive at all when it came to sharing what I wanted. This continued for years! One day, while discussing my past (vanilla) relationship, we realized that placing a toy out was my way of communicating, that I wasn't doing it to annoy him on purpose.

To would-be slaves with Asperger's, I'd advise: Tell your dominant everything that goes on in your head, even if it's embarrassing to you or it seems normal to you. Asperger's manifests itself differently in different people, so the only way your dominant can know your brain is to share. They are not mind-readers, even though I wish they were—that would be awesome!

Interview with Dr. Bob Rubel and his Owner Jen

Robert Rubel (Dr. Bob), is an educational sociologist and researcher by training. He has ten books currently in print, including four on Master/slave topics. He's been on both sides of the slash, and he (and his owner and co-presenter Jen Fairfield) were kind enough to talk to Raven about his ongoing struggle with Asperger's Syndrome and brain injury.

So Bob, I understand that you only figured out about your Asperger's fairly recently, in 2006.

Dr. Bob:
Are you interested in the story that triggered that?

Yes, please!

Dr. Bob:
I petitioned Karen as my Mistress in July of 2002, but within about eighteen months, we realized that we weren't sexually compatible. About twelve months later I met Melinda, and after about three months of "slow this down", she gave Mindy to me as my slave. So all three of us were united in family, but we had three separate homes. I lived with my second wife, Melinda lived with her young daughter, and Karen lived with her son and daughter, all in very different communities; it would take me forty-five minutes to drive to Karen's, and in the early stages it was forty-five minutes in a different direction to get to Melinda's. Over Memorial Day of 2006, we all moved in together and … well, I essentially had a heart attack over that same weekend.

Now, the reason that's relevant is that Melinda claims that my personality changed after the operation and with the meds; she said I was much more aggressive and less open and loving and friendly, and from this side of the skin I can't tell that. As we were just moving in, I had had some blow up with Melinda, and Karen pointed at me with a beckoning motion, which was a gesture she'd never done before, so I knew something serious was going on. She said, "Can you step outside onto the balcony?" So we went out there and she said, "You will lose her, you know." And I said, "What are we speaking about, Mistress?" And she said,

"You can't speak to her that way, or you will lose her." And I said, "What way would that be, Mistress?"

She said, "You have Asperger's Syndrome." I said, "And what's that, Mistress?" She said, "Why don't you go upstairs and look it up on Wikipedia?" So I did that, and I came down and said, "OK, I'm 90% that, now what?" She said, "Well, you might want to do some reading."

I said, "How long have you known this?" She said, "Oh, since about, two months after I met you." Which puts it to ... well, we started dating in March of 2002, so by May she had trouble discerning if I was simply eccentric or had Asperger's. But she's an Autism Spectrum Disorder Specialist for the school district with thirty years background as a credentialed speech therapist who deals with learning disabled kids. So she said, "I picked you because I knew I could manage you." So that's how that went, and that's really the beginning of the story.

But she didn't tell you at the very beginning?

Dr. Bob:

No, she said, "I'd never seen you react badly to anyone." Because our time together was having dinner with her twice a week, and on Wednesdays we would go out to a very, very rural dance hall and we we'd dance country-western a couple of hours. So it never came up. She's never triggered me; she doesn't do anything that would trigger me. However, my slave Melinda, had a hard time absorbing my behavior. I would have learned faster if she had had a way of pointing out that the behavior was abnormal, as Jen has done, which has driven me to certainly a year and a half of introspection and work.

Jen:

When we met—not met, when our relationship began, the very first night he handed me a list out of Temple Grandin's book I believe, that these are the characteristics, and he said, "There are ten of them, I've got eight of them." And I looked the list and was like, "Oh geez, I've got eight of them, too," so I never saw what he has a challenge. I always saw it as this is what you have, we're going to work through this. I read Temple Grandin's book, I read the

Twenty-Two Things a Woman Needs to Know book, I walked into this relationship with a lot of information. He has done a lot of work on himself in understanding what's going on, so the relationship I have with this Asperger's man is with a different Asperger's man than Melinda had. Plus I'm in a different role. With Melinda he was Master, so how much say does she have really to say, "You're acting weird"? Whereas I can definitely say, "You're acting weird."

So I want to hear about how you two manage that, but first I want to say, from your side of the skin, what were the issues that were hardest for your former slave?

Dr. Bob:

One of the hardest problems would come up almost every night. I care about orderliness more than cleanliness, and we dine semi-formally, and the dining room table is always set. It's easiest to draw the pattern for you. If this is the knife-and-fork setup, that's a water glass and that's a wine glass, and that's a wine glass and that's a water glass, and that's a water glass and that's a wine glass, and that's a water glass and they line up in all the directions. And if you're off a little bit, I've got a problem, because I get a physical reaction to something visually out of order. If you were to set three candles of different sizes on a shelf, many people would set them up in a row or something like that. This would be disturbing to me. I want the pattern to be a 2:3 ratio.

None of those problems affected her as a matter of daily living, so if I just said, "Mindy, just clean the house," and then the house was absolutely spotless and neat, and I'd come in and be uncomfortable with little things like that. And so then I was in a fairly grim loop where she hadn't done anything wrong, she was working like mad to please me, and I was still uncomfortable. So now I'm feeling guilty that I'm making such a big deal out of this, and I've also at the same time gotten slightly out of control. Once I start down an Asperger's meltdown spiral, she never could interrupt it. With Jen, we've developed a good work-around. Since having Melinda, we've come to realize that just interrupting me verbally doesn't work.

What I discovered with Melinda—and I used to talk about this in class a lot—was that we needed to have an emotional safe word, and that safe word was to call me Bob. She normally would only have called me "Master" or "Sir". But when I was in an Asperger's spiral, it didn't work. When I started the relationship with Jen, we had some upsets, so I decided to take a number three red billiard ball and have a friend of mine make the three into an eight. So now we have a red eight-ball, and it lives on our mantle. So if we've got company over, and we have pre-planned that we're going to do A, B, C, and D; and for whatever reason I have forgotten this, and something else seems to flow better for me and I'm off on another path. So we were supposed to be going here, and I'm somewhere else. In the past that has led to a blow-up, which became a real crisis because she had no way of stopping me. Now all she has to do is mention that red eight-ball, and why we have this red eight-ball, and that's a signal to me that I need to excuse ourselves from our company for a minute and find out where exactly I've gone wrong. because I won't even have noticed that I've gone wrong.

Jen:

And it doesn't have to be with company, it can just be the two of us. And we construct the evening and I can say I would like a sensual evening, and the next thing I know he's getting ready to do rough body play with me. I can bring up the eight-ball to say we're not going in the direction that we had intended. This works especially well if he's emotionally charged and I'm saying something and it's not sinking in, I can't get through, so I can bring up the eight-ball and it redirects him to stop and think.

Dr. Bob:

And we go from there to a talking stick, which is our standard. Talking stick is Level 1 problem solving. Red eight-ball is Level 10 problem solving. So, once I've been stopped with the red eight-ball, then I'll do some clearing techniques. Then it's good for me to have a "state change", in the NLP sense—a physical change of activity.

Now, we also have another workaround that I'd forgotten until just now, because of my short-term memory issues. If she wants to have certain experiences in the evening, we have a little white board with dry-erase markers, and when she has the idea she wants to do A, B, and C, we just write that down and stick that in the kitchen so that I don't lose track of it.

So how do you cope with the Asperger's need for precision and specificity in language and in orders, do you find that to be a pain in the ass, do you find that to be wonderful because you can get exactly what you want, or something in-between?

Jen:

Well, we have a little behavior modification that he's gone through. His former slave Melinda speaks in what Bob refers to as "Southern Indirect". So after living for eight years listening to Southern Indirect, he tries to translate everything to Southern Indirect. I can say, "I want A, B, and C," he comes up with, "A1, B2, C7," and I'm saying, "Why are we off? I said exactly what I want, why are we somehow slightly off?" And it's because he's used to trying to hear what the meaning is instead of hearing the words and just doing what they say.

Dr. Bob:

Let me explain a couple of things. First, my former slave grew up being told, or thought she'd been told, that it is rude to say things straight out. So here's the joke I do about this in class.

So we're at the dinner table, and she'd finished her plate and I was still eating a little bit and she looked over and said, "This is where we could use a sideboard, right here." And I said, "Sideboard? Why would we want a sideboard right here?" She said, "Well, that way we could have the food out here and it would be closer to the table for service."

And I said, "OK, I get that, but what's wrong with one of us getting up and going to the kitchen and getting more food?" And she said, "Well, that will take longer and my plate's empty." I said, "Just a minute. Are you saying that the phrase, 'This is where we should have a sideboard,' means you want a second helping?" She said, "Well, yes."

I said, "Just a minute. Let me go through this again. I want to go through the whole loop. And actually, I want to write it out." And I wrote it out, the whole thing, and that's what it was. But that kind of indirect is what I lived with. So the joke of it now between us is, if she were to say, "Oh look, the carpet is green," my reaction is, "Do I need to vacuum something, Mistress?"

Jen:

Whereas Jen grew up with military-officer Dad, y'know? I say everything that I mean, and I mean it now.

Dr. Bob:

Another *major* area I had was that Melinda's a RN paralegal, and she did nursing home defense preparation for an attorney for nineteen years. So she's used to thinking A, B, C, D, up to God knows where, and finally you reach the conclusion. But with my short-term memory difficulty, if you start giving me a bunch of sentences, I can hang onto your first sentence, I got your second sentence, but to pay attention to your third sentence I'm going to have to let go of part of the first sentence. And the way she would do this, by the time I got six or seven sentences in, I'd be triggered, I didn't know what in the hell she was talking about, and I'd get angry. When I finally figured this out, I'd say, "I need your request or your statement first, and then I need you to ask permission to give me the backup story. But I usually am not going to be interested in the backup story, and I don't need it, and it's frustrating to sit through." And that helped us quite a bit, but it took seven years into an eight-year relationship for us to get this far.

Jen:

And that's actually a problem we still have. My stories are shorter, but I may be six things into the story, and he's held onto the first three and is responding to the first three, and I'm saying, "Ok now, you're not exactly getting what I'm saying." So I'll go through the whole thing again, we get the same response. And I have not been able to give him the conclusion at the beginning because if it has any emotional loading to it, he can't hear me. He shuts down. The mouth is moving, the words are coming out, I hear the words, but there's nothing in there. So he needs that build-up to it, but you get to a certain point when the emotions come in and there's just this wall.

You mentioned that you have a traumatic brain injury also, and is that the cause of the memory issues?

Dr. Bob:

Oh yeah. In the first place, when I was eight years old I was riding my bike down a hill and there were grass clippings and … well, actually, my nose was removed from my face, and these teeth were knocked back in—all of these are a permanent bridge—and I had a hundred stitches on the roof of my mouth. I was completely out of it for a while. Now, in retrospect, I understand why I had so much trouble in school, and I now understand why when I was twenty-eight I began commenting that I could feel myself getting smarter. It's also how I end up with a doctorate with an SAT in English of 384. (Because 300 is 0, as I recall the SAT scores.) It's very hard for me to memorize something. I've put myself through NLP basic training and stopped at that point because I can't remember the patterns, to the point—I won't even turn it on now—but I listened to NLP training patterns when I'm driving and I still can't retain them. It's just too many words. So one theory on the memory is yes, it's physiological, and I've just got brain damage from connecting with a curb. The other is that my memory issues may be selective and emotionally linked to trauma as a child.

Are there any protocols that are in place for being memory aides for you, for helping you manage that? How do you guys work that in your relationship, that fact that you have memory issues and so forth?

Jen:

Well, I have an excellent memory, and what I struggle with in this relationship is if he were to open his life and share what's going on, I would be able to help him to remember to do things. For example, he got your call last night, said that he was going to call you today, and I'm ready to walk out the door and I said, "Now did you call Raven?"

Dr. Bob:

I hadn't written it down.

Jen:

And that's just a way for me to be able to help him. Now he's Asperger's, he compartmentalizes his life. Jen is struggling to fit into each compartment. He has this attitude of, "When I'm with Jen, this is the way our life is, then when I'm not with Jen, this is the way my life is." This means that there's a lot of what's going on in his life that I don't know, so thus I can't help him remember it. But other than that, he always has a paper, he's writing it down, he takes those notes, puts them into his computer, he organizes them, he looks at them every day, he can remember what needs to be done.

Dr. Bob:

And to some extent, there's a question of just how she wants to know about what Karen is going through with her grandkids? So I give her a general briefing. I'll provide an overview, but *I'm* not interested, so I'm not exactly sure why she'd be interested. But she is, and it's a very different way of working with the world.

We're still very much in a learning phase with our M/s relationship. We're figuring out how to better communicate with each other, and it's an ongoing process. But we're both people with a lot of life experience, and that helps.

Jen:

And for me, it's important to know that I am here helping this man to work through his issues and become a more effective person, and serve more effectively as well.

Interview with pais

pais (with help from her master Brian)

Brian and his slave pais were interviewed simultaneously, but pais's part of the interview is here, and Brian's is in the counterpart book Mastering Mind.

Tell us about yourself and your relationship.

pais:

We've been together over seven years, and been M/s for six and a half. It is a no-limits relationship, 24/7, and has been since it started. That's the short summary. Originally I was looking for a female sub, because my dominant of the time was uncomfortable with me playing with anyone other than a female sub.

Brian:

I was looking for a summer fling. I was about to move to Florida, and I didn't want to, and I was looking for anything that would make me feel better at that point. I only wanted a fuck buddy, so there was no reason for her partner to feel threatened.

pais:

So we both went into it thinking it was going to be short term ... you know, no strings attached. But within two months it was clear things were heading in a different direction.

Tell us about pais's conditions.

pais:

First, I have a thyroid condition. I was diagnosed with it as a thyroid condition in my early twenties, but they have apparently recently changed what is considered normal as far as thyroid levels go. I have had depression my whole childhood and adolescence, so my guess is that it was always the thyroid issue. I was diagnosed and on meds; it was pretty severe. When I was twenty-four I started on a thyroid medication which has changed my life, except that I still have all of these bad habits from having been depressed my whole life. And my thyroid gets continuously worse, so sometimes I have rough patches while the medication is being adjusted.

On top of that I'm ... well, I wouldn't really say Asperger's, as I've never really been diagnosed, I'm clearly not on the far end of the autistic disorder spectrum, but I do have some Aspie-type behaviors ... PDD-NOS. (*Note: Pervasive Developmental Disorder, Not Otherwise Specified.*) So I'm a little bit OCD, I have some sensory issues, I have a hard time with eye-contact. I have done some flapping and strange noises, although I have to really be under a lot of stress to get to that point. I have some difficulty with emotional display. That's really the biggest thing, but because I was depressed for so many years it's hard to know how much of that is because I was depressed and my whole emotional experience in childhood was skewed, or whether it's an autism-spectrum thing, or both.

I tend to have a lot of emotions, but I don't show it. I get overwhelmed. I get to a place where I cannot access language at all. I do that much less now, because we've done so much work on it, but sometimes he'll ask me a question, just a simple question, and I will literally have no way of getting the words from my brain to my mouth. And sometimes there are no words in my brain, but usually there's just no way of getting them out.

Brian:

Because of pais's issues, I've had to adapt how I work with her from day to day. In my head, there was a very serious amount of structure that I dreamed about. I'd say, "Not only is this what I want done, but this is how I would like it done." But we ran into a lot of conflicts about the way I would like the thing done not working for her in a way that she could manage successfully. Sometimes I wasn't very good at giving step-by-step, granular enough directions for how to get from point A to point B, either. Much of the time now, I just say, "This is what I want done, I don't care how you do it." On some days, when there's house cleaning to get done and other numerous tasks, I can just say, "Do your rounds," and she can do the routines she needs to do, which consists of going from room to room in a particular pattern. For me, that would drive me crazy, because it would feel like nothing is actually getting done. In actuality, everything is getting a little done at a time, and eventually everything is magically done at the end, so I've had to kind of trust that her process is going to work. If I want something done, I generally just jump in and do it myself, or say, "You need to finish that first before we move on to anything else because of X, Y, and Z." Another way has been me just getting better at saying, "I know this is going to be difficult for you, so here are the specific things I would like you to do," and her narrowing the scope of the problem down until it's something that's easier for her to handle in bite-size pieces.

pais:

One of our big communication difficulties has been that the more anxious he is about the things that I'm not saying, the harder it is for me to talk. So it is important for him to get to a place of saying, "Oh, she is going to be able to talk to me eventually, I just need to wait."

Brian:

And wait. And wait. And wait and wait and wait until she gets to the point where she's verbal again. I keep thinking, "She's never going to talk if I don't make her talk right now. She's never going to do it. We're going to sit here forever, and I have to go to work, and nothing will get solved!" She'll tell you herself that she can go for days without talking, for much longer than I'm comfortable with.

So for me, part of that has been to shift my focus, or shift my view of the situation from one of Dominance and submission, of "I'm going to make you move forward in this, I'm going to actively pull you," to one that's more parental, that's more like asking questions. "How are you feeling?" or "Can we move this forward?" It means being a little more gentle and slow, and still confident that I'm the authority figure and it's going to be OK, instead of being clearly anxious and upset. Since I am a parent and have two kids, it wasn't a far step. But it was a switch. We had a conversation where she said, "I would really function better if you could be a little more like a parent." And I said, "Oh, I know how to do that! Yay!"

pais:

It's about the tone of voice, the energy, the pauses, and just going slower. But that makes it more about what I need than what he needs, and I don't like that at all. I work hard at telling him what I need, but it's a struggle. I'd much rather not say anything, because I want it to be more about what he needs than what I need.

Brian:

Well, I want the end goal. I need to get to the end goal. But in this moment, right now, we need to start at this place where we are and deal with what is, and what's going to help her to get back to the place where I want us to get.

How do you cope with moments of, "Goddammit, I'm supposed to be the Master, why am I not getting what I want?"

Brian:

Oh, there have been those moments of feeling like I'm not getting what I want, but a good part of working around it has been understanding that I *am* getting what I want eventually, and she's working incredibly hard to give me what I want. I'm just not getting it in the *way* I want. But I think I've learned that the end goal is more important to me than the path to get there. Figuring that out has been a big step.

pais:

Separate from any kind of mental health stuff, my whole life I was basically looking for this relationship, so this is where I've always needed to be. When I got into a Master/slave relationship with Brian, I had a really deep sense of "fit". Happiness has never been a huge motivator for me, because I hadn't had a lot of it in my life, so a sense of fit was always kind of my goal. I never had that, so in this relationship I have been both happy and felt like I am in the right place. Brian has his own problems, and they are pretty major, yet in our relationship, my stuff has had so much more impact on the day-to-day functioning of our relationship. That's hard for me, because I want to be perfect robot slave and just make everything happen. "My feelings don't matter at all!" In fact, we've had periods in the beginning back when we were still figuring out how this was going to work, and I would go a week and not say I was upset about something, and he wouldn't necessarily have any idea. Because he's not a mind-reader, and I'm really good at just soldiering on.

Brian:

Until you hit the wall, right?

pais:

Right, but often I would hit the wall because you would be poking me! "What are you feeling? What's going on with you?" "I don't want to talk about it!" But one of my protocols is that I'm not allowed to have temper tantrums.

Brian:

We're actually at a place now where we're less structured than we had been about some of it. For a while we were processing every day, like enforced processing every night at bed time—which ended up being counterproductive in some ways, I think—but also we're just in a better place now. The enforced processing during that time was good in terms of making sure that there was an opportunity to say things, for her to say how she was feeling and get it out there. Then again, we had other counterproductive processing issues. She would say that thinking about being upset would cause her to go find reasons to be upset, even if she hadn't been upset in the first place. Now we're at a place where I understand the symptoms when she's actually got something going on that's going to affect her service and our relationship. I can let it go for a little while and see if it will resolve itself, but, there comes a time where we need to talk about it. There isn't any protocol specifically around that, aside from the fact that she needs to be honest and tell me what I want to know.

pais:

Because before I would say, "I'm upset, but if you just leave me alone it'll be fine." Which would work once in a while, but usually I would just escalate. I would go from,

"I don't want to say anything, perfect slaves don't complain, so I don't want to tell you anything about what's going on," to "Perfect slave is totally honest," Then I would feel like I had to say every negative thought that came into my head, and since my head was full of negative thoughts, it would take forever to say every negative thought. I had to figure out which were the negative thoughts that I could just file under "This Is Just How My Brain Works" and which were the ones that I needed to share. That was many years of just bouncing back from one extreme to the other.

Brian:

Trial and error… and error and error and error.

pais:

With a fair amount of whining in between. Now I know the rule is: "If it effects the relationship dynamic, I have to share it." Originally there were a lot of my problems that were affecting the dynamic, but I kept saying, "No, this doesn't affect the dynamic, I'm fine! Everything is fine!" I needed to get to a place of being able to say, "No, actually, this is affecting my service and I do need to share it, even though I don't want to." There are other rules too—I had some self-harming stuff before we met, then a little bit during our relationship, the beginning of our relationship, and there is a rule against that now. Although it had been so long that I'd forgotten that rule, and then I got stressed and I did a little self-harming recently, because it had been so long since it'd been relevant.

We don't really do a punishment context—or maybe my punishment is that I have to process for hours and hours! We did punishment once at the beginning, but it didn't go well. At that time his bedroom was set up so there was a place behind the dresser that he couldn't see on the bed. My punishment was that he sent me behind the dresser to sit for about fifteen minutes while he sat on the bed with his laptop, and I couldn't see him. And it took me months, probably more than a year, to get over that. Just getting sent behind the dresser. I felt like, "Well, this means you're going to send me away if you get upset with me, so you're probably just going to send me away eventually anyway." I'm going to cry now thinking about it!

Brian:

It triggered her abandonment issues. I think we could call that "calibration" at the beginning of the relationship.

pais:

We did both try to read up on my problems. I was in grad school; my last decision as a free person was my application to grad school to be a social worker. I'm also a trauma therapist, so I had a trauma focus in grad school. I started taking classes and realized, "Oh, OK, I have much more understanding of what's going on with me."

Brian:

For a long time in the beginning of our relationship I actually started reading up on the wrong things—learning about depression, for example—which was useful during the few times that she got depressed, but it wasn't actually until we started reading posts from Raven and Joshua about Josh's Aspie stuff that some of the other things started to really click and make sense. This is an issue that we have, too, in a different way, without having any specific diagnosis to work with. But it wasn't like I could find a manual that described pais perfectly.

pais:

Well, I was trying to give him a manual, but it was the manual that I wanted him to have as opposed to the real thing. I wanted it all to be true, but it wasn't. "If you just don't make me process things then everything will get better" was not true. "If you just ignore me for a week, then when you come back, I'll be fine" was not actually true. For example, last night I was cleaning the house, in my special pattern, and he asked some question about when I was going to be finished. I was upset because I was telling myself that I could be finished whenever he told me to be finished, but from his perspective he was trying to be helpful and say, "I know you've got your pattern, and I don't want interrupt your pattern." But I was thinking, "I don't think it's that bad; you can interrupt my pattern and I'll survive."

Brian:

Which is where we are now, but it's not where things have always been. So it can be tricky, and the lines move around, and we take it day by day. Her level of stress definitely plays a role. When she's really stressed about other things, then she gets much more rigid. It's been an issue with sex and play in the past; for a long time, I felt like what I could ask for was strongly contingent on the starting place that she was already in. If her stress is at a 9, then going to 10 is going to send her into a non-communicative space that severely limits sort of what you can do with play. I was more OK with that than she was. I feel like I can say, "No, I'm taking care of you, and we're not going to be doing something that's going to be bad for you and send you into that space." But then her response was "Nooo! Worst slave ever! It's not that bad! Do whatever you want!" But we'd tried that, and it didn't work out so well. So we went back to doing it my way, and I think that worked out better for everybody. I was honest about saying, "It's OK. It makes me feel good to know that I'm doing the right thing by you, and that I can feel confident I'm making a decision that can get us to a place where we'll be able to get out of bed in the morning without having an hour's worth of discussion first."

pais:

Yeah, I don't reset during sleep, so whatever state I fall asleep in is the state I wake up in the next morning. So if he puts me to bed and I'm a blubbering mess, I wake up a blubbering mess, and he still has to deal with it. Whereas he has a tendency to fall asleep right after sex and wake up reset in the morning and feel like "It's all good!" And I'm saying, "…I can't move."

In terms of the ongoing depression … I have growths on my thyroid, so as my thyroid functioning decreases, the effectiveness of the medication will slowly taper off, and I'll start to notice that I don't have a lot of energy, and it wasn't just that I didn't get enough sleep last week. I'll feel like the last two or three weeks I just haven't had energy. I don't really notice it as depression so much; it hasn't gotten to the point where it's felt internally like depression, although apparently it looks like it from the outside. When I was really depressed, I had to take time off of college because I couldn't get out of bed, so a little low energy doesn't feel really depressed to me.

Brian:

I've become highly attuned to her moods, so I notice it. From the outside it looks like mild depression. First it looks like being a little sad, and then getting increasingly sad on a bad trajectory over the course of some days. Then the next thing I know she doesn't want to do anything. But the last time that it happened, I noticed it pretty quickly, and she made an appointment and got her thyroid checked.

pais:

I'm taking four times the amount of medication I was taking ten years ago. It's not super fast, but I assume eventually that my thyroid will die entirely.

Brian:

And I'm prepared for that. It's a medical time bomb in our future. I knew it when I took her on.

pais:

But plenty of people have no thyroid at all and manage on replacement hormones, so ... Anyway, depression. What masters most need to know about depression is that you can't order someone with depression to be happy.

Brian:

I wish I'd known that, in the beginning. I ordered her to act more cheerful, and she did, but inside she was losing her mind. That was a bad interaction between the ASD stuff and the depression stuff. She would say, "Why don't you just tell me how to act? Tell me what you want. Tell me how you want me to behave." I said, "OK. Act cheerful." So she did a good job of acting cheerful; sometimes too good a job, and then I would have no idea what was actually going on with her for a week until she exploded over some minor thing, and I would be saying, "Where'd that come from?" Then we'd have to unwind a week's worth of accumulated grievances to get through.

pais:

I didn't know that I was capable of really being happy. I wish I had known that, because I think it would have been easier if I'd known that was actually an achievable goal. I think I undermined my happiness sometimes because I just didn't think I could actually get there.

How many of her medical decisions do you make?

Brian:

It's not easy, because even after years and years of transparency, she still sometimes doesn't give me enough information ... although sometimes she does give me too much. We keep trying to find the sweet spot which moves around from day to day. But I try to get as much information as I can get from her; then I run it through my own filters of how much of it is true, and how much of it just feels true, and I end up making the final decisions on pretty much everything. If she ever said to me, "I feel like I need to go to therapy," then she'd go to therapy. Clearly, if that is even coming up as a topic of serious conversation then there's no reason to mess around with it. I have nothing invested in her not going to therapy.

Do you always feel what is coming out of her as self-assessment is correct? Or do you feel like sometimes she's telling you something that she would really like to be true but you really don't think that it's true?

Brian:

Less now than in the past. I think we've slain most of our porn-fueled demons at this point. I'm sure there are still lingering areas that we're going to deal with forever, because the fantasy of life is not always the reality. But I know that she always tells me what she believes to be true, and she's usually pretty good at saying, "This feels true, but I don't know how true it actually is." So it's good to take a sample over time: "We can talk about it now when you're upset, and we'll talk about it in the morning when you're not upset, and we'll talk about it in the evening when you've had a little more time to think about it." But that's mostly for her benefit. I've actually got a pretty good sense of when she's lying to herself, but I usually like to walk her through the process. When I make a decision based on my own judgment rather than what she's told me, it's actually a good litmus test for how confident she is about her perceptions, because if she really believes very firmly that she's telling me the real truth, then I'll get some pushback. Whereas most of the times she'll just say, "OK." But it's pretty rare that she gives me pushback on something and is wrong about it. I can't think of a single time when she has really stuck to her guns and it's turned out not to be true.

On the other hand, I would say I have a really good track record of having hunches about whether she's lying to herself, although I only recently had a very good track record of believing my own judgment enough to put it into action. I had to learn to trust myself more than the words that were coming out of her, to trust my gut. In Myers-Briggs terms, I'm an INFJ, so everything for me is a hunch. I don't even understand all of my thought processes at times—they are sometimes very intuitive and touchy-feely—which is very hard for her to understand at times. But I think it works out OK, because she's somewhat drawn to the more feely-stuff, and it actually works well for me to have a sounding board that likes to have things laid out so that I can walk through them. I'm really good at taking complicated things and crunching them down and coming up with a solution, but really terrible about explaining the process of how I got there, or why the solution makes sense. So she's actually been super beneficial to my entire life, especially around my work where I do these complicated network things, and I'll be trying to explain to a roomful of engineers who are extremely logical people, "No, it'll just work. Why don't you understand? Just look at the thing!"

Have you ever sought counseling from a kink-aware professional since getting together?

pais:

When I stated grad school I was worried that it was going to be a huge trigger. I had had some anxiety and some panic attacks in college, and I was worried that some of that was going to start back up again. So I found a therapist and I went for a session to introduce myself and to say, "Here's my history and I'm starting grad school and I'm concerned." I had looked on the Kink Aware Professionals list and had found someone, but she was full up and she recommended this other person to me. The other therapist had said, "Oh, she's kink aware, you can go to her even though she's not on the list." So I went, and I said, "One thing you should know about me is that I'm in a TPE relationship." She said, "What's that?" and I said, "Well, it's, you know, Master/slave stuff. It's a power exchange." And she said, "What's that?" She had no idea what I was talking about. I gave something of an explanation, and she said, "Oh, I'll have to read more," but it didn't leave a great taste in my mouth. I ended up not needing to go back to her, which was good. I managed to get through my Master's degree without that. As a therapist, I say I'm not super comfortable finding a therapist and trying to explain my dynamic. I always say that if something happens and I got outed and I couldn't work with kids anymore, it makes sense that I would work with the M/s community, except then who would I socialize with? The community is not that big, and I still need a social life.

What advice would you have for two people already in a relationship who want to make it D/s or M/s, and the would-be s-type has these issues?

Brian:

A lot of it is being willing to be in the relationship that you're in. It's not going to change because you want it to. You are taking on someone who has problems that may budge or move, or they may not. If someone has a physical disability, it may get better, it may get worse, but it's going to be there. In the same way, just because it's not a disability that you can see doesn't mean you're going to be able to "dom it away". Also, life isn't porn. It's real stuff.

pais:

I work with kids with severe mental illnesses, and they're still people! I think the most important thing is not necessarily to say, "This is the person I love and this is the disability," because especially with people who have long-term mental illness, you can't separate them. I take my thyroid medication, so I'm not constantly depressed any more, but I'm still the person who grew up having depression my whole life. For some people the mental illness may be less of a part of their identity or how they function—for example like a bipolar syndrome that only shows up every couple of years—and you could possibly say, "This is the person I'm in the relationship with and then this is what they look like when the mental illness kicks in." But this is a human being, you know? Accept the whole package you're getting.

Brian:

Be honest with yourself about what you can handle. There have been other people we have started down the path of bringing into the relationship, and I've had to really take a hard look at them and say, "You have issues I cannot support you through." It's hard to do, but I have a lot of other responsibilities, and clearly this is going to be something that's going to take a lot of time and effort, and I just can't do that right now without sacrificing somebody else who I already have a commitment to. "Super Dom" cannot just fix every problem. If you have the feeling that, "I probably can't handle this," you probably can't handle it. And that's OK! It's OK to not be able to fix every submissive's mental health problems. I used to have a white knight thing about that.

pais:

Then it was my job to say, "Master... not a good one." We like to say that our crazies were broken in a way that our puzzle pieces line up very well.

ADD and BiPolar

slave elliott (with help from Master Fire)

Note: Master Fire and slave elliott are a female-dominant, male-slave couple with a very formal and specific way of speaking and writing, and they have requested that we retain this style for their twin interviews, in this book and Mastering Mind. *We have agreed to let their unusual grammatical conventions stand.*

Master Fire:

Our name is Master Fire, and We are the head of an M/s household affectionately known as "The House of Fire". We have had multiple members in our household in the past, but at the time of this writing, slave elliot is Our only slave. This slave has been collared for three years, and We have lived together for almost two, which began when we moved across the country for Our job. But first, a note about the pronouns in this essay: Our M/s relationships are spiritually driven and Our odd speech protocols are guided by our spiritual beliefs. We use the "royal We" form of speech while the slaves use "it". In this manner, no one in the household uses the egoic "I". While SM and sex are a great deal of fun and We enjoy having those in an Ms relationship when they happen, the dynamic isn't based on, and may not even contain, either. With slave elliot, We do not have a romantic or sexual relationship, due to the fact that our sexual orientations don't match. We are a straight woman and it is a gay man.

Our slave elliot has a similar set of major diagnoses to Our own (Type II Bipolar and ADD), but elliott's bipolar seems to be somewhat milder than ours, while its ADD is much worse. It has been able to completely replace its Western bipolar meds with natural remedies, and has to take much less and a smaller variety of them in order to be stable. The ADD, however, is only really effectively treated with a conventional medication, while Ours is treatable mostly with behavioral modification.

Like Us, elliot is most apt to become unbalanced when tired. A stable sleep pattern is crucial for bipolar balance, and so sometimes this means putting aside things We want it to do in order for it to get sleep. It also means not projecting Our sense of guilt about elliott not getting school work done, and making it call in sick when necessary. It is imperative that it get rest, and We make that the priority.

Our slave elliot's bipolar seems to manifest as feeling grumpy and depressed when in a depressive swing, and much more ADD when in a manic swing. However, it is very good at self-care and often self-corrects with little intervention from Us. Helpfully, it will often announce how it is feeling long before We even notice, and it self-corrects by taking naps, meditating or doing something fun.

Our biggest challenge is dealing with elliot's ADD. We find it mentally and emotionally stressful to have to continually deal with Our own manifestations of ADD, and feeling as if We should be doing all that for the slave, too, is a bit overwhelming. We feel guilty about not doing everything that We should do, even though We believe that as a spiritual being, elliot should be allowed to make its own mistakes. As of now, Our efforts have included an attempt at giving it a strict schedule to follow (which failed miserably) and refocusing it at night to make sure it gets its school work done. On occasion, We have to refocus it even more, such as making it get offline or stop playing a game, or give it orders about chores that need to be done that day. This level of refocusing and loose planning feels like a good level of management for Us to be doing; more makes us both feel as if we are in a parent-child relationship, which makes both of Us unhappy.

In our dynamic, We have full authority over all things, except when We are mentally incapable of giving orders from a place of good stewardship. *(Editor's Note: Master Fire's challenges will be discussed in the next book in this series, Mastering Mind.)* When we are together, elliot must ask permission for all actions, including taking meds and doing self-correction techniques. While we both know that We would never in Our right mind deny it these things, asking permission becomes an affirmation that We have authority. There are some actions over which it has been given standing orders, such as self-care when We are not physically present.

In the area of medical care, We have given several orders to elliot. First, We ordered it to see the same excellent doctor We see. He is a medical doctor who functions as our psychiatrist, and we chose him because his beliefs about herbal and Western medical treatments are in line with both of our beliefs. He is very supportive of natural remedies and always wants to try them first before trying a Western medicine. We all agree, however, that sometimes western medicine works best and should be used if needed. Second, We ordered elliot to marry Us, even though We are not romantically involved, so that We could provide medical insurance for it. Third, We ordered elliot, who is in training to become a clinical herbalist, to explore creating the medicine for the household, which is does as much as it can. For some medicines this means growing the plant itself, and for others it means ordering the bulk herb to create remedies from a reputable company. Lastly, We ordered elliot to be observant of Us and Our own state and to make Us aware of it, in a gentle way, as well as to suggest changes in remedies.

slave elliott:

This slave has been diagnosed with Bipolar Type II, with rapid cycling and mixed states as well as ADD. Its bipolar began to express around the age of 12; this slave mentions this because most people don't express their Bipolar disorder so young, but the boys in our family seem to get it early while the women more typically get an early adulthood onset. It feels that this is important to share because it was quite literally raised with the disorder through its teen years. The ADD wasn't caught early, as it is with most children, largely because it has a high I.Q. and at first the learning disability only seemed to affect its mental ability to do mathematics. Most children with ADD also tend to have problems with reading or reading comprehension, but it actually learned "on time" and was always ahead of its reading grade level.

To its master's frustration, this slave does have problems with domestic duties. Its Master is much more detail-oriented than it has ever been. Most of its own habits of clutter have stemmed from its ADD and the resultant "out of sight, out of mind" phenomenon. This slave has found that if it needs to remember things (like what it has to take to work every day), it will remember them much more consistently if it sees them when looking for other necessary things like the keys, wallet, etc. This slave has had countless days of locking itself out of the house as a kid, or forgetting a pencil for class, so it found this to be the best way to remember what to take. Unfortunately, this also reinforces a tendency to simply create piles or stacks which become more and more cluttered over time. This is how the "chaos" in its room is perpetuated, which bothers its OCD master. It doesn't really like this method, but would rather be able to find things it needs than spend all morning trying to find its work keys and end up being late to work. So as strange as it may sound, this is actually a coping mechanism, albeit a lazy one.

To overcome the learning disability aspects of the ADD, it takes a stimulant medication which helps its studies quite a bit, and turns math from infuriatingly frustrating to merely difficult but achievable. (However, it still requires a calculator to do the math in any realistic time frame.) The behavior aspects are still present with the medication, but the medication reduces their severity.

This slave maintains its own bipolar symptoms using herbal remedies that its psychiatrist approves. It has realized that while its symptoms can be very severe when allowed to accumulate, it responds very well to treatment, whether it be herbal or classic medicine. This slave was happy to toss out its old prescriptions after they expired because it responded so well to the herbal replacements. Other than medications, meditation, ensuring enough sleep, and not getting overstressed, this slave trained itself at an early age to notice mood patterns over time. Usually it can see how things change from day to day, and can compare them with the situation a week ago. When it feels strong emotion, it uses the rational and unemotional part of its mind to ask questions like, "What is this emotion in response to?" or "is this an appropriate level of emotion in response to said stimuli?" and so on. Usually, if it is actually experiencing bipolar-induced mood swings, the intense emotion will fail the first question; then it assesses which herb might affect this swing, and either reduces or increases it as appropriate. Of course, if its Master notices that its mood has gotten out of hand, She will mention it, and if needed it will take more drastic action. However, it has been decades since it has needed any more extreme measure than simple medicine adjustments.

Master Fire:

Our slaveboy has a really good handle on its emotional state. We think this stems from the fact that it actually started to do meditation exercises at a very young age before the bipolar began to manifest. While it still struggled a lot as a teen, We have a feeling that this would have been immensely worse had it not developed those skills early.

As much as chaos might frustrate Us, We understand that with elliot, this is just an essential part of its nature. It is that fact that makes Us smirk at the humor of Spirit—Higher Power—which has a way of sending things that challenge us. Chaos is a challenge for such a detailed and grounded person such as Ourself, but while We're often flustered, underneath that is gratitude.

It's true that elliot's ability to self-analyse is invaluable in our relationship. We don't think that We would manage nearly as well if it did not have this skill. It has helped Us realize that only people of a certain mindset and development are really appropriate for Us, whereas before We might have had the impulse to accept anyone, especially in an effort to "fix" them. This is a bad idea, and working with elliot and its quirks brought that to the surface, probably in a better way than through outright failure.

We must admit, however, that while We work to be accepting of elliot's coping mechanisms, We don't fully understand them. To Us, we imagine that if it would simply get into the habit of putting its keys (or whatever) in the same spot every time it got home, thereby creating consistent order, it would then always know where to find them. But We are learning that finding them isn't the issue; remembering them is the issue.

Dealing with a slave like elliott is all about the give and take of learning about another person's view of the world, the filters with which they view that world and the coping mechanisms they have. Our elliot, by having such a developed understanding of itself, is able to help Us develop this skills to do this job.

Rebellious Neurology

Brandon Hardy

Within the first few months of getting to know my now Master, he brought up the topic of ADD in an email. More specifically, if I noticed that I had it. I told him that I had been diagnosed with ADHD anout five years ago, although nobody (including myself) really believed it. There had been a lot of mental instability and chronic pain going on that explained it all away, so away it went! But he knows what ADD looks like—even though he didn't end up with it, it runs strong in his family—and I had all the tells. So unless there was another reason that I would become significantly *less* spazzy after I started throwing back notable amounts of prescribed amphetamines a few years later, it seems he was right.

Our dynamic has been developed with that in mind, amidst other health glitches. The standard my Master set is that he doesn't compromise with me, he compromises with reality, and part of my reality involves impaired brain activity. The assumption is that I want to be here and submit, so together we find ways to not only work around or with my ADHD, but ways to make it the lowest amount of hassle possible, or perhaps even a fun alternative.

ADD or ADHD?

Although I was diagnosed with ADHD in high school, it has to combat with other factors, such rather intense Chronic Fatigue Syndrome, which caused some doubt around the hyperactivity factor that makes up the "H". So I say that I have ADhD, as my hyperactivity is compromised enough that it shouldn't be capitalized. I'm usually just too flat-out exhausted or in pain to carry through with it. My fidgety behaviors have often been delegated to wiggly toes or chronic doodling, and I'm often unable to fight the impulse to fall asleep during activities that required me to sit still for long periods of time. So I will be referring to "ADHD" throughout this writing as it's my formal diagnosis, but do keep in mind that as most of these points don't address the "H", it's a matter of simplifying language rather than specifying these techniques for ADHD rather than ADD.

Our Attitude

First, a general statement. In my opinion, the most important thing to do when one has an s-type with a neurological quirk is to work at separating what's a wiring issue from what's actually disobedience. I have taken to joking with my Master in regards to both this and my chronic pain issues that I may have a "slave heart", but I don't always have a "slave nervous system". Much to the continuous distress of an authority-lover like myself, there are things that I always struggled with doing when told due to no lack of submission to those around me... and I can usually get easy commiseration from other people with ADHD in regards to all of them to one extent or another.

My Master knows that if I communicate issues that fall into these areas, then he's going up against faulty wiring, not me, and that makes it a lot easier to target the issue with minimal excess drama. Unlike what I had become used to—which was being treated as if these behaviors are a conscious decision on my part—it instead became about working together to make these behaviors more manageable.

As for my part as the s-type, I have reached a point where avoiding my ADHD symptoms is no longer an option. It's finally reached the top of my self-care list, and until it reached that point, it wasn't going to change. I need to be on board, motivated, and have the belief that I actually can get better in these areas of my life that I had been struggling with for as long as I can remember. I can be led to the water, but I have to be drinking of my own volition. Small steps are noted and celebrated to keep myself in that mindset, especially since a notable point people with ADHD struggle with is the ability to recognize personal progress. Therefore, just keep in mind while reading these explanations of how we've been finding ways to handle my ADHD that all we do relies on our trust in each other in these areas as a foundation.

The Anxiety

A good overarching (and often unaddressed) place to start is my rather pervasive anxiety. This is also the most aggravating for me because it's caused by things that make no sense, and if asked to verbalize what's going on in the moment, it causes more freaking out. In the past I had a rather severe anxiety disorder (caused by other biological factors that have since been remedied) and I always wrote it off as part of that, since anxiety disorders are rarely logical or confined to one form of expression. Even more recently, I still shrugged it off as leftovers. However, both my Master and my therapist informed me that actually, in certain areas this flavor of anxiety is typical for a person with ADHD. From my own experience and the anecdotal experience of others, I will say that the two times it shows the most is when I am trying to get things organized within a time limit (think: getting out the door for an appointment in a timely manner) and when trying to start a task or project (such as some sort of accursed paperwork). These things can heavily impact functionality in a service-based dynamic, such as the one I'm in.

The former problem is likely acutely familiar to you if you have ADHD, or spent a few school or work mornings watching someone with it. There are two easily recognizable themes that are combined in some variation: the Very Important Routine that is Always Followed (which I will touch on again later), and piles of things everywhere with a panicked individual rushing among them unable to find anything; then, noticing they're running late, deciding a shower really isn't *that* important, locking themselves out of the house while rushing out the door, and only noticing their lack of keys because they tried to run back in to snag their forgotten cell phone after making it halfway down the street.

Now note the "panicked individual" in the second theme. That right there is ADHD anxiety. For us, there's too many things to remember, too much stimuli, too many objects to sort through, that one thing I just forgot about while starting this other thing I'm now forgetting because I was trying to remember the first thing, *too much too much too much*. It's crazy-making. If you've ever noticed poor verbal impulse control paired with ADHD, it's because the output filter that is easily noticed as missing to whatever degree is also missing for input. Information that most people's brains would have caught in their filter (and thusly spared everyone else) instead comes straight on through as if it was just as important as everything else. I find that this can become either a case of distraction by irrelevant things (which can result in bouncing around from one before-I-leave goal to another) or just not noticing much of anything because there's too much to process (which can result in not being able to find all those things needed for successfully leaving). I've always considered myself lucky to make it out the door with finality after less than three runs back inside.

The latter manifestation of this anxiety in relation to projects is chronic avoidance. This looks simply like procrastination, when it's actually due to the panic that comes from facing down Beginning. No, I haven't got a clue what makes the anxiety keep happening, even with simple tasks I know I can do; and yes, it's probably about as annoying from my side as it is from yours. When faced with that panic, it becomes even more easy than usual to get completely distracted by trivial things, to the sadly repetitive surprise of seeing that hours have suddenly vanished into some meaningless activity. When trying to follow orders, this can sometimes seem like the s-type is simply not following them for some reason that's indiscernible to you both. This is very much a case of, "If I could've just done it, then I would have," and getting angry at a person with ADHD who does this will likely get you no coherent answer on what happened, as there probably isn't one for them to give. Quite frankly, I find it incredibly embarrassing that I can't always control this impulse, and will get caught up in it more to try and escape my own shame when I see it's caused upset to those around me in an annoying, self-feeding cycle—particularly when it involves someone as important to me as my Master.

What that has actually helped here the most has been patience on his part. This helps me not get caught in the cycle as easily, as I have less stress around the fact that sometimes I will mess up in this way, and he understands why. He spent a great deal of time getting me to internalize the sentiment that I can waste more time berating myself for being such a lousy s-type by my (not his) standards... or I can just get to doing what I'm supposed to be doing, as he'd really prefer that. Messing up happens, but not putting forth effort to fix it and try to find ways to keep it from happening again is a problem. This doesn't mean that I haven't faced consequences when the mistake has been particularly unfortunate, but he made it clear that making me taking responsibility is different than my dismissal as a person of any use.

There's also that he is very good at figuring out when things were due to disobedience or actually due to wiring. An important part of him being able to make that distinction was building up enough trust that I was committing (and able) to give him accurate information about my current state. Because life and health are ever changing, it has been crucial for him to make it blatantly OK to go up to him and say, "I thought I was going to be able to follow this order, but I misjudged and I'm having a really hard time." This is important because on the occasions I've got a particularly nice batch of symptoms going, all my anxiety is in play. So not only am I telling him what's going on, I'm telling every person who has ever thought I was lying to them or overdramatizing my struggles to avoid responsibility, as well as answering the part of myself that is ashamed that I can't pull it together and wonders if what all those others said is actually true. This is a glorious breeding ground to really get that anxiety into high gear, and finding ways to keep it out of approaching him with my shortcomings has been key. The best results have come from seeing him repeatedly stick to his word and not react the way many others have, which can only come from consistency over time.

Another thing he did (and still does) is ask for continual calibration of what to expect of me for tasks that would not result in a disaster if done incorrectly, inefficiently, or not at all, to see what he could trust giving me responsibility to do. This means that what would in another context be an admission to overall failure is now providing information to find ways to make it work, and continuing to build that trust through honesty. This includes my being able to accurately report on my ability, both mentally and physically. (I had to learn this skill as a patient, but in some cases, helping the s-type find ways to be self-aware enough to do that in the first place is a necessary first step.) Knowing that my assessment will be heard and worked with has been an absolutely freeing experience, so instead of putting my energy into proving that I'm not lying that I *really can't* do something, I can put that effort into working with or around that limitation.

Routine Building

Remember when I mentioned that Very Important Routine that is Always Followed? It's because routines are the bread and butter of many a functioning ADHD person. It's that one place where they always put their wallet, or that they take a vitamin immediately after breakfast with the last swallow of juice. Eventually, the task becomes more muscle memory than actually involving thought. The biggest problem with this is when it is interrupted or interfered with in some way, since we become so reliant on the routine that if it doesn't "just happen", then we aren't likely to remember to do it, then later on usually can't reliably recall if it happened at all (which is an issue for things like medication). I've heard many people joke about being distracted and messing up their routine by a well-meaning person reminding them in the middle of it to not forget the goal of that routine. It's a dangerous game.

When I was going out and about on a daily basis, I tied the activity of brushing my teeth in the morning into my "things to do before leaving" routine. All good and well. More recently, I am pretty housebound due to various factors, so my life doesn't include the "things to do before leaving" routine on anything near a daily basis. As I am still in the active process of rebuilding habits and standards for self-care after years of severe depression and physical limitations, it took me longer than it probably should have to realize that I was only brushing my teeth when my "things to do before bed" routine came into play. This meant that I had to find a new routine to set this into action, and this took a significant amount of effort and focus. Until I handle getting one good habit down, it's detrimental to add in another, regardless of how much I want to speed up the process. By my Master slowly and patiently increasing my responsibilities in both number and importance while taking into consideration my need to also spend that focus on establishing self-care patterns, he has not only given me a chance to build them into routine, but pointedly not set me up for failure. This has resulted in me being a better-functioning human being than I've managed at any other point in my life.

To minimize the likelihood of a new rule going in one ear and out the other, my Master always tries to communicate it in the most effective way possible. This usually means with the least amount of external distraction during face-to-face time, and the occasional non-reprimand style reminder as I make it routine. He also allows for grounding techniques (such as certain types of fidgeting) that help me pay attention so I don't just mentally drift away while he's trying to talk to me.

Dealing with Beginning

To get back to the earlier point of dealing with the barrier of getting started on one's own: The most across-the-board technique many people with ADHD (including myself) have used to make it less painful to start and stick with a task seems to be having background sound stimuli of some kind to keep it from being Too Quiet, which is really distractingly troublesome most of the time. This can be music, a movie, or something like that. Music can also help a great deal specifically with focus while driving, which I only recently discovered wasn't just a personal quirk.

The other technique is having another person present during the duration, or perhaps even just the beginning, of a task. By "present", I mean something as simple as sitting in a nearby chair while forms are filled out or a stressful phone call is made. Having another person there as a grounding presence and for spontaneous interaction (reciprocation is usually not required with these interaction, really) somehow makes things less overwhelming. Go figure, but it's certainly always been the case for me. If you as a Master are thinking of being that presence, it's important to make sure the dynamic is still in clear view when doing this. Many s-types feel uncomfortable receiving anything that seems like service from their M-types, and in some cases a sense of going against the dynamic can happen for all involved.

One way we've found to work with this is that my Master will often offer to provide "soundtrack". This means he'll read aloud to me or play his guitar while I do dishes, which is a magic combination. This only works because he already enjoys reading his favorite books to people, and he's a musician who enjoys jamming out to the delight of my inner-groupie. Both are already done as part of low-stress socializing during his usually hectic days, so it is very clear he isn't just placating me. Now it's just a more productive stretch of time. It's also important that we don't treat the activity as something that threatens the power dynamic or as something that exists outside of it. He has the right to say no to being my soundtrack when I ask, and to tell me to use another compensatory mechanism. Joking about the "captive audience" nature of the situation is a way we keep the power-dynamic in mind without stressing the point too much. (He has also threatened the classic "wearing a butt plug" and "being chained to the stove" solutions, and although he has yet to follow through on it, I'm willing to bet this would probably create the same type of mindset. And I obviously have no ulterior motives for putting those particular tips in an essay he's going to read.)

Sometimes he will offer to be my anchoring presence simply because he's a good person who wants to help me out (and it gets his order met), and it's my job to endeavor to find ways to make him helping me as un-taxing as possible. He is in no way obligated, but it's still his decision to do this and I have to respect it as such.

Navigating Sensory Issues

One aspect of ADHD that I've only learned of relatively recently is the potential for sensory issues. It's far more often brought up in regards to people on the Autistic

Disorder Spectrum, but many of us have it too. This is where a particular sound, texture, color, or so on causes the person experiencing it to tweak out for no other discernible reason.

When I learned of this, I suddenly recalled the futon my parents bought after our couch broke when I was seven. For whatever reason, the sound of that fabric being scratched was one of the most dreadful things I'd ever heard. Ever the thought of it still makes me twitchy, as do similar noises or the feel of fabrics prone to making that noise. When my mother would clean the futon, I would close myself off in the bathroom and rock back and forth with my hands over my ears making noises to block out the sound. My parents treated it as some over-dramatic tendency to be either ignored or taunted in turn, while I had to find ways to control my impulse to snap at someone or bodily keep them from making that noise. (Thankfully these impulses were so out of character that people mostly humored me.) Turns out this isn't extraordinary in the world of ADHD. I've recently taken to bringing this not-so-well-known fact up to my friends with ADHD. This resulted in one friend digging up a photo of herself as a toddler looking offended at her first cone of ice cream because she was disgusted by the texture, and yet another friend proceeding to compare notes of her childhood sensory issues with her husband, who has Asperger's Syndrome.

There really is not too much to be done about this except to work with it. Some power-exchange couples use it for sadomasochistic play, but even though I can be beaten bloody or scared past the point of verbal communication and still happily fetch my Master a drink afterwards, the idea of having to tolerate my sensory issues for a scene is horrific and would likely make me ridiculously spazzy for a while. Tread this ground carefully. (And I now *honestly* have no ulterior motives for putting this in an essay my Master is going to read.) My Master and his alpha boy, who has Asperger's Syndrome, use it occasionally to enforce their dynamic, in that my Master will reassert that he can still touch whenever he pleases despite his alpha boy having a bad sensory day and finding any physical sensation gross in the moment, and it's turned an otherwise unpleasant thing into a comfort. This is all dependent on the severity of the sensory issue or how often it comes up or affects day to day life. Just know that it is something other than the s-type being unreasonably fussy.

Vocal Impulsivity

I've already mentioned the issue of our filters being flawed for both input and output. If you've ever noted the rambling, tangenting talking habits of someone with ADHD, then you've been witness to this. It's as if there's this unreasonably excited person in the back of my mind, jumping up and down and being all manner of distracting to get my attention so that I'll share whatever it is they have to say. They won't shut up until I share what's gotten them all flaily, or sometimes it gets blurted out before I have a chance to stop them, or sometimes they even encourage me to ramble unintentionally. It can lead to accidentally taking over a conversation by filling in all the silences or constantly interrupting, and is all part of the vocal impulsivity control package. But it's not for lack of an interest in what other people are saying.

My Master works with it by reserving the right to tell me to shut up or to interrupt me when I've got the rambles going, which is actually wonderful as not only does it put the brakes on in those times I can't stop myself once I get rolling, it's also a lovely little reminder of his control. In group discussion settings, it is a requirement for me to bring a notebook and pen if I'm having a spazzy day so that I can write down thoughts that occur to me. By getting the thought out of me and onto paper, it cuts down on that urgent need to say that point and to determine with a more detached attitude if it needs to be shared at all. I've gotten to the point that I need the notebook less and less to keep things on the inside, but it's been a slowly learned skill.

Also, finding alternatives to speaking can be beneficial. I have issues with verbal communication that get compounded by ADHD. Sometimes my rambling is actually me trying out words to find a successful way to communicate my point, because I can't reliably do that in my head. So sometimes I will ask to write about something instead of talk about it. Due to this, I have discovered the amazing power of the Delete Key against the aforementioned rambling. It can go on for however long it does, but can be edited out before it even gets to the other person. This has simplified communication with my Master in many ways and given him an alternative with which to work.

Fighting the Hyper-Focus Control

For all the lack of attention that comes with a disorder whose very name quantifies it as being in deficit, there are times when something just clicks. We get sucked into something, such as a book or a project or a video game, in a way that takes an almost physical effort to detach oneself and reattach onto something that doesn't hold our interest to a similar degree. Sometimes this is born of those accidental avoidance tendencies, but certainly not always, and it usually holds more than the comparatively fleeting interest those topics usually have. This is called hyper-focus. I usually refer to it as "hyperdrive" in the privacy of my nerdy mind, and it's as if our brain suddenly burns through all of our focus-fuel in one mad dash towards our thing of (somewhat) choice.

It will sometimes take a few tries to get a person with ADHD to refocus onto a new topic, but it isn't for lack of trying on their part. Once again, patience is key. But through careful work, some ADHD people have figured out how to trip hyper-focus in themselves so that they can latch onto a project at will. The panic of a rapidly approaching deadline does help, but I'm talking about less harried methods. With a little work up, like a dog circling on a bed before plopping down, I can futz through a few other tasks to build up to flinging myself into a harder task. It's not only because it takes a lot of effort to get to the hyper-focus point, but because I know that once I get sucked in, I'm there for the long haul. To throw in another metaphor, it's like getting in the pool. Once I jump in, it's going to take a lot of time to leave, and my being wet and in swim gear is going to infringe on my ability to readily do something else.

My Master will repeatedly prod me about a time-sensitive task to remind me that I need to gear up and get to it. Like with what you're reading right now. He frequently mentioned it and gave me time to work on it, but let me figure out what pacing about I needed to do before jumping in and allowed for that, too. And I even managed to get it done in time!

Meds

For some people, medication helps. A lot. I'm one of those people, even if I can't take it daily due to other physical issues. The first time I took a full dose, it was like someone had turned the volume down inside of my head from an 11 to a 2, which ended up distracting me even more until I got used to it. It certainly didn't fix the problem, but it has made it significantly easier to implement my different coping mechanisms. Like when I caught myself being overpowering in a conversation, I thought, "Hmm, I should chill out." And I did. And it was really, really strange, because I hadn't realized that it could be this effortless. (Then I ended up interrupting the person to share this strange occurrence. It's an ongoing process.)

Even though my physical problems can cause symptoms similar to ADHD, not having to deal with them both at once can be a relief—although the chronic fatigue issues I have can exacerbate things. Where someone without ADHD takes medication like Adderall to stay awake, when I said the effect almost seemed backwards on me during a doctor's appointment, my primary care physician likened an exhausted person with ADHD taking Adderall to a drunk person drinking a lot of coffee. "You'll have some energy, yes, but you're still going to be drunk."

If your dynamic has this level of control, I highly recommend encouraging at least some trials in this arena. There is a lot of stigma around these meds that certainly caused me to avoid them if no one else, but my Master pushing the point led me to discovering a fantastically beneficial thing for my ability to function the best I can for him. A program such as *Mastering Your Adult ADHD* from the *Treatments That Work* series, which uses Cognitive Behavioral Therapy (or "The Other CBT") techniques to help not only the person with ADHD find ways to improve their quality of life, but also has place for a partner or family member to learn more, can be a fantastic addition to a medication regimen. And having someone who can order me to keep with the program when I wander off into outer space has certainly been nothing but beneficial.

I know that it takes some extra effort to handle an s-type who has a rebellious nervous system, since I know how hard it can be for us. But for some M-types, the payoff of handling those uprisings is worth it. As I have seen the improvements he has caused or inspired, it's done nothing but intensify my dedication and desire to keep bettering myself for my Master—and the ripple effect from that has strengthened our dynamic more than I can even quantify.

www.ingramcontent.com/pod-product-compliance
Lightning Source LLC
Chambersburg PA
CBHW020244290326
41930CB00038B/238